Casting a Movement

Casting a Movement brings together US-based actors, directors, educators, playwrights, and scholars to explore the cultural politics of casting.

Drawing on the notion of a "welcome table"—a space where artists of all backgrounds can come together as equals to create theater—the book's contributors discuss casting practices as they relate to varying communities and contexts, including Middle Eastern American theater, disability culture, multilingual performance, Native American theater, color-conscious and culturally conscious casting, and casting as a means to dismantle stereotypes. Syler and Banks suggest that casting is a way to invite more people to the table so that the full breadth of US identities can be reflected onstage, and that casting is inherently a political act; because an actor's embodied presence both communicates a dramatic narrative and evokes cultural assumptions associated with appearance, skin color, gender, sexuality, and ability, casting choices are never neutral. By bringing together a variety of artistic perspectives to discuss common goals and particular concerns related to casting, this volume features the insights and experiences of a broad range of practitioners and experts across the field.

As a resource-driven text suitable for both practitioners and academics, *Casting a Movement* seeks to frame and mobilize a social movement focused on casting, access, and representation.

Claire Syler is Assistant Professor of Theatre at the University of Missouri and previously the Education Director at the Nashville Shakespeare Festival. Her research focuses on the intersection of theater and education and has appeared in *HowlRound, Theatre, Dance and Performance Training, Theatre Topics*, and *Youth Theatre Journal*.

Daniel Banks is Co-director of DNAWORKS, an arts and service organization dedicated to using the arts as a catalyst for dialogue and healing, engaging topics of representation, identity, and heritage. He served on the faculties of Tisch School of the Arts, NYU, the M.A. in Applied Theatre, CUNY, and as Chair of Performing Arts, Institute of American Indian Arts, Santa Fe, NM. He is the editor of *Say Word! Voices from Hip Hop Theater* (University of Michigan).

Casting a Movement

The Welcome Table Initiative

Edited by
Claire Syler and Daniel Banks

Routledge
Taylor & Francis Group

LONDON AND NEW YORK

First published 2019
by Routledge
2 Park Square, Milton Park, Abingdon, Oxon OX14 4RN

and by Routledge
52 Vanderbilt Avenue, New York, NY 10017

Routledge is an imprint of the Taylor & Francis Group, an informa business

British Library Cataloguing in Publication Data
A catalogue record for this book is available from the British Library

Library of Congress Cataloging-in-Publication Data
Names: Syler, Claire, editor. | Banks, Daniel, 1965- editor.
Title: Casting a movement : the welcome table initiative / edited by Claire
Syler and Daniel Banks.
Description: Abingdon, Oxon ; New York, NY : Routledge, 2019.
Identifiers: LCCN 2019009028| ISBN 9781138594470
(hardback : alk. paper) | ISBN 9781138594777 (paperback : alk. paper) |
ISBN 9780429488221 (ebook)
Subjects: LCSH: Theater--Casting--United States. |
Theater and society--United States. | Minorities in the performing
arts--Employment--United States.
Classification: LCC PN2293.C38 C37 2019 | DDC 792.0973--dc23
LC record available at https://lccn.loc.gov/2019009028

ISBN: 978-1-138-59447-0 (hbk)
ISBN: 978-1-138-59477-7 (pbk)
ISBN: 978-0-429-48822-1 (ebk)

Typeset in Bembo
by Taylor & Francis Books

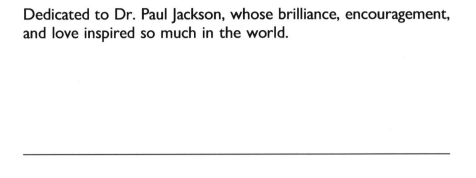

Dedicated to Dr. Paul Jackson, whose brilliance, encouragement, and love inspired so much in the world.

Contents

List of illustrations   x
Acknowledgments   xii
List of contributors   xiv

Foreword: From "I Love Your Freckles" to "Representation Matters"   1
LIESL TOMMY

Introduction   4
CLAIRE SYLER

The welcome table: Casting for an integrated society   12
DANIEL BANKS

PART I
Culturally conscious casting   31

1 The chasm between   33
   AYANNA THOMPSON

2 Playing with "race" in the new millennium   36
   JUSTIN EMEKA

3 Nevertheless, whiteness persisted   49
   BRIAN EUGENIO HERRERA

PART II
**Approaches to casting Middle Eastern American
theater**   55

4 Casting pearls before authenticity   57
   YUSSEF EL GUINDI

5 ReOrienting: A Middle Eastern American casting case study   60
TORANGE YEGHIAZARIAN

6 Casting Middle Eastern American theater: Cultural, academic, and
professional challenges   72
MICHAEL MALEK NAJJAR

PART III
Casting and disability culture   **83**

7 Casting disabled actors: Taking our rightful place onstage?   85
CHRISTINE BRUNO

8 The difference disability makes: Unique considerations in casting
performers with disabilities   88
CARRIE SANDAHL

9 A great and complicated thing: Reimagining disability   100
VICTORIA LEWIS

PART IV
Casting and multilingual performance   **113**

10 The sea will listen   115
CARIDAD SVICH

11 Setting a global table with multilingual theater   117
EUNICE S. FERREIRA

12 Creating emergent spaces: Casting, community-building, and
extended dramaturgy   131
ANN ELIZABETH ARMSTRONG

PART V
Casting contemporary Native American theater   **143**

13 Journey   145
TY DEFOE (GIIZHIG)

14 Native Voices at the Autry: Casting the room   147
JEAN BRUCE SCOTT AND RANDY REINHOLZ (CHOCTAW)

15 Decolonial practices for contemporary Native Theater   159
COURTNEY ELKIN MOHLER (SANTA BARBARA CHUMASH)

PART VI
Subverting stereotypes   171

16   Whose story is this to tell?   173
     MEI ANN TEO

17   Casting, cross-racial performance, and the work of creativity   176
     DORINNE KONDO

18   Artists of color/cross-racial casting   190
     DONATELLA GALELLA

PART VII
Casting across identities   201

19   Reaparecer   203
     ELAINE ÁVILA

20   *Collidescope 2.0*: Performing the "alien gaze"   207
     PRISCILLA PAGE

21   The spatio-temporal logics of *Collidescope*'s welcome table   220
     BRANDI WILKINS CATANESE

     Afterword   228
     DANIEL BANKS

     Index   235

Illustrations

Figures

2.1 The three witches inviting Macbeth. Production photo from *Macbeth* by William Shakespeare at Oberlin College in 2010. Directed by Justin Emeka.   38

2.2 Production photo from *Death of a Salesman* by Arthur Miller at Oberlin College in 2008. Petronia Paley as Linda Loman, Avery Brooks as Willy Loman. Directed by Justin Emeka.   41

2.3 Production photo from *Death of a Salesman* by Arthur Miller at Oberlin College in 2008. Marc Jablon as Charlie, Avery Brooks as Willy Loman. Directed by Justin Emeka.   43

9.1 The piano roll factory. Randolph Bourne (Clark Middleton) and Helen Clark Hummel (Ann Stocking) in John Belluso's *The Body of Bourne*, world premiere, Mark Taper Forum, 2000.   104

9.2 Cast of John Belluso's *The Body of Bourne*, world premiere, Mark Taper Forum, 2000.   106

9.3 Laura Hernandez as Lakisha Griffin in *One Day on the Road to the ADA*, University of Redlands, 2018.   109

11.1 Promotional photo with the four Odysseus and Penelope couples. Clockwise from top center: Molly Burdick, David Gyampo, Ted Randell, Julianna Quiroz, Daniella Deutsch, Grant Landau-Williams, Bella Rinskaya, and Christopher Naughton. *The Orphan Sea* by Caridad Svich, multilingual premiere directed by Eunice S. Ferreira, Skidmore College, 2016.   121

11.2 The ensemble performs the first choral movement "Crossings" in Arabic, Asante Twi, English, French, Mandarin, Portuguese, Russian and Spanish. *The Orphan Sea* by Caridad Svich, multilingual premiere directed by Eunice S. Ferreira, Skidmore College, 2016.   124

11.3 Julianna Quiroz, one of the four Penelopes, cries out in Spanish and English as she digs in the earth for the bones of Odysseus. *The Orphan Sea* by Caridad Svich, multilingual premiere directed by Eunice S. Ferreira, Skidmore College, 2016.   125

12.1 *Theatre for Youth* diversity wheel adapted by Stephani Etheridge
      Woodson.   136
14.1 2017 Oregon Shakespeare Festival production of *Off the Rails* by
      Randy Reinholz (Choctaw). Madame Overdone (Sheila Tousey)
      hatches a plan to free Isabel (Lily Gladstone) and Momaday
      (Shaun Taylor-Corbett) from Angelo's treachery.   153
14.2 2016 Native Voices at the Autry production of *They Don't Talk
      Back* by Frank Henry Kaash Katasse (Tlingit). Grandfather teaches
      Paul Sr. why "they don't talk back." Young Paul (Kholan Studi,
      in mask), Grandfather (Brian Wescott, in mask), and Paul, Sr.
      (Duane Minard).   156
15.1 A medicine wheel of Indigenous theatrical praxis.   161
15.2 Creative continuum.   164
17.1 Anna Deavere Smith as Mrs. Young Soon Han in *Twilight: Los
      Angeles, 1992*, world premiere at the Mark Taper Forum, Los
      Angeles, 1993.   181
17.2 Left–right: Jon Hoche; Daniel May (facing away); Kendyl Ito;
      Kristen Faith Oei; Maria-Christina Oliveras (obscured);
      Raymond J. Lee; Jaygee Macapugay and Geena Quintos in the
      world premiere of David Henry Hwang and Jeanine Tesori's *Soft
      Power* at Center Theatre Group/Ahmanson Theatre. Directed by
      Leigh Silverman and choreographed by Sam Pinkleton for CTG
      Ahmanson Theatre.   186
20.1 "Epilogue: Hands Up, Don't Shoot" (Michael Brown Memorial
      section) from *Collidescope: Adventures in Pre- and Post-Racial
      America* at University of Maryland, College Park, 2014. Directed
      by Ping Chong and Talvin Wilks.   209
20.2 "Scene 6: Politics and Race in America" (Fannie Lou Hamer
      section) from *Collidescope 2.0* at the University of Massachusetts-
      Amherst, 2016. Directed by Ping Chong and Talvin Wilks.   213
20.3 "Scene 10: On the Eve of the American Civil War" (The Civil
      War/Secession Ball section) from *Collidescope 3.0* at Wake Forest
      University, 2017. Directed by Ping Chong and Talvin Wilks.   217

Tables

I.1   Actions to expand casting practices in US theater.   8
5.1   ReOrient 2009 program.   65
5.2   ReOrient 2009 projected casting grid.   67
5.3   ReOrient 2009 cast list by play.   68

Acknowledgments

The shoulders on which we stand …

From Claire Syler

Daniel, thank you for your partnership, encouragement, kindness, and for being willing to schedule so many late-night calls after I put my children to bed (smile). You model generosity and grace with every utterance. It has been a pleasure and privilege to work alongside you. Much gratitude goes to my parents, Bill and Georganne Syler, whose fierce love and support shapes my every move. Thanks to my sister for her love and continued calls to check in. Deep thanks to my children, Harvey and Margot, who teach me more than I can ever teach them; your laughter, snuggles, and school schedule keep me going. Thanks to my husband and partner in all things, Chuck; you are the best decision I ever made. Big thanks to the Department of Theatre at the University of Missouri for supporting my research—most especially my Chair and advocate, Heather Carver, whose laughter makes everyone smile. Thanks to my teachers, collaborators, and friends: Gloria Baxter, John Yorke, Denice Hicks, Jon Royal, Bruce McConachie, Ellice Forman, Cindy Croot, David Peterson, Deirdre O'Rourke, Kristin O'Malley, Michelle Tyrene Johnson, Kara Braudis, Uncle Scott Lawrie, Megan Murphy-Chambers, and Jules Willcox. I stand on your shoulders.

From Daniel Banks

My sincere thanks to the workers and visionaries who contributed their voices to "The Welcome Table" article and to this volume; and to the generous readers who offered their feedback on/support for both of these projects: Gwendolyn Alker, Lisa Brenner, Amy Green, Kathy Ervin, Anne Hamilton, D. J. Hopkins, Maxinne Leighton, Roberta Levitow, Adam McKinney, Jim Peck, Kevin Vavasseur, and Talvin Wilks. Heartfelt appreciation goes to Beth Turner and *Black Masks* for inviting the first iteration of article, and Betsey Baun and SETC for encouraging me to continue developing these ideas.

While the number of people doing the important work of equity, access, and opportunity in the arts in the US is too great to print or discuss in this volume, my participation in the formulation of this collection has been deeply and specifically impacted by the preceding work and leadership of: Rachel Watanabe Batton, Clinton Turner Davis, Una Chaudhuri, Hal Scott, Ellen Holly, Emily Mann, John O'Neal, George C. Wolfe, Ngũgĩ wa Thiong'o, Margaret Wilkerson, Ellen Donkin, Baraka Sele, Roberta Uno, Emilya Cachapero, Marvin Sims, Glenda Dickerson, Susan Booth, and Kwame Kwei-Armah. Finally, tremendous credit goes to Claire Syler for her tireless work on this volume and commitment to advancing equity in theater. The consummate collaborator, Claire listened, processed, and acted with generosity and focus to realize this collection of extraordinary narratives and critical thinking. Thank you for thinking *beyond* the box with me and for your keen eye and insights.

This work is ongoing and the names and projects lifted up in this book are but a few of the wealth of work being done to decolonize US theater and ensure equity, access, and opportunity for all people. For any omissions, please forgive us.

From Claire and Daniel

Thank you to Ben Piggott, Laura Soppelsa, Hamish Ironside, Reanna Young, and Mat Willis at Routledge for your support of this project. Our deep appreciation to the book's incredible contributors who generously shared their knowledge, experience, and time. May our movement be cast and grow in ways beyond what we can imagine.

Contributors

Claire Syler is an Assistant Professor of Theatre at the University of Missouri. Previously, she was the Education Director at the Nashville Shakespeare Festival where she helped to bring classical performance to Middle Tennessee audiences through professional productions, performance residencies, and teaching artist visits. Claire's research focuses on the intersection of theater and education and her writing has appeared in *HowlRound*; *The Routledge Companion to Theatre, Performance and Cognitive Science, Theatre, Dance and Performance Training* (UK), *Theatre Topics*, and *Youth Theatre Journal*. She is an alumna of the University of Pittsburgh's PhD in Theatre and Performance Studies program and the University of Memphis's MFA in Directing program. When she is not in the classroom, rehearsal hall, or library, you can find her with her two kids, Harvey and Margot. She lives in Columbia, MO with her husband, Chuck.

Daniel Banks is the Co-director of DNAWORKS, an arts and service organization dedicated to using the arts as a catalyst for dialogue and healing, engaging topics of representation, identity and heritage. He is founder and director of the Hip Hop Theatre Initiative, promoting youth self-expression and leadership. Directing credits include: National Theatre of Uganda; Belarussian National Drama Theatre; Market Theatre, South Africa; Playhouse Square, Cleveland; and the NYC and DC Hip Hop Theatre Festivals. He has served on the faculties of Tisch School of the Arts, NYU; M.A. in Applied Theatre, CUNY; MFA in Contemporary Performance, Naropa University; and as Chair of Performing Arts, Institute of American Indian Arts, Santa Fe, NM. Among other publications, Daniel is editor of the critical anthology *Say Word! Voices from Hip Hop Theater* (University of Michigan).

Ann Elizabeth Armstrong is an Associate Professor of Theatre at Miami University in Oxford, Ohio. She has published on feminist pedagogy, theater for social change, and theater of the oppressed. She is a director, deviser, and applied theater facilitator and has created plays, walking tours, and a location-based app about Freedom Summer in 1964. The latter was awarded an NEH digital humanities grant (fsapp.lib.miamioh.edu) and was awarded most innovative program from the ALL IN Democracy Challenge. Her current book project, *Performing Freedom Summer*, examines relationships among a social movement's various performance practices and genealogies of applied theater and theater for social change.

Elaine Ávila is a Canadian/American playwright of Azorean descent and the Fulbright Scholar to Portugal in 2019. Her plays have premiered in the US, Canada, Europe, and Central America. Recent writing residencies/teaching appointments: Quest University, Pomona College, the Disquiet International Literary Program in Lisbon and the Playwrights Theatre Centre. Recently, her Portuguese plays have won many awards, including: Best New Musical, Disquiet Best Short Play Award, Mellon Foundation Award to write an environmental play, the Top Unproduced Latinx Plays List in the US and the SureFire List (top 23 plays) in Canada. Her collected plays are available at NoPassport Press.

Christine Bruno is an actor, teaching artist, and disability inclusion consultant, with an MFA in Acting and Directing from the New School, member of The Actors Studio, and was Disability Advocate for Inclusion in the Arts from 2005 until the organization's closure in December 2017. Selected credits include Bekah Brunstetter's *Public Servant*; *The Glass Menagerie; The Maids* (adaptation by José Rivera); *The Good Daughter*; the musicals *The Ugly Girl, Raspberry* (UK tours); *Screw You, Jimmy Choo!*, *Law & Order, The Homecoming,* iCreep; award-winning independent features *Flatbush Luck* and *This is Where We Live.* Distinctions and appointments include NY Local Board, SAG-AFTRA; Chair, NY SAG-AFTRA Performers with Disabilities (PWD) Committee; member, SAG-AFTRA National PWD and Actors' Equity EEOC Committees; Freelance Disability Consultant, Cultural Plan for the City of New York.

Brandi Wilkins Catanese is an Associate Professor at UC Berkeley in the Departments of African American Studies and Theater, Dance, and Performance Studies. She writes about contemporary black performance, broadly defined.

Ty Defoe (*Giizhig*), Grammy Award and Jonathan Larson Award winner, is from the Oneida and Ojibwe Nations of Wisconsin, and resides in NYC. Writer, lyricist, scorpio, and cultural pioneer. As an interdisciplinary artist, Ty has gained recognition in many circles around the world. His writing publications can be viewed in the *Pitkin Review, Woody Guthrie Anthology, Thorny Locust Magazine*, and *HowlRound*. Degrees from CalArts, Goddard College, NYU's Tisch. He/Him/They/We/Us—Tydefoe.com.

Yussef El Guindi's recent productions include *Hostages* at Radial Theater Project; *The Talented Ones* at Artists Repertory Theatre in Portland (Santa Barbara Independent Indy Award); *Our Enemies: Lively Scenes of Love and Combat* at Golden Thread Productions (American Theatre Critics

Association's M. Elizabeth Osborn Award); and *Threesome* at Portland Center Stage, ACT, and at 59E59 (Portland Drammy for Best Original Script). In January 2019, Bloomsbury published *The Selected Works of Yussef El Guindi*. Currently a Core Company playwright member at ACT in Seattle, 2018, and a Resident Artist at Golden Thread Productions.

Justin Emeka is a director who integrates traditions of the African Diaspora within classical and contemporary theater. His directing credits include: *A Midsummer Night's Dream* and *Romeo and Juliet* at the Classical Theater of Harlem; *Macbeth* at the University of Washington; *Julius X* at the Karamu House in Cleveland; and *Death of a Salesman* at Oberlin College. He authored the essay "Seeing Shakespeare through Brown Eyes" published in *Black Acting Methods: Critical Approaches*. Mr. Emeka is a member of the Stage Directors and Choreographers Society and is currently an Associate Professor of Theater and Africana Studies at Oberlin College.

Eunice S. Ferreira is an Assistant Professor of Theater at Skidmore College, Saratoga Springs, NY. As a scholar artist, her directing and research focus on the intersections of theatrical performance and issues of language, race, class, gender, culture, and national identity. She has published in *Theatre Journal, African Theatre 12: Shakespeare in & out of Africa,* and *Moving Worlds.* Her translation of *Alone Onstage (Sozinha no Palco),* in collaboration with Christina S. McMahon, is the first English-language publication of a play from the Cape Verde Islands. Her current book project is titled *Remapping Creole and Mixed Race Theater.*

Donatella Galella is an Assistant Professor of Theatre at the University of California, Riverside. She has previously written on race, racism, and casting in *Theatre Journal, Theatre Survey,* the *Journal of Dramatic Theory and Criticism,* and *The Disney Musical on Stage and Screen.* Her book *America in the Round: Capital, Race, and Nation at Washington, DC's Arena Stage* provides a critical history of one of the leading regional theaters in the United States.

Brian Eugenio Herrera is Associate Professor of Theater in the Lewis Center for the Arts at Princeton University. He is author of *The Latina/o Theatre Commons 2013 National Convening: A Narrative Report* (HowlRound 2015) and *Latin Numbers: Playing Latino in Twentieth-Century US Popular Performance* (Michigan 2015), which was awarded the George Jean Nathan Prize for Dramatic Criticism. He is also the Inaugural Resident Scholar for The Sol Project, an initiative dedicated to producing the work of Latinx playwrights in New York City and beyond.

Dorinne Kondo is Professor of American Studies and Anthropology at the University of Southern California. She is the author of *Crafting Selves: Power, Gender, and Discourses of Identity in a Japanese Workplace; About Face: Performing Race in Fashion and Theater;* and *Worldmaking: Race, Performance, and the*

Work of Creativity (Duke 2018). Kondo served as dramaturg for three world premieres of Anna Deavere Smith's plays. Kondo's plays include *(Dis)graceful(l) Conduct* (Mixed Blood Theatre's "We Don't Need No Stinking Dramas" national comedy playwriting award), *But Can He Dance?* (production, Asian American Repertory Theater), and *Seamless* (runner-up, Jane Chambers Award for women playwrights).

Victoria Lewis Editor *Beyond Victims and Villains: Contemporary Plays by Disabled Playwrights*. Recent publications: "Activating the Past: Performing Disability Rights in the Classroom"; "Hands Like Starfish/Feet Like Moons: Disabled Women's Theatre Collectives," in *Women, Collective Creation, and Devised Performance*; "From Mao to the Feeling Circle: the Limits and Endurance of Collective Creation," in *A History of Collective Creation*; and "Disability and Access: A Manifesto for Actor Training," in *The Politics of American Actor Training*. Victoria is the Founding Director of the Other Voices Project at the Mark Taper Forum and Professor of Theatre Arts at the University of Redlands.

Courtney Elkin Mohler (Santa Barbara Chumash) is an Assistant Professor of Theatre at Butler University where she directs for the department, teaches Theatre History and Performance Studies, and serves as a faculty mentor for the Social Justice and Diversity Core. Specializing in Native American Theater, Critical Race Theory, and Theatre for Social Justice, she has published articles in *Theatre Topics, Modern Drama, Ecumenica, Platform*, and *Text and Presentation* and is currently co-authoring *Critical Companion to Native American and First Nations Theatre and Performance – Indigenous Spaces* with Christy Stanlake and Jaye T. Darby. Mohler has directed, dramaturged, or acted in over 40 productions and works closely with Native Voices at the Autry in Los Angeles, California.

Michael Malek Najjar is an Associate Professor of Theatre Arts at the University of Oregon. He holds a PhD in Theatre and Performance Studies from UCLA and an MFA in Directing from York University. He is the author of *Arab American Drama, Film and Performance: A Critical Study, 1908 to the Present*, and editor of *The Selected Works of Yussef El Guindi, Four Arab American Plays: Works by Leila Buck, Jamil Khoury, Yussef El Guindi, and Lameece Issaq & Jacob Kader*, and co-editor of *Six Plays of the Israeli-Palestinian Conflict*. He serves on the Advisory Board for *Arab Stages*.

Priscilla Maria Page, MFA/PhD, teaches theater at UMass Amherst, where she directs the Multicultural Theater Certificate. Her research includes Latina/o/x Theater and Contemporary Native American Performance. Her essay "My World Made Real" is published in *El Grito Del Bronx and Other Plays* by Migdalia Cruz, NoPassport Press, 2010. In 2016, she published "Speedo Activism and the Aesthetics of Resistance" and "An Interview with Dr. Liza Ann Acosta" in Café Onda. She is a contributing co-editor for *Wings of Night Sky, Wings of Morning Light: A Play* and *A Circle of Responses* with Joy Harjo, Wesleyan Press, 2019.

Randy Reinholz, (Choctaw), Co-founder and Producing Artistic Director of Native Voices at the Autry is a professor at San Diego State University, where he served as Head of Acting (1997–2007), Director of the School of Theatre, Television, and Film (2007–2012), and Director of Community Engagement and Innovation for the College of Professional Studies and Fine Arts (2012–2015). His breakout play *Off The Rails* was produced at Native Voices at the Autry (2015) and the Oregon Shakespeare Festival (2017), Bill Rauch directing. He has produced and directed over seventy-five plays in the United States, Australia, Mexico, Canada, and Great Britain.

Carrie Sandahl is Associate Professor at the University of Illinois at Chicago in the Department of Disability and Human Development. She directs Chicago's Bodies of Work, an organization that supports the development of disability arts and culture. Her research and creative activity focus on disability identity in live performance and film. Sandahl's publications include a co-edited anthology, *Bodies in Commotion: Disability and Performance*, which garnered the Association for Theatre in Higher Education's award for Outstanding Book in Theatre Practice and Pedagogy (2006). She is collaborating on a documentary, *Code of the Freaks*, a critique of disability representations in cinema.

Jean Bruce Scott, Co-founder and Producing Executive Director of Native Voices at the Autry, has spent twenty-five years developing new plays, including more than 200 by Native American playwrights. She has produced twenty-six plays (including twenty-three world premieres) in thirty-nine productions, twenty-five New Play Festivals, nine Short Play Festivals, fifteen Playwright Retreats, national and international tours, and hundreds of play readings. She has received a McKnight Fellowship, a MAP Grant, Playwrights Arena's Lee Melville Award, serves on the Leadership Board of the Theatrical Producers League of Los Angeles, Large Theatres, and is a member of New York's National Theatre Conference.

Caridad Svich is a playwright and theater-maker. She received a 2018 Tanne Foundation Award, 2018 Ellen Stewart Award for Career Achievement in Professional Theatre from ATHE, 2013 Edgerton Foundation New Play Award, 2012 OBIE for Lifetime Achievement, and 2011 American Theatre Critics Association Primus Prize. She has edited several books on theater and performance, including *Fifty Playwrights on Their Craft* (Bloomsbury Methuen Drama, 2017). She is associate editor at *Contemporary Theatre Review* for Routledge UK. Her works are published by Intellect Books, Seagull Books and more. She is founder of NoPassport theater alliance and press.

Mei Ann Teo is a theater-maker and filmmaker who works at the intersection of artistic/civic/contemplative practice to shift culture towards justice and compassion. As a director/deviser/dramaturg, she collaborates across genres, including multi-form performance and music theater. Her work is seen at theaters and festivals internationally including Singapore, China, and Europe. She has served as an educator, from heading a drama program at Pacific Union College to being Assistant Professor of Directing and Dramaturgy at Hampshire College. She is the Producing Artistic Director of Musical Theatre Factory, a Resident Company of Playwrights Horizons.

Ayanna Thompson is Director of the Arizona Center for Medieval & Renaissance Studies (ACMRS) at Arizona State University. She is the author of *Shakespeare in the Theatre: Peter Sellars* (Arden Bloomsbury 2018), *Teaching Shakespeare with Purpose: A Student-Centered Approach* (Arden Bloomsbury 2016), *Passing Strange: Shakespeare, Race, and Contemporary America* (Oxford University Press 2011), and *Performing Race and Torture on the Early Modern Stage* (Routledge 2008). She wrote the new introduction for the revised Arden3 *Othello* (Arden 2016), and is the editor of *Weyward Macbeth: Intersections of Race and Performance* (Palgrave 2010) and *Colorblind Shakespeare: New Perspectives on Race and Performance* (Routledge 2006).

Liesl Tommy is a Tony-nominated and Obie/Lortel award-winning director whose Broadway production of Danai Gurira's *Eclipsed* starring Lupita Nyong'o garnered six Tony nominations. She has two feature films in the works, RESPECT starring Jennifer Hudson about the life of icon Aretha Franklin, and the film adaption of Trevor Noah's book *Born a Crime,* starring Lupita Nyong'o. Her television directing credits include: *Queen Sugar, Insecure, The Walking Dead, Dietland* and *Jessica Jones.* Recent off-Broadway credits include: Public Theater: *Party People, The Good Negro*; Signature Theatre: *Appropriate* (Obie Award); MCC Theater: *Relevance*; and Vineyard Theatre: *Kid Victory.* Awards include: Obie Award; Lucille Lortel Award; The Lee Reynolds Award; Pioneer of the Arts Award; Lillian Hellman Award; Alan Schneider Award; NEA/TCG Directors Grant; and the inaugural Susan Stroman Award from the Vineyard Theatre. Liesl is a Program Associate at The Sundance Institute and Associate Artist at Berkeley Repertory. She is a proud native of Cape Town, South Africa.

Torange Yeghiazarian is the Founding Artistic Director of Golden Thread Productions, the first American theater company focused on the Middle East, where she launched such visionary programs as ReOrient Festival, New Threads, Fairytale Players, and What do the Women Say? A playwright, director, and translator, Torange has been published in *The Drama Review, American Theatre Magazine, AmerAsia Journal,* and contributed to *Encyclopedia of Women & Islamic Cultures* and *Cambridge World Encyclopedia of Stage Actors.* Born in Iran and of Armenian heritage, Torange holds a Master's degree in Theatre Arts from San Francisco.

Foreword: From "I Love Your Freckles" to "Representation Matters"

Liesl Tommy

Many times in my life as a director, whether in regional theater, on Broadway, or Off-Broadway, I found myself as the "first" version of me in a building—meaning the first woman of color director in an institution. And every now and then I ran into a woman or a person of color in a department at the institution who looked at me like I was a unicorn; and they came up to me and invariably put their hand on my shoulder or arm, or took my hand and, with eyes full of emotion, they said, "I love your freckles" or "I love your hair." And I just smiled and replied, "thank you"; and then we chatted about what they do in the building.

As a person of color, I knew what these statements meant—it was someone saying, "I'm so glad to see someone who, in some way, looks like me here in leadership." I knew that they were rooting for me. And, to be honest, that was not always the case with the rest of the staff. Because often I was hired by a new artistic director trying to change the way that the institution had been doing business or hiring, and I was on the front line of that change. So there may have been hostility or the sense that I was some sort of "diversity hire" and that I was going to screw it up or be incompetent (because that is often the perception of "diversity hires"). In these situations, I was always navigating two tiers of exchange—the "I love your freckles/I love your hair" exchange and the "you better prove it to us" exchange.

This past year something changed. (And my story now includes directing film and television as well.) The same people who, ten years ago, would have come up to me and said, "I love your freckles"—someone in accounting in a production office, or a production assistant—now comes up to me, takes my hand, or put their hand on my shoulder or my forearm, and they say, "I am so happy that you are here, it is so exciting—representation matters." What that means to me is that, now, more and more, people have the language to express the joy, pride, and solidarity that these individuals felt when ten years ago they said, "I love your freckles." Now there is actual, specific language they can use—"It is so important that you are here—representation matters." And it matters enough that they will come up to a stranger and express it.

I find it encouraging, this level of sophistication that we are finding in terminology—and our ability to dissect how bias functions as well as the behavior of people who are in positions of power. Because we have language now that is widely available like "white fragility," "toxic masculinity," "settler colonialism," and other nuanced language that is so powerful as we gather forces for our movement.

Thinking about the phrase "the welcome table" and the wonderful chapters in this book, I am struck by how incredibly important it is to let people know about the long history and legacy of the work of creating equity in US theater. For many of us, when we are in the thick of creating theater or even just entering into the field, it can feel like there is so much to change and that we are starting from scratch and doing it alone. And we can forget that there are many people who have come before us and done really transformative work.

We also have to be rigorous about this work—none of us is exempt from doing it. And there is a certain amount of humility and discomfort that we have to embrace. It requires learning new language, thinking differently—one can feel on the defensive, that it is too much. Yes, it can be uncomfortable; but change is uncomfortable. And it is also uncomfortable to feel like you do not know, or to feel like you are out of step. But the solution to that is to get in step—and the way to do that is to listen …

Change is currently happening through what artists on the ground are doing everywhere. That is how people in power shift casting, hiring, and programming practices; they learn from artists. We who are on the ground, making demands, are leading the grassroots movements in our field. The reason so many of us are tired and feel as if we need to step away is because being active participants in a grassroots struggle is a serious undertaking and requires life force. I regularly find myself spending extra time with the publicity, education, and marketing departments to contextualize my work—and that means many more meetings, outreach events, interviews, and radio spots to make sure there is a broad representation of the city in which I am working in the audience. All of this work takes time that is not directing the play. For those of us who approach our work in the theater with a commitment to community, it feels like we are doing three jobs, and that we have been doing three jobs for many years. Sometimes theaters are so open and excited about these efforts; and sometimes not. The challenge is how to make people care about something they don't care about—equitable representation on the stage and in the audience—but that is central to the survival of our art-form and the field.

Being the vanguard of changing your field is the same as being the vanguard of changing society—it requires that much commitment and mental, physical, and psychic energy. Burnout is a real issue. Figuring out how to make our field sustainable for everyone is the biggest challenge of this moment. And the most important change that is happening now in the US theater, in my opinion, is the number of people of color and women running theaters and becoming producers—at least those leaders who are rigorously studying questions of dismantling white supremacy in the workplace. That is how the table becomes welcome. People must be questioning what they understand to be the status quo on a daily basis in a meaningful way. So many people in the theater think of themselves as progressive and the "good people," but their programming, casting, and hiring processes, to those of us on the ground, say something very different.

We as a field cannot dismantle a complex system that is embedded in every part of the art form and our lives—from our training to our practices—if we are not willing to look at the structures and systems that we have been supporting for decades. There are so many more ways to open ourselves up and investigate our own biases in the twenty-first century. Until people do this critical work and look within themselves and their communities for honest rigorous exchange about equity and access, there is not going to be systemic change, meaning equitable access and opportunity for all.

We can't take this progress for granted—I now understand that I did not experience a "feeling" when I experienced racism—I actually experienced racism. We now have more resources to identify the structures in place that are racist, sexist, ableist, classist, and/or homophobic. There is going to be a relentless wave of change, and every step we take to craft the field that we want has history and innovation—the chapters in this book help to document the breadth of that progress and that we are not alone in this work. Welcome, everyone, to the table of your US theater—you are not guests; all this belongs to you.

Introduction

Claire Syler

In this book, Daniel Banks and I bring together US-based actors, directors, educators, playwrights, and scholars to ask:

> *What are the many ways theater practitioners can think about casting to provide more access to opportunity and broader representation on our stages, and what are the politics of these choices?*

Implicit in this question is an aspirational premise. We suggest that casting is a way to invite more people to the table so that the full breadth of US identities can be reflected onstage. This premise also suggests that casting is inherently a political act. Because an actor's embodied presence both communicates a dramatic narrative and evokes cultural assumptions associated with skin color, gender, sexuality, and ability, casting choices are never neutral. Like the contributors of this book, our goal is to expand the theater beyond its bias towards dominant cultural groups, which include, but are not limited to, Eurocentric, able-bodied, and male-dominated narratives.

The origins of this anthology reside in an article, a partnership, and a desire to create a resource for all those interested in casting. In 2013, co-editor Daniel Banks wrote "The Welcome Table: Casting for an Integrated Society" for *Theatre Topics* (Banks 2013). The article offers a re-viewing of the terms, ideas, and practices that often define casting in US theater. Drawing on sociological and historical research, as well as his professional directing experience, Daniel identifies how the dominant discourses surrounding casting (e.g. "non-traditional casting" or "color-blind casting") often undermine practitioners' progressive aims. To develop the dialogue, Daniel proposes the notion of a "welcome table"—a space where artists of all cultural backgrounds can come together as equals to discuss casting as it relates to varying communities and contexts.

As a theater academic, I teach, direct, and help to plan university theater seasons; I also research the relationship between casting and undergraduates' emerging racial-ethnic identity development (Syler with Chen 2017). Prior to my academic role, I was the education director of the Nashville Shakespeare Festival. Working in a canonical medium in a Southern US city helped me to understand the criticality of casting. When casting a production of *Macbeth* that would tour rural Tennessee, for example, our company considered the different meanings that body forth from the title character's casting. Given the South's history of violence towards Black men, to cast an African American actor as the murderous Macbeth could contribute to stereotypical depictions of Black men as "threatening." But, alternatively, why should actors of African heritage be kept from performing an iconic, challenging, and career-building role? Furthermore, could Macbeth's representation be re-contextualized by the casting of Lady Macbeth, Banquo, and Duncan? Questions like these compelled me to study casting.

In 2016 Daniel and I partnered to convene a panel anchored by "The Welcome Table" at the Association for Theatre in Higher Education conference in Chicago.[1] Our proposal asked panelists to discuss the opportunities, challenges, and successes they encountered when inviting artists to a welcome table. The session was well-attended and the panelists relayed rich case studies of practice.[2] Contributor Ann Elizabeth Armstrong, for instance, detailed fourteen years of casting and devised performance work at Miami University, which she described as "confronting white hegemony on campus." Other speakers discussed how casting can be employed to draw attention to cultural contexts, defy stereotypes, and engage audiences in conversations concerning representation. Collectively, the panelists' case studies challenged engrained assumptions that casting is largely an apolitical, instinct-driven practice—similar to what contributor Brian Herrera calls "the mythos of casting," which is sure to deliver "the best actor for the role" (Herrera 2015a, 1).

The audience's response to the panel was energetic; questions and comments kept coming long after the panel should have concluded: "How can I introduce my colleagues to these ideas?" "What if the audience is resistant?" "How have students responded?" It was as if the panelists' case studies compelled our colleagues in attendance to map their own experiences, contexts, and goals onto the performance examples, allowing the dialogue to flow freely. The panel struck a chord, perhaps because the panelists shared a commitment to employ casting in critical and intentional ways.

Building on these efforts, Daniel and I set out to create a resource for individuals who, like the panel audience, want to discuss casting as it relates to access and equity. To develop the richest text possible, we believed that casting should be explored from a range of cultural perspectives, as different communities have different priorities and histories of (mis)representation. Additionally, we wanted a variety of artistic perspectives—actors, directors, educators, playwrights, and scholars—to speak to casting practices from their professional contexts and standpoints. Here, we took the notion of dialogue seriously. We encouraged each contributor to write in a register that was most familiar to them and, to emulate the turn-taking of conversation, we designed a dialogic structure for the anthology.

This book is composed of seven multi-voiced parts. For consistency, each part features the same format:

- A *prologue* briefly poses an idea related to performance and casting.
- A *case study* thickly describes a casting project or scenario.
- An *epilogue* contextualizes a historical or theoretical idea embedded in the case study.

In general, the prologues are personal and immediate; the case studies tell a story and theory of practice; and the epilogues extend key points from the case studies in a kind of dramaturgical baton-pass. Interestingly, while each part presents a linear conversation, the dialogue-driven processes that gave rise to each part were more circuitous. Case study authors wrote first and shared their initial drafts with prologue and epilogue authors who wrote in response. The dialogic structure of this book aligns with its broader premise to welcome more people to the table. Through dialogue, multiple perspectives can be heard, ideas can be revised, and new terms can be drafted. Dialogue can propel movement.

Movement building

Discussions focused on the political and economic stakes of casting in US theater are not new.[3] Across the book's seven parts, the contributors reference a range of discourses and cultural events—some generated *by* the field of theater (e.g. August Wilson's 1996 speech "The Ground on Which I Stand") and others that happened *to* the field of theater (e.g. September 11, 2001)— all of which have influenced casting and representation in US performance. In an attempt to trace *some* of the formative antecedents referenced throughout this book, the following timeline (Table I.1) identifies key events when theater workers took action to change casting practices. Not meant to be comprehensive, the timeline begins at a mid-twentieth century moment when desegregation—and the possibilities of integration—begins to reshape cultural institutions.[4] These are some of the actions upon which our movement builds.

These events demonstrate concerted, longstanding efforts made by theater artists working from a range of cultural perspectives to expand casting practices in US theater. Put together, they represent what scholar of social movements Suzanne Staggenborg (2016, 4) calls a "repertoire of collective action" joined by a common purpose to de-center dominant casting practices. Building on these and other events, this book brings together multiple stakeholders from varying facets of the theater community to discuss common goals and particular concerns related to casting. As a resource-driven text, it seeks to frame and mobilize a social movement focused on casting, access, and representation.

The title of Daniel's article and the phrase used throughout this book, "the welcome table," offers our movement a framing perspective with multiple meanings. First, it proposes a communal space where people of all cultures, backgrounds, and histories can sit together as equals. Next, it offers a flexible form. Whether it is in the shape of this book, a conference panel, a theater audience, or a production meeting, a welcome table can be formed any place theater artists meet to discuss casting as a way to invite more people to the table in critical and intentional ways. Finally, every welcome table teeters between the past and the future. Conversations about casting should consider past performance traditions so that future practice might responsively (re)shape ideas. Daniel's essay provides an example of this kind of historical situatedness. Since the article's publication in 2013, new events in the casting timeline have transpired and new political climates have unfolded. To sit together at a welcome table is to be aware of the ever-changing landscape to which performance responds and with which it partakes.

Setting the table

There are multiple ways to engage *Casting a Movement*. Readers are invited to chart their own paths through the book parts, setting their own tables along the way. As mentioned previously, each part features a dialogic format—a prologue, case study, and epilogue written by different authors.

Part I, "Culturally Conscious Casting," examines how casting can be an intentionally interpretative practice. Ayanna Thompson's prologue encourages an expansive understanding of culturally conscious casting in classical performance, arguing that casting practices can have bearing upon audience development and actor training. Director Justin Emeka's case study extends many of these ideas by relaying production examples of *Macbeth* and *Death of a Salesman,* wherein he cast actors of color in roles originally imagined for white performers. In an epilogue, Brian Herrera examines how, despite the advent of "integrated" and later culturally conscious casting in the second half of the twentieth century, contemporary theater is frequently "white washed" with actors of European heritage performing roles not intended for white characters.

Part II, "Approaches to Casting Middle Eastern American Theater," discusses casting and Middle Eastern American performance. In his prologue, playwright Yussef El-Guindi challenges the US theater's reception of Middle Eastern-focused plays and critiques the emphasis placed on "authenticity" when it comes to casting characters of Middle Eastern heritage. Torange Yeghiazarian continues these themes in a case study that describes why she founded Golden Thread Productions, the US's first professional company dedicated to the Middle East as a whole. Yeghiazarian details the multiple features considered when casting actors to perform in the company's signature offering, the ReOrient Festival of short plays. Michael Malek Najjar's epilogue concludes the part with a powerful discussion of five factors that shape the representation, casting, and performance of Middle Eastern characters onstage and on screen.

Table 1.1 Actions to expand casting practices in US theater.

1956	New York Shakespeare Festival initiates "integrated casting" featuring multiethnic casts (see "The Welcome Table," Banks 2013)
1959	Actors' Equity Association sponsors the first "Integration Showcase" (Chapter 3)
1968	The Oriental Actors of America picket and submit legal cases against the use of yellowface in NYC productions (Chapter 18)
1968	The Non-Traditional Casting Project (NTCP) is established to identify and find solutions for issues of inequity and racism in theater, film, and television (Banks 2013; Chapter 3)
1989	The Other Voices Project, dedicated to training disabled theater artists, is established at the Mark Taper Forum Theatre in Los Angeles (Chapter 9)
1991	*Miss Saigon* premieres on Broadway and protests erupt as white actor Jonathan Pryce performs the role of the Engineer, who is of mixed Vietnamese and French heritage, in yellowface (Chapter 3; Chapter 17)
1992	Performing across gender and ethnic identities, Anna Deavere Smith's *Twilight: Los Angeles, 1992* opens at the Mark Taper Forum in Los Angeles (Chapter 17; Chapter 18)
1992	Ping Chong + Company begins *Undesireable Elements*, an ongoing, community-specific performance project exploring the identities of individuals who live outside of the US's dominant culture (Chapter 21)
1994	Native Voices begins as a place for Native playwrights to gather and develop new work at Illinois State University (Chapter 14; Chapter 15)
1996	August Wilson delivers "The Ground on Which I Stand" and decries "colorblind casting" (Banks 2013; Chapter 2; Chapter 6)
2006	The NTCP changes its name to the Alliance for Inclusion in the Arts (Banks 2013)
2011	Asian American Performers Action Coalition (AAPAC) is founded (Banks 2013)
2015	*Hamilton: An American Musical* opens on Broadway with a cast of Black and Brown actors performing the US's white "founding fathers" (Chapter 18)

Part III, "Casting and Disability Culture," considers how disability is and is not represented onstage and in the media. Disability advocate and actor Christine Bruno begins the conversation by discussing a key contradiction—the high number of disabled people in the US and the relative lack of disabled actors represented in performance. Scholar and activist Carrie Sandahl develops this premise by identifying how disability often functions dramaturgically as a device to be solved or cured, rather than depicted as cultural experience; Sandahl concludes her case study by offering theater makers considerations when casting performers with disabilities. Victoria Lewis's epilogue draws on her rich professional experience as a performer, writer, and scholar whose career has consistently created space for disability on professional stages as well as in university settings.

Part IV, "Casting and Multilingual Performance," examines casting in the context of a multilingual production of Caridad Svich's play *The Orphan Sea* at

Skidmore College. In her prologue, Svich poetically introduces the Odysseus myth her play is based upon—a tale about language, movement, and shifting identities. Eunice Ferreira's case study describes how, as the play's director, she set a "global welcome table" by casting multilingual Skidmore students who opened up linguistic borders through performance. Ann Elizabeth Armstrong's epilogue, in turn, identifies the "emergent strategies" undergirding Ferreira's casting, rehearsal, and production processes—work that resonates with Armstrong's own community-based performance efforts at Miami University.

Part V, "Casting Contemporary Native American Theater," explores casting and contemporary Indigenous theater making. Performance artist Ty Defoe (*Giizhig*) begins the dialogue with a personal meditation on place, identity, and self-knowledge experienced through performance. In a case study, Jean Bruce Scott and Randy Reinholz (Choctaw) discuss co-creating Native Voices at the Autry, a twenty-five-year-old professional theater company "devoted to developing and producing new works for the stage by Native American, Alaska Native, and First Nations playwrights" and offer readers important ideas concerning the company's approach to casting and Native self-identification (Autry Museum n.d.). Like the performance work created at Native Voices at the Autry, Courtney Elkin Mohler's (Santa Barbara Chumash) epilogue theorizes how "Indigenous theatrical praxis" is a force of decolonization in a nation organized by settler colonialism.

Part VI, "Subverting Stereotypes," investigates how cross-racial casting can identify and critique stereotypes. In her prologue, Mei Ann Teo poses questions concerning who should tell certain cultural stories and stresses the importance of including cultural knowledge bearers in production processes. Dorinne Kondo's case study picks up these ideas by theorizing the creative labor and creative vision at work in high-profile productions that feature cross-racial and cross-gender performance, such as Anna Deavere Smith's *Twilight: Los Angeles, 1992* and David Henry Hwang's *Yellow Face*. Historicizing the politics of casting, Donatella Galella's epilogue helps to explain the cultural impact of cross-racial casting, as well as the power dynamics always at play in such work.

Part VII, "Casting Across Identities," discusses the rigors of casting actors to perform across identities in the context of a multi-site performance project conceived by Ping Chong and Talvin Wilks—*Collidescope: Adventures in Pre- and Post-Racial America*. Playwright Elaine Ávila begins the part with a reflection on the hybridity of identity, often lodged in language, song, geography, and performance. In a case study, Priscilla Page describes how staging *Collidescope 2.0* at UMass Amherst in Spring 2016 contributed to a campus program designed to honor the region's "Art, Legacy, & Community." Brandi Wilkins Catanese's epilogue analyzes the performance work undertaken at UMass Amherst, putting it in conversation with the aspirational ethos of the welcome table.

The book concludes with an afterword by co-editor, Daniel Banks, who reminds readers to attend critically to language. Oftentimes, for those engaged in social justice efforts, a leader's language serves to build the welcome table model of collaborative consensus building and power sharing. This language, then, deserves attention. Are there terms or phrases that need to be revised or omitted all together? The afterword also offers readers a series of generative themes that ripple across the contributors' varying discussions of casting. These themes provide a powerful synthesis of the book's chapters, emphasizing concerns that deal with cultural competency, intersectionality, and histories of representation.

As the conversations staged throughout this book seek to make clear, there is no single way to practice casting. The shifting contextual, cultural, and material variables of each casting scenario shape its various enactments. What can unify disparate acts, however, is a collective desire to deploy casting (and its conferment of power and access) in ways that critically and intentionally confront our field's historical biases. The contributors in this book demonstrate how the material outcomes of such casting approaches are likely to operate at varying grain sizes of activity—from interpersonal relationship-building to the creation of new companies to shifts in established theaters' season selections or leaders. Collectively, we are creating change. Collectively, we are casting a movement. Will you join us at the table?

Notes

1   Under the Strategic Planning Committee, this panel was the first of a two-part series on casting, both of which relied on "The Welcome Table" as an organizing frame. Daniel and I co-convened the first panel, "Casting as Critical Practice, Part 1: Working with a Welcome Table." Dr. David Peterson organized the second panel, "Casting as Critical Practice, Part 2: Putting Bodies to Work."
2   The panelists included Ann Elizabeth Armstrong, Elizabeth Brown-Guillory, Kathryn Ervin, Eunice S. Ferreira, and Lisa Jackson-Schebetta. Daniel and I co-moderated.
3   Many of the book's contributors have written important texts that examine casting and representation; see, for example, Ayanna Thompson's *Colorblind Shakespeare* (Thompson 2006), Brandi Wilkins Catanese's *The Problem of the Color[blind]* (Catanese 2011), Brian Herrera's *Latin Numbers* (Herrera 2015b), and Donatella Gallela's *America in the Round* (Gallela 2019).
4   Officially, the US military desegregated in 1948 and the US educational system desegregated in 1954.

Bibliography

Armstrong, Ann Elizabeth. 2016. "Confronting White Hegemony on Campus." Paper presented at ATHE, Chicago, IL, August.
Autry Museum. n.d. "About Native Voices." Accessed January 9, 2019. https://theautry.org/events/signature-programs/native-voices/about-native-voices
Banks, Daniel. 2013. "The Welcome Table: Casting for an Integrated Society." *Theatre Topics*, 23(1) (March): 1–18.
Catanese, Brandi Wilkins. 2011. *The Problem of the Color[blind]: Racial Transgression and the Politics of Black Performance*. Ann Arbor, MI: University of Michigan Press.
Gallela, Donatella. 2019. *America in the Round: Capital, Race, and Nation at Washington DC's Arena Stage*. Iowa City, IA: University of Iowa Press.

Herrera, Brian Eugenio. 2015a. "The Best Actor for the Role, or the Mythos of Casting in American Popular Performance." *Journal of American Drama and Theatre*, 27(2): 1–11.

—. 2015b. *Latin Numbers: Playing Latino in Twentieth-Century in US Popular Performance*. Ann Arbor, MI: University of Michigan Press.

Staggenborg, Suzanne. 2015. *Social Movements*. New York: Oxford University Press.

Syler, Claire, with Anna Chen. 2017. "Casting Youth/Developing Identity: Casting and Racial and Ethnic Identity Development." *Youth Theatre Journal* 31(2): 92–104.

Thompson, Ayanna. 2006. *Colorblind Shakespeare: New Perspectives on Race and Performance*. New York: Routledge.

The welcome table: Casting for an integrated society

Daniel Banks

> I'm gonna sit at the welcome table
> I'm gonna sit at the welcome table one of these days, Halleluyah
> I'm gonna sit at the welcome table
> Gonna sit at the welcome table one of these days.
>
> —Spiritual

James Baldwin titled his unfinished, final play *The Welcome Table*, describing legendary performer Josephine Baker's home and her practice of adopting young people of all backgrounds, cultures, and ethnicities into her family.[1] As I complete work on this essay in November 2012, several events coincide, confirming that it is a significant moment to be reexamining questions of representation and plurality in US theater. First, President Barack Obama was reelected due, in part, to the overwhelming support of African American (93%), Asian American (73%), and Latino (71%) voters (Robinson 2012). In addition, both the Theatre Communications Group (TCG), the "national organization for the American theater," and the Actors' Equity Association (AEA), the professional union for stage actors, have launched initiatives to explore this topic. The TCG held its Fall Forum on Governance titled "Leading the Charge" because, as Executive Director Teresa Eyring explains, the organization "decided that we must bring trustees and theater leadership more deeply into a thought process around diversity and how we make concrete strides in thought and practice—as individuals, as organizations, and as an artistic ecosystem."[2] And, in the lead article on the front page of its October/November newsletter, the AEA reasserts its commitment to "access" and "opportunity," both artistically and legally, having participated in the twentieth Federation of Actors World Congress in September where the topic was discussed in depth. The Broadway League has also introduced an EEO (Equal Employment Opportunity) committee to examine hiring practices across the industry (McColl 2012). There is clearly a renewed commitment to making US theater more of a welcome table, with room and food enough for all.

I propose that the first step in a sustainable future for our beloved profession and art lies in reexamining the terminology that defines contemporary practices.

In some cases, this language serves as an obstacle to more complex narratives about US society; in other cases, the words are misnomers. I have great respect for the work done in the arenas of "non-traditional" and "color-blind" casting; at the same time, I have concerns about the continued use of these and similar terms. Although the introduction of these concepts ignited a crucial process of change in the industry, the terms themselves have now ossified a collective imaginary within the theater, which works against their original progressive intentions and inhibits practices from changing. In this essay, I will discuss the current language used in US theater casting, cite examples of work that defy the assumptions embedded in that language, and propose strategies for engaging audiences in dialogue around these important sociological concerns. By troubling the authority of this language, I hope to create even greater possibilities for casting, while shifting a national dialogue around identity and identification.

Fictions

> Your fictions become history.
>
> —Barbara Kruger (1983)

The AEA introduced the language of non-traditional casting because, as Harry Newman, founder of the Non-Traditional Casting Project (NTCP), writes: "A four-year study … completed in January 1986 revealed that over 90 percent of all the professional theater produced in this country—from stock and dinner theater to the avant-garde to Broadway—was staged with all-Caucasian casts" (Newman 1989, 23). In the past twenty-six years, these numbers have not improved significantly. The Asian American Performers Action Coalition (AAPAC) was founded in 2011 to "expand the perception of Asian American performers in order to increase their access to and representation on New York City's stages" (Bandhu 2012, 36). In a five-year study of 493 shows in the New York area from the 2006–2007 to the 2010–2011 seasons, the AAPAC discovered that 80 percent of all shows were cast with European heritage actors.[3]

Regrettably, many of the challenges that the NTCP worked hard to address still exist, as evidenced by these numbers and several high-profile casting controversies during the past few years.[4] For the purposes of this essay I focus on the aspects of so-called "non-traditional" casting pertaining to actors of color, often referred to as "mixed-race," "cross-race," "race-blind" or "color-blind," and "race-conscious" casting. No less important, however, are questions of gender and ability, which similarly need to be addressed.

In *Ways of Seeing*, John Berger writes that "[t]he way we see things is affected by what we know or what we believe … We never look at just one thing; we are always looking at the relation between things and ourselves" (Berger 1972, 8–9). Thus what a person sees—or thinks they see—is based on how that individual knows the world.[5] The language they then use to represent that worldview both describes their conception of the world while simultaneously codifying it—as linguist J. L. Austin writes, "By saying something we do something" (Austin 1962, 94). The reproduction, or performance, of this understanding is, as Judith Butler writes, the "ritualized repetition" of certain social norms, which impacts the ways identities are culturally apprehended (Butler 1993, 2). It is through the "forcible reiteration" of these "hegemonic norms" on both societal and theatrical stages that identities, and hence beliefs, are "produced" (2, 107).

This theory of "performativity" is directly connected to how in the West we "know" race via the writings of Swedish botanist Carl Linnaeus (1707–78) and German anthropologist Johann Blumenbach (1752–1840). These individuals created arbitrary systems of racial classification that have infused today's language with their biases about the different "humors," or attributes, of peoples across the planet and where they fit into a supposed hierarchy of humanity.[5] In order to create lasting change in the national imaginary of "race," the premise behind these eighteenth-century belief systems needs to be exposed and reevaluated.

Today's scientists contest the authority of race as a discourse or fact. Professor of evolutionary biology Joseph Graves states that, due to constant "gene flow" over human history, there is no "biological rationale" for the argument that people belong to different races. He explains that "[p]ossibly only six genes determine the color of a person's skin out of between 30,000 and 40,000" (Graves, quoted in Villarosa 2002). Thus there is arguably more in-group DNA difference in hair or eye color than between groups based on skin color, despite the ways in which many cultures have focused on skin tone as the determining classificatory feature.

In addition, although contemporary sociology has demonstrated "race" to be a social construction, the term continues to have currency.[6] An over-reliance on a discourse of "race" results in a conflation of such concepts as culture, ethnicity, color, class, and heritage. Because of the continued discussion of race in US society, *racialism* (accepting and acting according to a system of so-called racial difference) and *racism* (discrimination according to presumed race, often based on appearance) are ever present. Newman writes of the US theater in 1986, evoking today's challenges: "Since so much of our knowledge, understanding, and compassion for the world is shaped by theater, film, and television, the absence of full and satisfying roles (in the largest meaning of the word) for these disenfranchised artists has had the insidious effect of reinforcing a view of a homogeneous American society that has never been more than a fantasy" (Newman 1989, 23). Unequal casting perpetuates sociological and biological fictions, which create a form of "law" in the cultural imaginary. However, the language often used to challenge these fictions operates within the same system of racialist assumptions and biases. Therefore, in order to avoid perpetuating misperceptions, the theater needs to change its language. And, as language changes, thought and practice can expand.

Language

Although the terms "nontraditional casting" and "color-blind casting" are used widely in US theater, their efficacy is limited. Ayanna Thompson, in *Colorblind Shakespeare,* writes that the "theoretical underpinnings" of color-blind casting are "unstable" (Thompson 2006, 6) because, as she challenges: "What constitutes a blindness to race?" (11), suggesting that it is not possible to overlook a person's heritage. Jocelyn Brown, in her talk at the 2012 Black Theatre Network conference in Atlanta, explains that "the phrase [color-blind casting] has mushroomed to enormous proportions. Use of the term has become problematic. To complicate matters further, much of what is labeled color-blind theater is, in actuality, color-conscious theater" (Brown 2012, 3). Unless productions do as most major symphony orchestras and audition people behind a curtain, color-blind casting is neither possible nor desirable.

Similar to Thompson, veteran theater director Clinton Turner Davis, in "Non-Traditional Casting: An Open Letter," challenges:

> This strategy of avoiding race—"I don't care if you are black, brown, white, yellow, red, green, or purple; I try to get along with everybody," or "When I look at you, I don't see color ..." embeds meaningful differences among non-meaningful ones. When was the last time you saw a purple person?
> (Davis 1997)

To erase color is to erase identity and legacy; to recognize and appreciate our differences is to know and honor one another's histories and stories.[7]

Brown advocates, as I do, for a more complex casting practice—building an integrated cast of actors from multiple ethnic backgrounds. This approach, Brown explains, "allows practitioners to assist society in imagining a multi-representation of cultures, to impact world views, and it allows for collaboration through balanced artistic cultural exchange" (Brown 2012, 11). With a more complex understanding of history and sociology (especially one that does not conflate color, culture, ethnicity, and class), more casting options are available, and thus an audience is reminded or informed of the multiple intersecting narratives of our society. This shift in focus is not about being "color blind" or "color conscious"; rather, it is a commitment to, as the AAPAC states, "reflect[ing] the racial diversity of the real world we live in" (Bandhu 2012, 36).

The term "nontraditional casting" has a different challenge. The NTCP opened its doors in 1986 to advocate for the non-traditional casting policy introduced by the AEA:

> To address the lack of participation of their black, Hispanic, Asian, and native American [*sic*] membership, AE conceived of non-traditional

casting, which they formally defined as the casting of ethnic and female performers in roles where race, ethnicity, or gender are not germane to the character's or play's development. (The NTCP later expanded this definition to include performers with disabilities.)

(Newman 1989, 24)

The NTCP's work and services were critical in expanding opportunities for marginalized theater artists and exposing audiences to a broader vision for theater in the United States. The organization's industry-changing activism includes hosting symposia and meetings, out of which emerged compelling documentation of theater workers' experiences, and maintaining "artist files"—a database used widely by the theater, film, and television industries. Nevertheless, Newman concedes:

Although there are drawbacks to the phrase, we at the NTCP adopted it as part of our title because it had already gained a measure of currency in the industry and because it seemed provocative … Our organizational goal is obsolescence … In time we hope that—like our organization—the phrase will disappear, and 'non-traditional' casting will become the performing arts' new tradition.

(Newman 1989, 24)

The NTCP did, in fact, change its name in 2006 to the Alliance for Inclusion in the Arts (AIA). Executive Director Sharon Jensen explains that

we believed the new name better reflected the scope of our work and mission. For example, even though since 1990 we had seen the issues of diversity and inclusion as comprehensive (meaning affecting not only casting and the consideration of a diverse pool of actors, but also extending to writers, directors, designers, the artistic leadership and staffing of theaters, boards of directors, and audiences), many did not understand this about us and still thought we were focused solely on issues of casting. Virtually overnight, with our new name, theater, film and television professionals had an expanded and accurate understanding of our work.[8]

While the AIA continues to advocate for all artists in the performing and media arts, it is no longer tethered to the notion of non-traditional casting, which, as Angela Pao, in *No Safe Spaces: Re-casting Race, Ethnicity, and Nationality in American Theater*, explains "relies on and reinforces conceptions of racial categories that are defined by visual and visible distinctions" (Pao 2010, 178). To illustrate this latter point, I offer a few examples that, rather than perpetuating the fiction and impermeability of notions of "race," stage a more complex conversation about identity.

Expectations

I first found myself formally discussing non-traditional casting on a panel at New York University in 1997 after my production there of Marc Blitzstein's *The Cradle Will Rock*. [9] Although the panel had "nontraditional casting" in its title, I explained that such casting was neither my intention nor what I had actually done, even though the cast was from a broad range of ethnicities. For example, people questioned my casting an African heritage actor as Mr. Mister and European heritage-looking actors as his children (Mrs. Mister was played by an actor of South Asian Indian heritage). Viewers, by which I mean both audience members and people involved in production (extrapolating from Thompson's formulation "the sociology of viewing," discussed below), calling this "nontraditional casting" raised several important issues. First, I repeatedly received the comment that there would be no African American in Mr. Mister's position as a successful businessman in the 1930s. However, this analysis is historically inaccurate. There has long been an African American bourgeoisie in the United States. In addition, predating the original production of *Cradle* by ten years, Franklin Delano Roosevelt relied on his "Black Cabinet" of appointed advisors comprised of university presidents, lawyers, ministers, and businessmen. Blitzstein intended that the play have an ethnically mixed cast, which is how it was cast by Orson Welles and John Houseman in its first iteration in 1937 (albeit only some members of the chorus were of color) (Gordon 1989, 137–138). These facts are important pieces of American history that defy certain racialist assumptions.

Nor was my casting strategy "color-blind" or "color conscious." Thompson invokes the "sociology of viewing" (Thompson 2006, 12) to describe, as Berger does, that specific beliefs influence the way people see. I did not attempt to make a statement by my choice of actor for Mr. Mister. Blitzstein himself did not designate ethnicity or color in the script and, to me, this actor was an appropriate historical choice, as well as the best actor who auditioned for the part. The "sociology of viewing" reveals that "truth" or "realism" in casting is actually only relative to an individual's personal experience of the world.

Along these lines, the second misperception about my casting of *Cradle* was that an African heritage man would not have European heritage-looking children. The variety of skin tone within one family has been explored throughout history, notably in James Weldon Johnson's *Autobiography of an Ex-Colored Man* (1912); *Passing* by Nella Larsen (1929); Langston Hughes's poetry, short fiction, and plays; and in numerous publications since. [10] However, different cultural and ethnic groups have differing experiences of this spectrum of familial skin color, while oftentimes unproblematically accepting the variety of eye or hair color. This divergence in sociological experience and viewing, therefore, made my casting choices seem experimental or "unrealistic" to some viewers—what Newman calls "you don't conform to my expectations" (Newman 1989, 33)—while familiar and "realistic" to others.

I received similar reactions to my casting an African heritage actor in the role of the supposedly Jewish protagonist of Max Frisch's *Andorra* in 1993. *Andorra* is a parable about fascism, an allegorical text set in a fictitious place (albeit of a real name). What some people had difficulty believing was that, according to the conceit of the narrative, this particular actor could be viewed as Jewish (a misperception of the ethnic plurality of a world religion). Ironically, a week before opening, the actor cast as Andri for his skill and stature among his peers revealed that he was biologically Jewish, even though that was not how he self-identified. My goal in this production, also with a multiethnic cast, was to create theater that would invite as many people as possible to the "welcome table"—especially an audience that is as eager as I am to see the complexity of our society on the stage. And the choice of individuals cast made perfect sense to me conceptually and sociologically, based on my own cultural experiences.

I offer two other examples that reveal the limitations of current casting language given the semiotics of today's ethno-social realities:

1   Using the current nomenclature, how would casting actor Wentworth Miller from *Prison Break*, whose father is African heritage, be characterized in the following roles: Othello? Happy in *Death of a Salesman*? Or Lymon in *The Piano Lesson*? Is any of these examples non-traditional or color-blind casting?

2   In her autobiography *Just Lucky I Guess*, published in 2002 when she was 81 years old, Carol Channing revealed that her grandmother was African heritage. Therefore it might seem that casting an African heritage actress as Dolly Levi in the stage version of *Hello Dolly* is, in fact, the most "traditional" choice for the US stage. However, when Pearl Bailey played the role to great acclaim on Broadway from 1967 to 1969, the production was recast with an African heritage cast to "make sense" of Bailey in the role, and productions do not generally cast Dolly in this way.[11]

In the above two examples, the casting issue becomes not just the actor's heritage, but the actor's appearance. In fact, in creating its report, the AAPAC had to rely on a similar logic to collect data: demographics were determined by "visual observation," unless "interviews, articles or bios online showed evidence of self-identification with another racial or ethnic group even when that racial identity was not readily apparent" (Bandhu 2012, 34). What this ultimately means is that its casting data point predominantly to the lack of Asian-, African-, Hispanic-, Native American-, and Arab heritage-*looking* actors on the New York stage.

Since "USers" live in a multiethnic society, we cannot rely on the visual to know a person's identity, or, more importantly, how they identify.[12] The visual sign is only as accurate as the person reading it. The inability to determine an actor's cultural and/or ethnic heritage based on their appearance demonstrates that the notion of race is a conflation and assumption of the impermeable linkage of visual identifiers and heritage. How "non-traditional" or "color-blind" would a production with actors of color be considered if audiences could not read the actors as being from historically marginalized groups? This lack of legibility of identity illustrates Thompson's point about the "instability" of race and means that language based on a system of racialism is no longer practicable. The next step is initiating a dialogue with audiences to provide accurate historical information about the stories being told and to introduce new language to describe their sociologies.

Rethinking tradition

Audience members questioning casting choices that do not conform to their own societal expectations is an understandable concern for theaters on both philosophical and economic levels. Jack Marshall, artistic director of the American Century Theatre in Arlington, Virginia, worries that so-called non-traditional casting practices risk "sacrificing the audience's enjoyment and understanding of a show to political objectives" (Marshall 2007). Similarly, a patron of Trinity Rep in Providence, Rhode Island, suggests that color-blind casting "interferes with the believability of the story" and wants casting to make "biological sense." Certain casting choices in *A Christmas Carol* "distracted" her, and she opines that Trinity Rep is "so blind to race that they defy science" (quoted in Lonati 2012). The process of change in US theater and society will advance as institutions continue to work with audiences to negotiate their ambivalences and misperceptions. Might audience members have a different response if they understood that these choices were not experimental practices, but an actual representation of their own society?

The history of casting Shakespeare on the US stage serves as a valuable example of the ways in which current casting language, such as "non-traditional casting," has created sociological fictions that cause confusion for viewers. For example, the African Grove Theatre was founded in New York City in 1821 while the practice of chattel slavery was still legal in New York State. The company of African heritage artists is especially known for its performances of Shakespeare. The first professional European heritage production of Shakespeare in the United States is usually cited as Thomas Kean's *Richard III* in 1750 (Boardman and Hischak 2004, 560). There were thus approximately only seventy-one years in US history of Shakespeare being performed solely by European heritage actors and, as of this writing, 191 years of actors of African heritage performing Shakespeare. The word "traditional" indexes something that is in the very body and history of the country. Actors of color performing Shakespeare on the US stage are thus an integral part of US theater tradition.

How then to inform audiences both productively and creatively as to the histories that may expand their sociologies of viewing? The Alliance Theatre in Atlanta has worked to transform its audience members' experiences and expectations by enjoining all of its staff members to think about audience engagement. Artistic Director Susan Booth explains that

> We've always been a theater of and for its community, and we can only achieve that aim through rigorous dialogue with as full a cohort of our community as possible. The resulting difference is shared ownership of the place and its work—we become stewards of the theater, rather than distanced purveyors of canonical culture.[13]

The theater's strategies include a symposium series in partnership with the Emory University Center for Ethics, where actors participate in pre-show dialogues about the issues in certain plays; post-show discussions; newsletters and program notes; dramaturgical lobby boards; carefully chosen marketing copy; and a "Living Room" series where plays under consideration are read to select audiences for discussion and community response. The theater also has a full-time engagement associate who, according to Director of New Projects Celise Kalke, is the "fulcrum" for all the activities across the different departments.

Kalke relates an inspiring story about how an audience's expectations can shift over a short period of time, explaining that, when she first arrived at the Alliance seven years ago, the audience's response to integrated casting for *A Christmas Carol* was

> sometimes curious and critical. So we developed talking points for discussion leaders focusing on the make-up of Dickens' London as an international multi-cultural city and that the reason to revisit a classic is to develop connections between the material and day-to-day life in Atlanta. At the same time, our other programming began to feature more and more local actors, so our audience was having more exposure to the *Christmas Carol* actors throughout the season. Therefore when we said *Christmas Carol* featured the best actors for each role, our audience knew that was true from their own experience. Not that we didn't say these things in 2005, we just said them more consistently. The result was the multi-ethnic casting quickly becoming a non-issue for the Alliance audience. And when we did an African-American production of *God of Carnage*, the trust that this choice grew out of wanting to feature the Atlanta casting pool and bring the best show possible to Atlanta, for an Atlanta audience, was complete. We [received] no questions about the choice.[14]

Thus, at the Alliance, transparency about artistic choices and consistent signposting of these decisions happen openly as part of a larger dialogue with the community. Similarly, on a panel at the June 2012 TCG conference, Kwame Kwei-Armah, artistic director of Centerstage in Baltimore, stressed the importance of building "artistic relationships" with the community. He described a process of audience engagement and artistic decision-making in which the "organization needs the same artistic flexibility as the artistic process" and remains "intellectually nimble enough" to make changes in a plan when there is a compelling reason to change course (Kwei-Armah 2012).

There seems to be a groundswell of thinking that matches Booth's and Kwei-Armah's philosophies. At previous TCG conferences, I had heard leadership express concerns that discussing artistic and planning decisions with patrons could open the door to a subscriber base feeling it could predetermine programming. Kwei-Armah and others at his session, however, demonstrated a conviction that this type of dialogue is actually crucial to a theater's health. In addition to newsletters and humanities events, which offer patrons the opportunity to engage more deeply with artistic decisions, some theaters offer pre-show discussions to help create the context for viewing a performance. DNAWORKS, the organization I co-founded, facilitates community dialogues before and/or after performances so that audience members can hear about one another's experiences and witness other sociologies of viewing within their own communities. Despite how financially stretched institutions are in today's economy, I have experienced how all these engagement strategies—organized and carried out in concert *with* communities—result in audience building and retention, with patrons as stakeholders in shifting institutional practices and philosophies.

For example, how might it change audience perceptions of integrated Shakespeare productions to know about their historical precedents, such as US-born actor Ira Aldridge, who was dubbed the "African Roscius" for his virtuosic performances in England of King Lear starting in 1827 (albeit problematically in White-face)? And that he also played, to great acclaim, Macbeth, Shylock, Othello, and Aaron the Moor in integrated casts? Once an audience knows this rich history, it is no longer necessary to invoke a terminology rooted in affirmative action suggesting that a production is doing something "special" for actors of color.

Unhistorically calling integrated casting "non-traditional" marks certain actors as casting problems to be solved, echoing W. E. B. Du Bois's searing question in his 1903 work *The Souls of Black Folk* (Du Bois 1996, 101): "How does it feel to be a problem?" And it simultaneously obscures the long history and tradition of African heritage actors performing European classical roles. Gayatri Spivak (1999, 2) uses the term "sanctioned ignorance" to point to unchallenged intolerance and bias. Newman also addresses these moments of disconnect:

> Our challenge was to get our colleagues to recognize that the conventions which guide their choices (or non-choices) are adopted attitudes. Or, to put it as our central question: How do we get the decision-makers in the

arts—our nation's image-makers—to take responsibility for the images
they are presenting, or in many cases not presenting?

(Newman 1989, 24)

Clearly and consistently challenging moments of "sanctioned ignorance" is
central to moving the theater forward and creating parity of opportunity.

Crossing lines and moving forward

During the Community Keynote Forum I facilitated at the 2008 Southeastern Theatre Conference (SETC), the gathering of close to 800 college
and high school teachers, students, and artistic leaders from the Southeast
region shared casting experiences and future hopes with one another. The
controversial subject came up of cross-cultural casting in the direction not
usually practiced—specifically, whether it was acceptable to cast across color
and culture in performing August Wilson's plays and other roles written for
actors of color. Over the course of the session, there was a growing consensus that, in theory, one day casting could happen in all directions, but
not until there was equal opportunity for all artists. In other words, the
playing field is still not level. Participants also discussed this casting practice,
with varying degrees of comfort or accord, as something that could possibly
happen in the classroom as a part of acting training to explore playing
across culture and ethnicity.[15]

Several acting students of color reported that they had only been cast in departmental shows as maids and in background roles. While I have heard it explained
that a student simply was not talented or advanced enough for a lead role, there is
an extant body of dramatic literature large enough to provide roles of all sizes that
do not play into colonial patterns of segregation. Contemporary writers Naomi
Iizuka, Caridad Svich, and Charles Mee, among others, write texts that often have
no fixed ethnicity attached to characters and are open to the complexity of today's
increasingly mixed heritage youth and society. Similarly, the genres of Hip Hop
Theater and devised theater offer more flexible casting options. What curricular
changes could happen so that the first priority in planning an academic season is for
directors to choose plays to fit the talents of all the students and give them room for
personal and professional growth? One strategy that has worked for me when I
guest direct is to visit the department, meet the student population, and spend time
at the school before choosing the play. I want to ensure that the project not only
serves the students in the given program, but also the cultural climate of the institution that will be the primary audience for the piece. If the play has already been
chosen and it does not meet these criteria, I propose a different text.

Other possible approaches for making educational stages more of a welcome table include involving students in play selection and casting. While it
may be several generations until US society is fully integrated, younger
artists and current students lend a vital perspective, as they have a different

generational experience of identity and belonging. Noted dramaturg Anne Hamilton explains:

> What has happened in the last 26 years that has irrevocably forced our need to change is the coming of age of the first generation of mixed-heritage children of those people born after the Supreme Court decision of *Loving v. Virginia* (1967) [in which the anti-miscegenation laws still valid in sixteen states were deemed unconstitutional]. With intermarriage and co-education of all races and integrated neighborhoods comes the changing landscape of people being comfortable around each other.[16]

In addition, institutions may choose to implement initiatives that offer instructors more resources, and support them in staying current with shifts in society and the industry. For example, team-teaching relieves one person of needing to know all aspects of the field. Similarly, departmental retreats, teach-ins, professional-development seminars, and access to organizations like the Faculty Research Network can provide access to people from other areas of the university or the industry to offer supplementary training in teaching literature and rethinking pedagogy. Departments can also mobilize community resources, and teachers can partner with community leaders to expand their curricula and knowledge bases.

At the SETC forum, an early career artist from North Carolina shared that he hoped to create a theater company where it was known and expected that actors would play roles from different identity locations than the playwright intended. In Pao's terms, this is an example of "sharing the hypothesis," where a theater initiates a dialogue with its audience on the specific aesthetics and politics of a production or mission (Pao 2010, 102). This proposal led to a passionate conversation about the inherent quality of theater: that it is not "real" and always asks the audience to make leaps and engage on an imaginative level. To reduce theater to what is "expected" or "safe" plays against the attributes of the art and diminishes the audience's participation in the making of meaning. Theatre builds understanding on a human level by inviting its audience into a constant negotiation between self and society. To insist on theater's theatricality—that is, its nonliteral, non "realistic" qualities—is to do the cultural work that will lead to better inter-group relationships.

The Detroit Repertory Theatre (DRT) is an example of a company that, since 1956, has engaged its audiences in such a process. Similar to what the SETC participant proposed, DRT utilizes what company member Milfordean Luster calls "race and ethnicity transcendent casting," meaning that the company will cast the best person for the part "unless the role specifically calls for a certain ethnicity." In one case, Luster—herself African heritage—was able to play what was perhaps intended to be a role for a European heritage-looking actor, since it was not explicitly stated in the script. Luster explains that the DRT does not consider what it does as color-blind casting, and I would argue that this is a perfect example of how, by retiring this terminology and "sharing the hypothesis" with an audience, a company has created progressive socio-artistic change.[17]

Rocking the boat

Throughout this essay I have referred to "integrated" casting, knowingly signifying on a national history that is not unrelated to this conversation. As a whole, US society is still uncomfortably segregated; for example, a *New York Times* headline on May 20, 2012, reads "Jim Crow Is Dead, Segregation Lives On." This distance inhibits us from knowing one another's histories, cultures, families, and identities on a deeper level. It is understandable therefore that, as a microcosm of that society and producer of culture within it, theater also struggles with integration. Nevertheless, what will be the future of US theater if it does not resist segregation—onstage, backstage, in its administrative offices, and in the audience—and truly become a welcome place for all USers to gather and share in the ritual of witnessing stories that are vital to the country's collective well-being?

The term "integrated casting" has precedence, most notably at the New York Shakespeare Festival under Joseph Papp's direction. As Pao relates, "the company's policies were described in terms of integration and desegregation, never in terms of color-blindness" (Pao 2010, 46). Is it possible, given the almost two-century history of African heritage actors performing Shakespeare, that the issue challenging some audience members regarding the question of an actor's ethnicity (both in Shakespeare and other productions) is seeing these productions with an integrated cast? Throughout US theater history, spanning from minstrelsy to award-winning Broadway musicals, performances with African heritage casts have had tremendous crossover popularity and commercial success—therefore, the point of concern cannot be the presence of people of color onstage. Why, then, does the theater industry continue to recomplicate the dramaturgy of productions by using segregating language to justify integrated casting? I suspect that this accommodation is for the benefit of viewers who experience integration as something unfamiliar, not part of their daily lives, and for whom seeing an integrated society onstage creates a kind of cognitive dissonance. If societal segregation is the obstacle to an integrated theater field, bringing this conversation clearly to the fore will provide an important opportunity for communities to reexamine their thinking and biases.

As a step toward both theatrical and societal integration, I also recommend putting pressure on the words "diversity" and "inclusion." "Diversity" implies there is an unmarked "normal" position on the one hand and, on the other, a marked "alternative" that is different from the norm—in other words, "diverse" as compared to whom or what? Similarly, "inclusion" and "inclusive" suggest that one group has the power to invite another group to the table and "allow" that group entry. This language is not innocuous—it enacts micro-aggressions on populations that have historically been denied access to resources and advancement, while suggesting detrimental expectations of privilege and entitlement to others. One fundamental step toward sitting together as equals at a welcome table is finding a way to discuss the plurality of our nation without using language embedded with social and economic hierarchies.

The questions of language, casting, and representation are not without their own inherent contradictions. Unless a person is playing themself in an auto-biographical performance, all theater is cross-casting of some sort. For decades, people advocating for better representational practices on the US stage have queried why a person with a different color skin than a playwright intended should be any less believable than a person born in a different century or on a different continent. As a result of the "sociology of viewing," some "crossings" are more acceptable than others to certain viewers.

Nevertheless, the complex dynamics of African heritage actors inhabiting parts written for European heritage actors have sparked an on-going debate. Some theorists—most notably August Wilson in his landmark 1996 keynote speech "The Ground on Which I Stand"—proffer that this casting asks a person of African heritage to "become" or attempt to "pass" for White, while others insist that, because of the semiotics of skin, the character immediately becomes Black in the audience's eye.[18] I am inclined to say that how such casting is read depends on many factors, including the identities of the other cast members and the geographical location of the production (as different regions have different sociologies of viewing), and that no two viewers will see any actor onstage in the exact same way.

While I concur with the argument that productions be discouraged from the tokenism of casting only a few select people of color in order to appear desegregated, I am nevertheless conflicted about the proposition that actors of color should be discouraged from performing in European classics. The pro-cess of acculturation is at the heart of US sociology and is the conundrum that all peoples coming to this country, whether voluntary or forced, have faced: assimilating, remaining culturally specific, or a combination of the two. The suggestion that people of color who adopt the speech patterns or class aspirations of the dominant culture, either in their personal lives or onstage, are somehow denying their heritage echoes the nineteenth-century political divide between Frederick Douglass and Booker T. Washington of resistance versus accommodation. The intensity of these positions reflects the long and unresolved history of societal racism and racialism in this country; at the same time, today's artists work to strike their own balance. As Michael Kahn said at the 1986 NTCP symposium: "An actor is an independent being and therefore has a right to turn down a role" (Kahn, quoted in Davis and Newman 1988, 31). I would also like to add that an actor is a creative being, and we are driven by and drawn to work for reasons that go much deeper than we may ever understand.

Another important element of an integrated theater field is culturally or ethnically specific theater. Institutions dedicated to the literature, traditions, and research of a particular culture still play a valuable role, both as one of a broader range of employment opportunities for theater workers from that culture or ethnic heritage, as well as a place where individuals can get crucial training in a specialized area of the field. This proposition touches on strongly debated philosophical questions that need further discussion, especially regarding the ways in which funding across the industry determines institutional survival. Nevertheless, the central structural notion is that, if all theaters are integrated at all levels of leadership, administration, and production, the theater field as a whole could operate more fluidly in multiple, intersecting circles and not be isolated into self-contained entities and aesthetics.

After the debates, after the renaming of terms, after the struggle to be heard and represented accurately, what theater artists have in common is a passion for and compulsion to tell human stories—good juicy stories, stories with unexpected twists, captivating characters, pathos, history, and evocative language—and to be able to inhabit the words of genius writers respectfully and artfully. What would have happened if actors like Aldridge, Canada Lee, Ellen Holly, or Earle Hyman had banned themselves from European classics? World theater history would have been deprived of a profound chapter.

As Eyring writes about the theme for TCG's Fall Forum on Governance, echoing my framing of this essay with Austin's and Butler's theories:

> as a theater community, we often view ourselves as good guys with a strong sense of justice, and we typically seek to investigate issues in our society, to help inspire reflection and change. But perhaps we are not facing the fact that we all have biases—and that some of our biases are based on race. And that these biases, which are often ingrained/institutionalized in our society, may be part of the reason why we also have trouble bringing about a more diverse and inclusive theater community—in terms of race, gender, ability and all the many intersections of difference ... Our theater field could be, *should* be modeling a better, more inclusive world—not replicating weaknesses in our society.[19]

As artists and as cultural workers it is our unique opportunity and responsibility to challenge society's blind spots, to notice the missing fullness of our society on our stages, and to trouble the notion that any family configuration would be "unrealistic," given the heterogeneity of our world. Some initial questions that I propose to guide the steps of directors, designers, casting people, producers, teachers, scholars, critics, and social activists as we move into a new era of theater-making and representation include: What do we need to learn about cultures different from our own to ensure that the theater accurately reflects the richness and fullness of our country's cultural, historical, physical, and epidermal landscape? Where are we inadvertently making that richness fit inside the narrow confines of an idea we have inherited, which was originally introduced to keep us separate? And finally, a crucial discussion for further exploration: What kind of training—in academic, institutional, and commercial settings—will be necessary for all parties to become fluent in the current sociologies and literatures of our nation? Reconsidering the language around casting reveals equally important questions about segregation and discrimination in other aspects of US theater, including the hiring of directors and designers and institutional leadership. As a theater community and profession, as we discuss these questions we can continue to address persistent inequalities and challenges in representation.

The playing field clearly needs to be balanced before US theater can seriously entertain a conversation about a "universal" casting policy; and audiences also need a broader understanding of history and the sociology of their own viewing in order to "read" artists' intentions more critically as we attempt to balance that field. At the same time, in the theater—at its best—we work to move others, be moved ourselves, and understand one another better. I agree with Newman that, if this is our unselfish goal, then someday casting will just be casting and everyone will have an equal seat at the welcome table—a metaphor for heaven in the spiritual quoted above. A colleague of mine asked if this utopian view of theater is "what we actually do?" My answer, inspired by Josephine Baker, is: "If it's not, let us begin today."

Notes

1 Copyright © 2013 The Johns Hopkins University Press. This article first appeared in *Theatre Topics*, volume 23 issue 1, March 2013, pages 1–18.

2 Teresa Eyring, email message to the author, November 26, 2012.

3 Although AEA's study was nationwide, given that New York has the highest number of union stage actors of any city in the country, it is reasonable to use these numbers as an indication of what is happening across the industry. In addition, since the question of casting is primarily about the visual perception of a person's identity and, as discussed below, genetic research indicates that at this point in US history most bloodlines are mixed, I choose the term "heritage" to indicate the predominant visible component of a person's identity within US culture. I acknowledge the inescapable ambivalence of using identificatory language in an essay that challenges the limitations of such language; however, I have done my best to represent people ethnically in the way they choose to represent themselves, while not using terms that presume unified cultural or political affiliations.

4 See, for example, the cases of Steven Adly Guirgis's play *The Motherf**ker with the Hat* at TheatreWorks in Hartford, Connecticut, in 2011 and *The Nightingale* at La Jolla Playhouse in California during the summer of 2012 (respectively, El Blog de HOLA 2012 and Ng 2012), as well as actress Erin Quill's www.fairyprincessdiaries.com blog about discrimination of actors of color in the theater.

5 For a detailed history and explanation of Linnaeus's and Blumenbach's beliefs, see Gould (1994).

6 Writers on race as a social construction include Peter Jackson and Jan Penrose (1993); Michael Omi and Howard Winant (1994); and Robyn Wiegman (1995).

7   See *Colorblind* by Tim Wise (2010) for a discussion of sociological studies demonstrating the color-based bias and assumptions in the United States, and *The Problem of the Color[blind]: Racial Transgression and the Politics of Black Performance* by Brandi Wilkins Catanese (2011) for more in-depth analyses of the limitations of the terms theatrically and sociologically.
8   Sharon Jensen, email message to the author, November 8, 2012.
9   Sections of this essay are revisions of my article "A Director's Work: Re-Thinking Non-Traditional Casting" (Banks 2003), and from the Community Keynote Forum I led at the Southeastern Theatre Conference in Chattanooga, TN, on 7 March 2008.
10 See, for example, *Life on the Color Line: The True Story of a White Boy Who Discovered He Was Black* by Gregory Howard Williams (1996) and *Caucasia* by Danzy Senna (1999), among many others. In addition, numerous narratives of enslaved people of African heritage describe the ability to escape and integrate into free society due to their light skin tone that was viewed as "White."
11 In chapter 6 of *No Safe Spaces*, Pao (2010) also discusses Levi's ethnicity and how it has been interpreted in numerous productions.
12 I use the term "USer," since the United States is only one of many American nations.
13 Susan Booth, email message to the author, November 21, 2102.
14 Celise Kalke, email message to the author, November 21, 2012.
15 See Melinda Wilson's *Theatre Topics* article for an example of how she cross-culturally cast *Joe Turner's Come and Gone* (Wilson 2009).
16 Anne Hamilton, email message to the author, November 24, 2012.
17 Milfordean Luster, email message to the author, September 15, 2012. Another prominent theater that has pioneered this work is Mixed Blood in Minneapolis, founded by Artistic Director Jack Reuler in 1976.
18 Jocelyn Brown (2012) and Melinda Wilson (2009), respectively, argue each of these points.
19 Teresa Eyring, email message to the author, November 26, 2012.

Bibliography

Austin, J. L. 1962. *How to Do Things with Words*. Cambridge, MA: Harvard University.

Bandhu, Pun. 2012. *Ethnic Representation on New York City Stages*. New York: The Asian American Performers Action Coalition.

Banks, Daniel. 2003. "A Director's Work: Re-Thinking Non-Traditional Casting." *Black Masks*, 16(2): 7–8, 15.

Berger, John. 1972. *Ways of Seeing*. New York: Penguin.

Boardman, Gerald, and Thomas S. Hischak, eds. 2004. *The Oxford Companion to American Theatre*, 3rd ed. Oxford: Oxford University.

Brown, Jocelyn A. 2012. "Color-blind Casting: To Be or Not To Be." Paper read at Black Theatre Network, Atlanta, July 29, 2012.

Butler, Judith. 1993. *Bodies that Matter: On the Discursive Limits of Sex*. New York: Routledge.

Catanese, Brandi Wilkins. 2011. *The Problem of the Color[blind]: Racial Transgression and the Politics of Black Performance*. Ann Arbor, MI: University of Michigan Press.

Davis, Clinton Turner. 1997. "Non-Traditional Casting: An Open Letter." www.performingartsconvention.org/diversity/id=50 (accessed November 13, 2012).

Davis, Clinton Turner, and Harry Newman, eds. 1988. *Beyond Tradition: Transcripts from the First National Symposium on Non-Traditional Casting*. New York: Non-Traditional Casting Project.

Du Bois, W. E. B. 1996. *The Souls of Black Folk: The Oxford W. E. B. Du Bois Reader*, edited by Eric J. Sundquist. New York: Oxford University.

Gordon, Eric A. 1989. *Marc the Music: The Life and Work of Eric Blitzstein*. New York: St. Martin's.

Gould, Stephen J. 1994. "The Geometer of Race." *Discover*, 15(11): 64–69.

El Blog de HOLA. 2011. "HOLA Denounces Casting in Stephen Adly Guirgis' Play THE MOTHERF★★CKER WITH THE HAT at TheaterWorks in Hartford, Connecticut." http://elblogdehola.blogspot.com/2011/12/hola-denounces-casting-in-stephen-adly.html (accessed November 15, 2012).

Jackson, Peter and Jan Penrose, eds. 1993. *Constructions of Race, Place and Nation*. Minneapolis, MN: University of Minnesota.

Kruger, Barbara. 1983. Untitled (Your fictions become history). Mixed-media owned by Milwaukee Art Museum.

Kwei-Armah, Kwame. 2012. "Artistic Decision-Making: Weighing the Balance in a Complicated World." Panel discussion at Theatre Communications Group, Boston, MA, June 23.

Lonati, Alex. 2012. "Thoughts on Theater: Colorblind Casting." July 14. http://wers.org/2012/07/14/thoughts-on-theater-colorblind-casting.

Marshall, Jack. 2007. "Non-traditional Casting." www.americancentury.org/essay_non-traditionalcasting.php (accessed November 13, 2012).

McColl, Mary. 2012. "Diversity and Inclusion are Focus of Worldwide Concern: Equity Continues to Fight for Access, Opportunity." *Equity News*, 97(8). www.actorsequity.org/docs/news/en_08_2012.pdf (accessed November 27, 2012).

Newman, Harry. 1989. "Holding Back: The Theatre's Resistance to Non-Traditional Casting." *TDR: The Drama Review*, 33(3): 22–36.

Ng, David. 2012. "Heated Exchanges at La Jolla Playhouse over Multicultural Casting." *Los Angeles Times*, July 23. http://articles.latimes.com/2012/jul/23/entertainment/la-et-cm-heated-exchanges-at-la-jolla-playhouse-over-nightingale-casting-20120722.

Omi, Michael and Howard Winant. 1994. *Racial Formation in the United States: From the 1960's to the 1990's*. New York: Routledge.

Pao, Angela C. 2010. *No Safe Spaces: Re-casting Race, Ethnicity, and Nationality in American Theater*. Ann Arbor: University of Michigan.

Robinson, Eugene. 2012. "A New American Speaks." *Washington Post*. November 8. www.washingtonpost.com/opinions/eugene-robinson-a-new-america-delivers-its-verdict/2012/11/08/ae348d12-29e8-11e2-96b6-8e6a7524553f_story.html.

Senna, Danzy. 1999. *Caucasia*. New York: Riverhead Books.

Spivak, Gayatri Chakravorty. 1999. *A Critique of Postcolonial Reason: Toward a History of the Vanishing Present*. Cambridge, MA: Harvard University.

Thompson, Ayanna, ed. 2006. *Colorblind Shakespeare*. New York: Routledge.

Villarosa, Linda. 2002. "Beyond Black and White in Biology and Medicine." *New York Times*, January 1. www.nytimes.com/2002/01/01/health/a-conversation-with-joseph-graves-beyond-black-and-white-in-biology-and-medicine.html?pagewanted=all&src=pm.

Wiegman, Robyn. 1995. *American Anatomies: Theorizing Race and Gender*. Durham, NC: Duke University.

Williams, Gregory Howard. 1996. *Life on the Color Line: The True Story of a White Boy Who Discovered He Was Black*. New York: Plume.

Wilson, August. 1996. *The Ground on Which I Stand*. New York: Theatre Communications Group.

Wilson, Melinda. 2009. "Joe Turner's Come and Gone: An Experiment in 'Race Conscious' Casting." *Theatre Topics*, 19(1): 39–49.

Wise, Tim. 2010. *Colorblind: The Rise of Post-Racial Politics and the Retreat from Racial Equity*. San Francisco, CA: City Lights.

Part I

Culturally conscious casting

Chapter 1

The chasm between

Ayanna Thompson

In May 2018, co-editor Claire Syler talked with Ayanna Thompson about casting, race, classical theater, and education. Thompson is a leading scholar of Shakespeare and classical performance, and her edited collection, *Colorblind Shakespeare* (Thompson 2006), analyzes the practice of colorblind casting and Shakespearean performance. Thompson's work has inspired a variety of artists and scholars, and her ideas inform "The Welcome Table: Casting for an Integrated Society" (Banks 2013).

When I worked on the anthology *Colorblind Shakespeare*, which is now over a decade ago, I thought that, finally, we'll have this dialogue about colorblind casting and Shakespearean performance and then it'll be done. I thought if I addressed the book to actors and directors and some Shakespeare scholars that that would be enough. And it just wasn't. It started a dialogue about casting and Shakespeare. But the anthology didn't achieve what I assumed it would achieve—a definitive end to the debates—and I think part of it was my own limitations. I hadn't clearly worked out good defining terms that would be clear. And also, at that point, I didn't really take into consideration the audience's role in how performance works. I was focused on the production end of performance and not focused enough on the reception end. So my work has somewhat veered toward reception—and part of that got me thinking more clearly about the role that education plays in preparing audiences to understand Shakespeare. Because it's not enough if we have forward thinking actors, directors, and theater companies. If your audience doesn't understand what's going on, or your audience comes in with a different set of expectations, or your audience is highly resistant to whatever discourse you want to put forward onstage, then ultimately the production won't be as successful. I kept circling around non-traditional casting and realized, "Oh, more informed dialogues about race and performance can only be achieved if we alter the way we teach Shakespeare."

So that's how I ended up thinking about the science of learning, the new generation of learners, and their expectations about not only their education, but the ways they are approaching race and dialogues around race. I think, in many ways, it is an incoherent dialogue. Because, on the one hand, students espouse a rhetoric of colorblindness and a "can't we be done with that kind of thing" perspective. And then, on the other hand, they really, really crave honest, clearly articulated dialogues about race and racial difference. It took me a while to see that everything I'm interested in around casting and race and classical productions means that we have to take into account education—we have to take into account audience development and then we have to take into account the production side. So we can't ignore any of those components because, otherwise, the performance will fail. And I've seen many productions that have great lofty goals and ultimately fail because one of those components is missing.

Take the example of Prospero from *The Tempest*. Theatrically, revenge looks really different when expressed by different bodies. *The Tempest* has a different cultural valence if it is a White Prospero or Black Prospero or Asian Prospero and taking into account the gender identity of the actor. The whole idea of exacting revenge and being powerful with the tools of books and magic together have different meanings depending on the body cast in the role. And I think that's the part of the dialogue that, for me coming up in the Shakespeare world, was missing. Because I never assume that one's body can be read in a colorblind fashion, I felt that I was constantly seeing a different play than my fellow audience members who seemed reluctant to admit that the race of the bodies onstage mattered. So, at some point, I decided to acknowledge it publicly in my work—"I'm experiencing something differently in my reception than the rest of the audience." And so what does that mean? Can there be a dialogue about those different ways of seeing? Because there are moments when people don't see "race."

This recognition is why I was excited to co-write *Teaching Shakespeare with Purpose* with education specialist Laura Turchi because, when I talked to professional actors and asked them about their training—"What discourses did you have when you were being trained? Did you only have 'colorblind' productions in your training?"—the answer was, "Yes." Unless it's *A Raisin in the Sun* or August Wilson. But then I responded, "That didn't really set you up for a career, did it?" So the big "aha" moment I had was, "Why aren't educators using those moments when incorporating performance into the classroom? Whether it is with juniors and seniors in high school, or even freshmen and sophomores in college—let alone specific actor training programs—why aren't instructors using classroom performance opportunities to say to students, "Yes, your body matters—your body matters in any performance that you're going to do"? Can the class have a collective dialogue about how students want their embodied presence, or not want it, to matter in this specific context?

It's incredibly important to give students the tools to decide, collectively, what kind of casting practices they want to use in their educational settings. And to acknowledge that classroom casting doesn't have to be what students think casting should be in every setting—like professional or amateur productions. In fact, it is empowering for students to realize that the casting practices they want to experiment with in the classroom do not have to replicate and/or replace what they have experienced in professional settings. But, in this classroom and in this moment, how do students want bodies to be taken into account or not? This kind of question can allow for a much richer discussion with students about interpretation and meaning-making—and this question also allows for a discussion about the difference between the intention of a production and the reception of a production. In other words, through the practice of casting in the classroom, students will alternate between being the ones with the vision of the intention and being the ones watching and interpreting the decisions others have made. Because, of course, the chasm between a production's intention and its reception can be quite large at times. It's incredibly illuminating when students realize that what they assumed would be a clear intention is not received in that fashion.

Bibliography

Banks, Daniel. 2013. "The Welcome Table: Casting for an Integrated Society." *Theatre Topics*, 23(1) (March): 1–18.

Thompson, Ayanna. 2006. *Colorblind Shakespeare: New Perspectives on Race and Performance*. New York: Routledge.

Thompson, Ayanna, and Laura Turchi. 2016. *Teaching Shakespeare with Purpose: A Student-Centred Approach*. London: Bloomsbury Arden Shakespeare.

Chapter 2

Playing with "race" in the new millennium

Justin Emeka

When I was accepted into graduate school for directing, I received a suggested reading list of plays and authors that terrified me. I was not terrified by the amount of reading, but by the number of White authors I might be expected to direct. Although I liked some of the plays, culturally speaking, I did not feel much connection to these texts and I resisted the idea of using them to develop my skills as a director. I feared that they might somehow force me to compromise my passion and/or purpose as a Black artist.

The fear must have been on my face when they introduced me during orientation because, afterwards, I was approached by one of the professors who had helped recruit me. She invited me to her office and told me, "Don't be scared, Justin. You are here because of the strength of your individuality, not in spite of it. I know that you know who you are, and so you will never lose yourself inside this education. In fact, I believe that you will find a way for it to make you stronger." Her words and conviction gave me the confidence I needed to begin to read the plays from that suggested reading list and learn to see the possibilities for staging them through the cultural lens of my own legacy.

Three years later, I directed my thesis production of William Shakespeare's *Macbeth*, re-imagining my production in the South just after the Civil War. Though I kept Shakespeare's language, characters, and plot largely intact, I created a unique backstory using historical research and set the action in and around a once majestic plantation house. In my interpretation, Macbeth was a White Northern general completing a brutal military campaign to win the war. Lady Macbeth was a Southern belle, with whom he had recently fallen in love and married. Although she sincerely loved Macbeth, Lady Macbeth despised the Northern King Duncan, a charismatic Lincoln-like figure, whose demise she was eager to plot. Macbeth's best friend and comrade in arms, Banquo, was a Black Union soldier. Although equal to Macbeth in intelligence, merit, and experience, Banquo remained under Macbeth's command. The witches were newly freed African slaves who still lived an impoverished life as servants in the house and in the fields. At night, they were sustained by their ancestral rhythms and spiritual faith that allowed them to see beyond the present and into the past and future. Through ritual and possession, the witches foretold Macbeth's ascent to the throne, as well as the ultimate succession of Banquo's seed—Black kings claiming power for many generations to come.

As a result of the success of that production over twelve years ago, I have continued to develop productions throughout my career that re-imagine the function of "race" in plays such as *Death of a Salesman, A Midsummer Night's Dream, The Glass Menagerie*, and *Romeo and Juliet*. My purpose with this essay is to illustrate how I developed my process as a director for re-imagining race while incorporating Black and Brown actors in "classical" plays by White or European authors. I accomplish this approach by:

- re-interpreting the text through a Black or Brown experience;
- finding ways to support that interpretation with creative and historical cultural references;
- and using archetypes to help actors shape characters that can transform the expectations of both artists and audiences.

Through this process I create new opportunities that can provide actors of color access to a legacy of Eurocentric theater that, for many years, has remained culturally exclusive. As theaters and schools work to find ways to engage contemporary audiences by being more inclusive, in addition to producing plays by writers of color, it is also important to invite different cultural lenses into the process of staging plays by White authors that continue to be widely studied and produced year after year. In doing so, audiences and artists discover important new perspectives, new relevance, and new possibilities in performing great texts from the past.

Recognizing "race"

In "The Welcome Table: Casting for an Integrated Society," Daniel Banks argues, "because of the continued discussion of race in US society, racialism (accepting and acting according to a system of so-called racial difference) and racism (discrimination according to presumed race, often based on appearance) are ever present" (Banks 2013, 3). Race is an abstract and elusive idea which makes it challenging for many people to discuss. Sometimes race is a reference to physical features such as skin color or hair texture or lip fullness; sometimes race is a reference to place of birth or parents' birth; sometimes race is a reference to language, religion, or behavior. Within the context of this essay, I use the term "Black people" broadly and inclusively to refer to all those with African ancestry. I use the term "Brown people" to refer to communities from the Americas and Asia that have had limited or no access to systemic "White privilege."

Scientifically, it has been proven that there are only extremely small genetic differences that separate us as human beings or warrant the racial distinctions

Figure 2.1 The three witches inviting Macbeth. Production photo from *Macbeth* by
     William Shakespeare at Oberlin College in 2010. Directed by Justin Emeka.
Photo by John T. Seyfried.

that we have come to rely on in distinguishing the world's population. That is
to say, scientifically, there is only one race—the human race (Bonilla-Silva
2010, 8). Nevertheless, from generation to generation, race has continued to
play a significant role in how people in the United States construct identity
and, in turn, as a concept, race greatly informs how and who theaters cast in
their season of plays. Therefore, placing Black and Brown bodies in roles originally imagined for White actors potentially raises complex questions that
actors, directors, and audiences must learn to address.

In 1996 August Wilson delivered his famous address, "The Ground on
Which I Stand," to the Theatre Communications Group National Conference
in Princeton, NJ, where he vehemently denounced the casting of Black actors
in so called "colorblind" productions:

> Colorblind casting is an aberrant idea that has never had any validity other
> than as a tool of the Cultural Imperialists who view American culture,
> rooted in the icons of European culture, as beyond reproach in its perfec-
> tion … For a Black actor to stand on the stage as part of a social milieu
> that has denied him his gods, his culture, his humanity, his mores, his ideas
> of himself and the world he lives in, is to be in league with a thousand
> nay-sayers who wish to corrupt the vigor and spirit of his heart.
>
> (Wilson 2001, 22)

When I first read a transcription of August Wilson's address shortly after he delivered it, I had recently graduated from college and was struggling to find my place and purpose in the US theater. Wilson's words helped me realize that part of my struggle as a Black artist was the result of inheriting a canon of "classical" plays written by White men that mainly explore and celebrate some variation of White life. Thinking on my own experience growing up as an actor of color in "colorblind" high school productions, I realized how Black and Brown actors were often consciously and/or sub-consciously conditioned to hide their ethnicities in rehearsal rooms in order to fit into the world of the play. This process usually began in the audition, where the handful of Black actors had to tactfully adjust their speech and mannerisms so as not to be seen as "too Black"—they did this so they might have the opportunity to exist in the worlds of plays such as *Our Town, The Music Man, The Man Who Came to Dinner,* or *Hamlet.* This was especially true with Shakespeare, where actors' eagerness to fit in can even lead them to try and take on a bit of a British accent in their speech. As Ayanna Thompson notes in her work *Passing Strange: Shakespeare, Race, and Contemporary America*:

> Shakespeare can oppress the people because the promotion of his universality makes White Western culture the norm from which everything else is a lesser deviation … it is often assumed that Shakespeare's plays are not only universal and timeless, but also humanizing and civilizing.
>
> (Thompson 2011, 6)

Recognizing this struggle, I wanted to find creative ways to explore and celebrate Blackness onstage. My first instinct was to explore the works of August Wilson as well as other US-American Black authors such as Lorraine Hansberry, Alice Childress, Amiri Baraka, and Adrienne Kennedy; then I also read African and Caribbean Black authors such as Ama Ata Aidoo, Derek Walcott, and Wole Soyinka. I began to discover how diverse Blackness actually is and became inspired by the various ways Black theater artists represented themselves on stage through unique forms such as ntozake shange's choreopoems and Aimé Césaire's *A Tempest*, a retelling of Shakespeare's *The Tempest*. I began to realize my problem with "colorblind" casting had to do with employing Black actors to perform roles written for White actors without incorporating Black culture. Ultimately, I decided to try and resolve my dilemma by directing.

As a director in graduate school, I became interested in casting Black actors to help craft a Black social milieu on stage in my favorite plays written by White playwrights. I thought about how some of my favorite jazz musicians— such as John Coltrane—were able to redefine songs through their own cultural aesthetic, like "My Favorite Things" and other Broadway tunes written by White composers. In this way, they were able to develop their own artistry while also introducing new possibilities for how music is played and appreciated. In a similar fashion, I wanted to encourage a new style of theater that redefines the cultural identities of characters within the canon of "classical" plays by White authors. Theater has the ability to teach audiences to see beyond what actually is—and to dream about what can be. Over the years, I have directed many productions that provided opportunities to develop my unique directorial approaches by redefining "race." One of my most significant early experiences was directing Arthur Miller's *Death of a Salesman.*

Redefining "race"

In 2008 I was invited by Oberlin College president Marvin Krislov to direct a multi-racial production of *Death of a Salesman* with a cast of half students and half Actors' Equity Association actors (i.e., professional union). *Death of a Salesman* was always one of my favorite plays because it illustrates, through the story of Willy Loman, the tragic nightmare that can exist within the American Dream. The main action of the play involves the struggle to define one's own identity in a world where a man's worth is defined by his ability to make money. As a Black man in the United States, I felt I had a special appreciation for Willy's attempts to be fully recognized in his society while trying to build a lasting legacy for his family. Featuring the renowned stage and screen actor Avery Brooks in the role of Willy Loman, I envisioned the Lomans as a Black family and began historical research to help me flesh out the concept of the play.

First, I needed to create a new backstory for Willy Loman as a charismatic, African-American traveling salesman in the 1940s and 1950s. I searched for stories or examples that could help ground my creative vision in reality and found a book by Stephanie Capparell, *The Real Pepsi Challenge* (2007), which detailed how the Pepsi-Cola company used African-American salesmen in the 1940s as a way to open up new markets to try and gain an advantage over their competitor, Coca-Cola. Although the play never mentions exactly what Willy sells, I used this as inspiration and decided Willy had made a career for himself by opening small, over-looked markets in African-American communities for a large, predominately White sales company. I wondered who might have been one of Willy's heroes when I came across Booker T. Washington's speech at the Atlanta Exposition in 1896. Washington articulated a philosophy of Black mobility by gaining trust and employment from White people. He felt it was far more important for Black people to learn a good trade and be liked as opposed to going to college and fighting for social equality. I realized Willy reflected a similar philosophy that the best way for him and his sons to get ahead was by building character through trades and services as opposed to academics and scholarship. As I read the following speech from Willy to his two sons, Biff and Happy, I recognized great potential in Booker T. Washington being a strong influence in Willy's life:

Figure 2.2 Production photo from *Death of a Salesman* by Arthur Miller at Oberlin College in 2008. Petronia Paley as Linda Loman, Avery Brooks as Willy Loman. Directed by Justin Emeka.
Photo by John T. Seyfried.

WILLY: Bernard can get the best marks in school, y'understand, but when he gets out you are going to be five times ahead of him ... Because the man who makes an appearance in the business world, the man who creates personal interest, is the man who gets ahead. Be liked and you will never want.

(Miller 1980, 23)

Next door to the Lomans lives Charley and his son Bernard. Willy and Charley are good friends; but they are also locked in a subtle but profound competition with one another that is established in their first scene together in which they discuss the fate of their sons while trying to beat each other playing cards. To highlight the complexities of their relationship, I did not want Charley to be Black. I wanted Charley and his son to reflect the experience of another marginalized ethnic group in America that, at the time, may have confronted similar challenges as Black Americans, but was able to overcome them to achieve more socio-economic mobility. In my research, I found the book *Strangers and Neighbors: Relations between Blacks and Jews in America*, edited by Maurianne Adams and John Bracy, which helped me trace the historical alliance between Black and Jewish communities as well as conflicts around accusations of Jewish racism or Black anti-Semitism (Adams and Bracy 1999).

I conceived of Charley as a Jewish immigrant who fled Poland during the invasion of Hitler's Third Reich at the beginning World War II. Charley and Willy's friendship originally emerged out of the convenience of being neighbors. However, Willy always saw himself as ahead of Charley, because Willy believed himself to be more "American" than his Jewish friend. Yet, over the years, as Charley and his son Bernard climb the socio-economic ladder while Willy and his sons struggle to find their place in the world, Willy's respect for Charley becomes muddled with resentment. When faced with financial hardships, Willy's pride will not allow him to accept "hand-outs" from Charley or be in a position where he must accept the fact that he is worth less than Charley in the United States:

WILLY: I can't work for you, Charley.
CHARLEY: What're you, jealous of me?
WILLY: I can't work for you, that's all, don't ask me why.
CHARLEY: You been jealous of me your whole life, you damned fool!

(Miller 1980, 71)

Willy struggles his whole adult life to understand how Charley, an immigrant, so easily passes him by economically. His inability to find an answer for himself creates an estranged relationship between Willy and his own country.

Willy is haunted by an acute "double consciousness," as described by W.E.B. Du Bois in 1903, that results from being Black and American, trying to navigate two worlds, two loyalties, two sensibilities (Du Bois 1996, 17). Having served his purpose for his company, he is of little use to the next generation of the company's leadership. Willy is caught between the reality of who he wants to be in "America"—how he wants to be seen—and the reality of who he is in the United States and how he is actually seen—which is not at all:

Figure 2.3 Production photo from *Death of a Salesman* by Arthur Miller at Oberlin
        College in 2008. Marc Jablon as Charlie, Avery Brooks as Willy Loman.
        Directed by Justin Emeka.
Photo by John T. Seyfried.

WILLY: You know the trouble is Linda, people don't seem to take to me ... I
    know it when I walk in. They seem to laugh at me ... I don't know the
    reason for it, but they just pass me by. I'm not noticed.

(Miller 1980, 26)

Willy's obsession with gaining success in a White world creates a strange
emulation of "Whiteness" and, in an attempt to find validation, he engages in a
secret affair with a White woman that would haunt him for the rest of his life.

Though it involves laughter and simple pleasures, it is not merely a simple fascination between a Black man and a White woman but also a momentary connection between two individuals who are alienated in their own realities:

WILLY: You picked me?
WOMAN: I did. I've been sitting at that desk watching all the salesmen go by, day in and day out. But you've got such a sense of humor, and I think you're a wonderful man ... My sisters'll be scandalized.

(Miller 1980, 27)

Willy's emulation of whiteness also creates an acute sense of "colorism." Alice Walker states in *In Search of Our Mothers' Gardens: Womanist Prose* that colorism "is the prejudicial or preferential treatment of people within the same race based on the color of their skin tone" (Walker 1983, 280). In this production, colorism impacts Willy's relationship with his two sons—Biff has lighter skin and Happy has darker skin. Both sons desperately seek their father's approval, yet Willy favors Biff, convinced of his destined success, and pays little attention to Happy, who ultimately seeks self-love through womanizing and material things. Young Biff enjoys his privileged status until he catches his father cheating on his mother with a White woman. In that pivotal moment Biff realizes his father's profound weakness and is shattered by a sense of betrayal in his father and his own self-image. Biff's life and identity are sent into a tailspin as he struggles to figure out who he is now.

In the climactic scene, Biff forces the family to speak truthfully and confront the illusion that holds them all captive:

BIFF: You're going to hear the truth, what you are and what I am.
LINDA: Stop it!!
BIFF: The man don't know who we are! The man is gonna know! We never told the truth for ten minutes in this house! ... I am not a leader of men, Willy, and neither are you. You were never anything but a hard-working drummer who landed in the ash can like all the rest of them ... I'm not bringing home any prizes any more, and you're not going to stop waiting for me to bring them home ... Pop, I'm nothing! I'm nothing, pop. Can't you understand that? There's no spite in it any more. I'm just what I am, that's all.

(Miller 1980, 95–96)

In the end, Willy takes his own life as his last attempt to try and help his family gain access to a world that rejects him. At his funeral, as the family reflects on the significance of Willy's troubled legacy, Biff leaves after coming to the conclusion, "He had the wrong dreams. All, all, wrong ... He never knew who he was" (Miller 1980, 100). Linda, Willy's wife, is left alone onstage by herself to make sense of their fate. In the final line of the play she ironically decries: "We're free ... We're free ... We're free" (101).

Once I completed my initial concept illuminating the story and major themes of the play through Afrocentric cultural perspectives, the next challenge was to guide the refinement of the concept in rehearsal with actors, for it is the actors who ultimately are responsible for transforming "race" within the play.

Transforming "race"

Each production introduces me to different casts that bring unique personalities, skills, and challenges to the process. From production to production there is no exact blueprint for how to guide actors from first rehearsal to opening night. However, it is important to develop a working understanding of the company members as individuals and artists; and secondly, it is helpful to provide good reference and direction that rouses the best of their creative abilities.

One of the most important techniques I use while working with actors of color to help them see themselves inside a role is to find archetypal references that allow each actor to embrace their character within their own cultural spectrum. I learned this early in my career while directing a production of *The Glass Menagerie* with a Black actor in the role of Tom. About two weeks into rehearsals, although the actor was doing reasonably well in his emotional work, I could tell there was something inhibiting his ability to embody the role fully. One night after rehearsal he confessed that he was still really struggling to see himself inside the part. He was a big fan of Tennessee Williams and knew the play was autobiographical, so he could not stop hearing Tennessee Williams's voice inside his head as he spoke the lines. Every time he opened his mouth, he said he felt a little ridiculous.

We spoke for some time, as I was trying to assess if he had any personal hang-ups about embracing my concept that Tom was a Black, sexually repressed, gay man in the 1950s who longed to abandon his mother and sister to pursue his dreams as a writer. Although the actor had no problem embracing those circumstances, when he spoke he felt out of place in Tennessee Williams's reflection. Finally, after about two hours of talking, I asked him, "Have you ever heard James Baldwin speak?" (the actor looked a lot like James Baldwin). And as soon as I asked it, a light came on in his head and he said, "Of course!" He went home and spent the next morning listening to James Baldwin interviews. When he came back the next day to rehearsal, he was glowing and, almost miraculously, was able to find his own voice. I was amazed how quickly his acting was elevated. I realized he needed a reference that would give him permission to embrace the role for himself culturally. By referencing James Baldwin's voice, it allowed him to find his own voice while speaking the words of Tennessee Williams. I realized how important it can be in building a character to find images and voices of people in which the actors can see their own likeness. Without such references, it can create serious psychological barriers that keep them from being able to fully embody their roles.

Building from these insights, on the first day of rehearsal I try to fill the room with historical and artistic images that I use to help create my concept—particularly those images that resemble the appearance of my actors in the room. I make a point early on in the process to lead a discussion with the company about "race"—and how it impacts the actors' identities offstage—to help build a cohesive understanding for how race will inform their character work onstage. Our ability to talk about race within the artistic process requires us to discuss it from different points of view, even different periods in time.

In my process, recognizing Blackness in a character is not to prescribe a particular behavior to that character, but rather to provide an important point of entry for both the actor and the audience. Some actors get it immediately, while others have a hard time and need more reference and direction. Actors of color who grew up in predominately White communities may not feel an instinctual relationship to any Black and Brown cultures and subsequently lack confidence in their ability to identify "authentic" cultural references to draw from. Some Black and Brown actors, who have little to no experience with material by White authors, may also have aversions to working on these texts. In most cases, creating a strong sense of community among the cast will greatly enable the actors to overcome their own apprehensions and take risks by building off of each other.

All peoples have legacies and dreams within their cultural memories that may be applied to stimulate innovation and inspiration in the classical theater of other cultures. In my work I invite actors to help fill the room with references for the characters that are rooted in the company members' own cultural experiences and imaginations. I encourage all the actors to bring into the rehearsal room different songs, dances, music, books, artwork, objects, and/or stories that they believe reflect something unique about the characters and/or world we are creating. In this way actors can begin to help serve as valuable references for each other. For instance, in my production of *Macbeth*, an actor playing one of the witches was also an African dancer. One day she taught the company a dance that she felt reflected the "energy" of the witches. I could tell it was the first time one of the other actors playing a witch had ever danced like that and I could sense how she was frustrated and perhaps a little ashamed by her inability to catch on immediately. But, as the whole cast continued to encourage and support each other, she became more comfortable. As she became freer inside the dance, she gained a new confidence that transformed her presence inside the rehearsal room.

The next day another actor, playing the Porter, brought in a traditional Afro-Brazilian instrument called the *berimbau* that he thought the porter might play in his spare time. On a break he began to play. Drawn to the sound of the instrument, the actor who had initially struggled the day before began to do the dance as the Porter-actor continued to play. The other witches joined in. Seeing them work together, I realized the potential of creating a more developed relationship between the Porter and the witches, imagining that they were all servants on different parts of the Macbeth plantation. We began using the *berimbau* to construct melodies with the witches' lines that became chants. As we moved into staging, I created transitions with the Porter inconspicuously playing rhythms on his *berimbau*. Then, in the climactic scene between Macbeth and the witches, we heard the Porter playing his instrument in the distance while the witches danced and chanted in time to his rhythm, "Double, double toil and trouble; / Fire burn, and cauldron bubble" (4.1.10–11).

In conclusion

Theater is fluid, and the cultural aesthetics from production to production are not fixed nor prescribed. The world of the play is uniquely crafted by the artists involved with each production. By reimagining the presence of Black and Brown life within the context of Eurocentric plays, I use theater as a tool to teach people to look for Black and Brown life where they have been trained by omission to ignore it. As our world changes, I believe we are living in exciting times that demand all theater artists to re-imagine how we see ourselves both onstage and off. Living in a nation that promotes an ideal of racial, ethnic, and cultural diversity—yet in action is still segregated in so many ways—there is a growing movement to find ways to fearlessly address issues of race through casting in a way that invites more participation from historically marginalized communities.

Ultimately, I want my work to help teach audiences and artists to embrace the creative possibility that there is no place on this planet nor time in history where it is impossible to imagine the contributions and presence of Black and Brown peoples. If contemporary audiences can sit in a movie theater and believe in White, Black, and Brown, English-speaking people living on spaceships a long time ago, throughout galaxies far, far away, then surely they can come to embrace a Black or Brown Prince in a fictionalized Denmark struggling with the dilemma of whether "to be or not to be."

Bibliography

Adams, Maurianne, and John H. Bracey. 1999. *Strangers and Neighbors: Relations between Blacks and Jews in the United States*. Amherst, MA: University of Massachusetts Press.

Banks, Daniel. 2013. "The Welcome Table: Casting for an Integrated Society." *Theatre Topics*, 23(1) (March): 1–18.

Bonilla-Silva, Eduardo. 2010. *Racism without Racists: Color-blind Racism and Racial Inequality in Contemporary America*. Lanham, MD: Rowman & Littlefield.

Capparell, Stephanie. 2007. *The Real Pepsi Challenge: The Inspirational Story of Breaking the Color Barrier in American Business*. New York: Free Press.

Du Bois, W. E. B. 1996. *The Souls of Black Folk Essays and Sketches*. Charlottesville, VA: University of Virginia Library.

Miller, Arthur. 1980. *Death of a Salesman: A Play in Two Acts*. New York: Dramatists Play Service.

Shakespeare, William. 1993. *Macbeth*. New York: Dover Publications.

Thompson, Ayanna. 2011. *Passing Strange: Shakespeare, Race, and Contemporary America*. Oxford: Oxford University Press.

Walker, Alice. 1983. *In Search of Our Mothers' Gardens: Womanist Prose*. San Diego, CA: Harcourt Brace Jovanovich.

Wilson, August. 2001. *The Ground on Which I Stand*. New York: Theatre Communications Group.

Chapter 3

Nevertheless, whiteness persisted

Brian Eugenio Herrera

On an unseasonably steamy evening in early October 2017, a few dozen people—actors, playwrights and others—gathered in a basement theater in New York's Greenwich Village to laugh about whitewashing.

Whitewashing, in a theatrical context, names the not-uncommon practice of casting a white actor to portray a character who is not—or is not necessarily—white.

This occasion to laugh at whitewashing was the most recent installment of *CastAndLoose Live!*, a pop-up performance series produced by actor-advocate Lynne Marie Rosenberg and based on her *CastAndLoose* blog.[1] The premise of *CastAndLoose*—in both its live and digital formats—is the same. Rosenberg curates a stream of unedited excerpts from actual casting notices, occasionally adding a bit of sardonic commentary. Whether read aloud by actors on a stage or by someone scanning their social media stream, the flow of selected excerpts on *CastAndLoose* invites the audience to confront—through laughter—the everyday instances of sexism, racism, and other bad habits that permeate the casting process, especially in projects operating without the services of reputable casting professionals. *CastAndLoose* offers gallows humor for striving artists and those who love them.

Rosenberg's wry explication of casting notices underscores how casting is always simultaneously an act of interpretation and an allocation of resources. The assignment of this particular actor to that specific role is, quite often, an inceptive interpretive gesture—a mechanism for making performance happen, and a way to manifest meaning within performance. These two aspects of casting—making performance and manifesting meaning—readily become so twined as to appear as singular, even inevitable. Rosenberg deploys comedy to mock the insulting cruelties routinized within the mechanisms of the casting process and to display, in ways both hilarious and horrifying, the meanings scripted by these—usually anonymously authored—casting notices that fill the inboxes of working actors on a daily basis.

The October 2017 presentation of *CastAndLoose Live!* carried the title "Not So Buenos Aires," with Rosenberg's selection of that evening's excerpts highlighting casting notices that described Latinx characters and actors. The first half of the evening-length presentation featured a half-dozen established Latinx actors—including Annie Henk, Liza Colón-Zayas, Jorge Chacón, and Gilbert Cruz, among others—reading casting notices, selected and organized thematically by Rosenberg (who also provided arch contextualizing commentary). In the evening's second half, the same actors read short scenes and monologues written by contemporary Latinx playwrights—including Migdalia Cruz, Guadalís del Carmen, Matthew Barbot, and Hilary Bettis, among others—that were devised in response to the same casting notices featured in the first half of the show.[2] The title for *CastAndLoose Live!*'s October 2017 show, "Not So Buenos Aires," nodded pointedly to the event's inspiration—a recent production of the musical *Evita* staged by a Boston-area company, the North Shore Music Theatre, in which no Latinx actors were cast in principal roles.

The controversy around North Shore's "whitewashing" of *Evita* stirred first in early September when Luis Eduardo Mora, writing on *OnStage Blog*, called attention not only to North Shore's casting of the production but also their deletion of critical comments from their Facebook page. Mora's report soon caught the attention of actor-advocate Lauren Villegas, whose own initiative "Project Am I Right?" was instigated in early 2016 when a Chicago-area theatre staged a similarly nearly Latinx-less *Evita*. Villegas joined Mora and others using social media to call for North Shore Music Theatre to account not only for their casting of the show but also the theatre's silencing of criticism.

North Shore's public response did little to quell the rising storm of controversy around its *Evita*. Producing artistic director Kevin P. Hill, writing on his personal Facebook page, offered the first attempt: "As the recipient of the Rosetta LeNoire Award for non-traditional casting, NSMT has always encouraged performers of all ethnicities to audition for our productions." As arts advocate Howard Sherman confirmed, when reporting Hill's initial statement on the *ArtsIntegrity* webpage, North Shore Music Theatre received this award from Actors Equity in 2003, when the theatre was operating under entirely different management. The next public rebuttal came from North Shore's owner/operator Bill Hanney. "I do colorblind casting," Hanney told the *Boston Globe*. "Our focus was not to find a Latino. It was to find the right Eva, Che, Peron…" A few days later, when pressed by radio station WBUR to explain the theatre's decision to block critics (like Villegas) on social media, Hanney was emphatic. "We're not going to put up with the kind of BS from people who just want to cause trouble."

But what some might think of as troublemaking, others might consider activism or advocacy. Hanney's unwillingness to engage his critics in traditional media only amplified national interest in the controversy, especially on social media. Using their respective platforms, Villegas, Rosenberg and others circulated each new article and, within days, North Shore Music Theatre had become the most recent exemplar of American theatre's persistent "whitewashing" problem.

As a term of social critique, "whitewashing" first gained notable prominence around 2010 when authors of young adult fiction, in tandem with readers, librarians and advocates, began using social media to call out the insidious pattern among publishers of featuring white-seeming figures on the covers of books featuring non-white protagonists. That same year, when the film adaptation of *The Last Airbender* featured white actors in roles originally scripted as characters of color, the term leapt readily into the social media driven outcry that followed. The term took a bit longer to enter the theatrical lexicon. (The term is, perhaps notably, mostly missing from the social media driven outcry that attended the casting of white actors as Puerto Rican characters in the 2011 TheatreWorks production of Stephen Adly Guirgus's *The Motherfucker with the Hat* in Hartford, Connecticut.) However, by 2016, when two productions in Chicago—Marriott Theatre's *Evita* and Porchlight Theatre's *In the Heights*—came under similar scrutiny, the term (or hashtag) whitewashing punctuated most reports whether in traditional or social media.

The practice of "whitewashing" offends for three main overlapping reasons. First, assigning white actors to roles scripted as characters of particular "non-white" backgrounds erases the potential contributions of actors of color in shows that might benefit from their collaborative presence and cultural expertise. Next, inviting white actors to portray characters that are not white predisposes the production toward rehearsing practices of racial imitation and mimicry and thereby adding yet another inaccurate or inauthentic depiction to the already overstuffed catalog of misrepresentation. Finally, hiring white actors instead of actors of color perpetuates the gross inequity of opportunity confronting actors of color in an industry that tends to default "white" unless otherwise instructed. In short, whitewashing perpetrates erasure, promotes inauthenticity and perpetuates privilege.

Whitewashing's critique of invisibility, inauthenticity and inequity is by no means new. Indeed, these three points of contention have animated actor-led advocacy and activism for the last seventy-five years. During the 1940s and 1950s, subcommittees within all the major actors' unions began to advocate for equitable access to employment opportunities for non-white union members. Deploying the principle of desegregation, the Actors' Equity "Committee on Negro Integration in the Theatre" (within which Rosetta LeNoire was a longstanding contributing member) emphasized access to opportunity for, first, actors of African descent before broadening its mandate to include all actors who were not white, leading to the first "Integration Showcase" in 1959. This principle of integration—or simply hiring non-white actors in roles previously not accessible to them—effected a measure of change but, within a generation or so, it became clear that the American theatre persisted in assigning most roles to white actors.

In the second half of the twentieth century, "integrated" casting became an essential bridge between the commercial and not-for-profit institutional theatres and the emerging community-based theatres creating work "by, for and about" people of color. Though various innovative "cross-racial" casting techniques had been deployed by artistic leaders in professional, amateur, educational and activist contexts in the United States since at least the 1820s, the rise of the non-profit theatrical industrial complex in the 1960s marshalled these varied approaches into what I have elsewhere called "the incoherent tradition of non-traditional casting" (Herrera 2018, 229). In particular, as leaders of two of the most dynamic institutional theatres of the 1960s and 1970s, Joseph Papp (of the New York Shakespeare Festival) and Zelda Fichlander (of Washington DC's Arena Stage) became particularly influential proponents of this constellation of ostensibly inclusive casting practices in which non-white actors might be hired to play characters previously presumed to be white, but not explicitly scripted as such. This constellation of casting practices—in which an actor of African descent might portray Hamlet, opposite an Ophelia of Asian descent, or where Antigone might be black, while her sister, Ismene, might be a Latina, or where a multicultural ensemble might sort of inhabit all roles in a family—over time came to called "non-traditional casting."

So, in the 1980s, amid widespread backlash against programs and policies (like school bussing and affirmative action) designed to effect desegregation, Actors' Equity's Non-Traditional Casting Project (NTCP) adopted an advocacy strategy to boost awareness of this newly aggregated constellation of casting techniques. The NTCP continued its advocacy for greater access to opportunity for minority performers but also emphatically affirmed the myriad creative ways that the casting process might be leveraged to build a more multicultural American theatre. The NTCP's advocacy for "non-traditional" casting practices provided an enduring vocabulary for a new actor-led advocacy movement consolidated amid the crucible of the 1991 *Miss Saigon* protests. Soon, variants of "non-traditional casting" were rapidly, but selectively, adopted by and adapted within a broad range of not-for-profit and educational theatres across the nation. For institutional theatres (whether not-for-profit or educational), these "non-traditional" casting practices leveraged the actor's capacity (their talent, their skill, their bodily presence) to serve as a creative bridge between the aesthetic traditions of the Western theatrical canon and the rising contemporary interest in greater visibility, representation and diversity on the American stage. The promise of these practices stirred the imaginations of theatermakers of all backgrounds (but perhaps especially actors and directors of color) and stoked hopes that the American theatre might be simultaneously sustained and transformed welcoming a more diverse ensemble to the stage.

In the last decades of the twentieth century, the transformative industrial and aesthetic shifts of American theatre begun in the 1960s had institutionalized these "inclusive" casting practices that so relied on the bodies of actors of color even as they also privileged the director's capacity to "overwrite" the Western theatrical canon within and through the promise of diversity. Yet such casting techniques "make sense" as a simultaneously social and aesthetic intervention only in a theatrical structure wherein the director's assignment of a particular role "non-traditionally" spins a distinctive interpretation of the dramatic work. In short, such casting practices prioritize the director's authority to "overwrite" the script and to conspicuously deploy actors of color to rehabilitate an otherwise exclusive canon. For directors of color (like Kenny Leon, Lileana Blaine-Cruz and Justin Emeka), and for those historically white theatres (like the Oregon Shakespeare Festival under the artistic leadership of Bill Rauch), the repertoire of practice rehearsed by non-traditional casting could prove a powerful tool in creating space for the meaningful contributions of artists of color. Even so, the ascendant creative structure of the not-for-profit institutional theatres— which so prized the director's capacity to overwrite the script—thereby also fortified a consolidation of power (in the hands, in the eyes, in the imagination) of the director to decide when inclusive casting practices would and could be used. By the turn of the twenty-first century, the thoroughly rehearsed "interventions" of non-traditional casting had ossified into familiar conventions within any theatre-maker's repertoire and had confirmed that, even when guided by the clearest principles and the best of intentions, "non-traditional casting" had been assimilated into the American theatre's most-longstanding tradition of prioritizing whiteness.

If unions were the place where actor-advocates discovered solidarity and community in the middle decades of the twentieth century, the twenty-first century showed social media to be the incubator for a new generation of actor-led advocacy initiatives. Independent actor-led initiatives like *Project Am I Right?* and *CastAndLoose* sought to disrupt the bad habits of casting convention, especially with regard to racial inequity and misrepresentation. While not dismissing either the principle or process orientations of their forbears, this social media era of actor-led advocacy rather added a critical new strategy: public accountability. These new models of actor-led advocacy maximize social media's unprecedented capacity to disrupt the hierarchies and proprieties of industrial habit to send a message directly to decision-makers. In so doing, they also galvanize a nimble network of supporters aligned with their cause. Rosenberg's *CastAndLoose* scrutinizes the routine horrors of the casting notice and beseeches those writing casting calls (and, by extension, those creating content) to "do better" when inviting actors into the process of collaboration. Villegas's *Project Am I Right?* shifts the scrutiny to working actors themselves by challenging all actors to understand that they are accountable for the choices they make when accepting the industry's invitation to audition for or accept a role. Villegas's project challenges actors to follow the familiar exhortation to "know your type" to its most ethical conclusion, while Rosenberg's demands that attention be paid to one of the most essential but least considered mechanisms of the hiring process, the casting notice itself. Like the actors leading advocacy initiatives preceding them, both Villegas and Rosenberg have been warned that their stance would likely hurt their careers and, unlike their predecessors who mostly worked from within actor unions, both Villegas and

Rosenberg continue their independent advocacy projects using social media as both tool and platform without the support or protection potentially provided by a larger organization.

Though a product of the twenty-first century's social media turn, protests against whitewashing are not especially new. Initiatives like *Project Am I Right?* and *CastAndLoose* join, in principle and in process, a longstanding tradition of actor-led advocacy efforts to demand accountability of an American theatre that persists in privileging whiteness in its search for the best actor for the role.

Notes

1 Rosenberg began both the *CastAndLoose* tumblr and pop-up performance series in 2014. In 2017, Rosenberg adapted the format of the live show so that each would scrutinize the ways casting notices misrepresented specific identity categories (Asian and Pacific Islander, Latinx, Trans/Non-Binary). In this new format, Rosenberg used the occasion of the live performance to also invite emerging and established writers from the relevant communities to develop short plays and monologues in response to her selection of casting notices. The same group of six to eight actors (all self-identified as part of the relevant communities) would perform both the notices and the playlets, with Rosenberg serving as host. See Lynne Marie Rosenberg, *CastAndLoose*, March 2016–present at http://castandloose.tumblr.com (accessed July 12, 2018).

2 I should note that, when the show was restaged at Joe's Pub in early 2018, I joined the list of contributing writers with my monologue "Busty Gabriela Speaks" performed by Zabryna Guevara. *CastAndLoose Live! Not So Buenos Aires*, by Lynne Marie Rosenberg, Joe's Pub, The Public Theater, New York, January 28, 2018; see also the video capture of the performance at www.youtube.com/watch?v= N6HffCamxEI (accessed July 12, 2018).

Bibliography

Aucoin, Don. 2017. "Casting Controversy Surrounds North Shore Music Theatre's 'Evita.'" *The Boston Globe*, September 11. www.bostonglobe.com/arts/theater/dance/2017/09/10/casting-controversy-surrounds-north-shore-music-theatre-evita/CEGGy70vnRZoAlVOIYzoEL/story.html [accessed July 12, 2018].

Herrera, Brian Eugenio. 2018. "Looking at *Hamilton* from Inside the Broadway Bubble." In *Historians on Hamilton: How a Blockbuster Musical is Restaging America's Past*, edited by Renee C. Romano and Claire Bond Potter, 222–245. New Brunswick, NJ: Rutgers University Press.

Mora, Luis Eduardo. 2017. "And the Whitewashing Kept Rolling In: Controversy Over 'Evita' Casting at MA Theatre." September 6. www.onstageblog.com/columns/2017/9/6/and-the-whitewashing-kept-rolling-in-controversy-over-evita-casting-at-ma-theatre [accessed July 12, 2018].

Sherman, Howard. 2017. "At North Shore Music Theatre, An Absence of Race, Ethnicity and Understanding Prevails." September 14. www.artsintegrity.org/at-north-shore-music-theatre-an-absence-of-race-ethnicity-and-understanding-prevails [accessed July 12, 2018].

Villegas, Lauren. 2018. Project Am I Right? March 2016–present. http://projectamiright.tumblr.com [accessed July 12, 2018].

Part II

Approaches to casting Middle Eastern American theater

Chapter 4

Casting pearls before authenticity

Yussef El Guindi

I am today, in the US, unfortunately, having to field the same emotional havoc triggered by anti-Arab and anti-Muslim sentiments that I experienced as an Arab/Muslim kid growing up in the UK. In the latter country it was all about blood and soil. Not being of their blood or soil, I was regarded as an interloper (to put it politely).

In the US today, I feel myself being nudged further into the margins by governmental policies, political rhetoric, and the hostility generated by both. Where once, as a US naturalized citizen, I thought I occupied an aspirational ideal—many different peoples coming together to form an exceptional bond of shared values—I now feel those values—as compromised and poorly expressed in actual policies as they have been in the past—dissipating at an accelerated rate, replaced by what I thought I had left behind: notions of blood and soil. I once again feel like an interloper.

But not just an interloper in the general environment of politics and the dominant narratives of mainstream discourse, but also in the supposedly safe space of my chosen profession: theater. In this growing warm embrace of marginalized voices that seems to be taking place in US theater, Arabs and Muslims still seem to be ever so slightly unembraceable.

But let's say some maverick artistic director decides to push back against that drum beat of racist and Islamophobic thinking and stage a play that depicts a more nuanced picture of the peoples of that region, and their diasporic brethren, that artistic director then has to confront the thorny issue of "authentic" casting.

The impulse to cast authentically is to be applauded. The talent pool of good Middle Eastern actors has definitely increased over recent years—at least in certain large cities like New York and Los Angeles—but not so in other cities. And in those cities that have no Middle Eastern actors, or maybe one actor who's still acquiring his or her acting chops and isn't quite up to the challenge, what is a theater to do? Decide not to do the play because they can't cast authentically, or …?

An Arab American friend of mine said to me many years ago: "You're writing plays for actors who don't yet exist." At the time, those rare theaters who staged plays by Middle Eastern playwrights wouldn't worry too much about casting a Middle Eastern role with a non–Middle Eastern actor. I didn't either. We would look for Arab actors but, if none were found, we selected good actors who could "pass". We cast from a wide pool of ethnicities: African American, Latinx, South Asians, and southern Mediterranean folk. If you were right for the part, with solid acting chops, and could kinda sorta pass as Middle Eastern, you were in.

And I wasn't going to privilege a so-so actor of Middle Eastern descent over an outstanding non–Middle Eastern actor who could bring the role and play to life. I sometimes bent that rule and agreed to cast a novice, still-wobbly-on-stage Arab/Arab American actor, if only because I have an interest in enlarging that pool of Middle Eastern actors. And actors have to get experience and learn their craft somewhere.

But I must admit to being a bit resentful sometimes of having to make that choice. White playwrights get to choose from a wide array of talented actors. Why do I have to make compromises when it comes to casting? Why was I being put in the position of having to engage in "social work" (as one critic labeled a play of mine) or act as a mentor, and not just an artist plying his craft. I know that sounds rather selfish, but shouldn't my focus be on trying to realize what's on the page in the best manner possible? Wouldn't that raise the profile of our stories, and our place in the wider cultural conversations, presenting quality work in all areas of the production, so the audience doesn't feel like they're attending out of obligation to some liberal idea of exposing themselves to different cultures and perspectives? Which is a great impulse, but can also feel more like homework than entertainment.

Torange Yeghiazarian in her essay asks, "When does authenticity get in the way of creativity?" (Chapter 5). Here's one example of how it can: because of this emphasis on "authentic" casting now, and because of the current paucity of Middle Eastern actors, I am now fudging, where I can, the Arab backgrounds of my characters. If there is no particular need to draw attention to their ethnic background I won't. They may just be vaguely Muslim. And because Muslims hail from all parts of the world, there is a larger pool of actors to choose from. More, I realize I am beginning to unconsciously phase out or blunt Arab-centric stories. Why put even more obstacles to my plays getting produced by giving theaters headaches about casting?

So, in this case, authenticity threatens to erase the telling of Arab/Arab American stories.

The word "authentic" begs for a longer essay devoted exclusively to dissecting exactly what that word means. But let me end by describing the tangled little web "authenticity" can create. A play of mine, *The Talented Ones*, was recently criticized by a reviewer for not naming the ethnicities of the immigrants in that play. This is one play where I felt I didn't have to name the ethnic backgrounds of the characters. *I* knew where they came from (the actors who played these two characters were Mexican American and Vietnamese American). But I didn't name races or put clues in the play because there was no dramaturgical need to, and for the reasons I mentioned above. This was a problem for the reviewer. Most of her critique centered around that omission. But is it such a dramaturgical problem when that problem can be solved with the addition of *one line*: naming the racial background of my characters? And if the reviewer were to respond and say she would want more than just having their race identified, then what would that more be: have the characters speak in accents? Have them wear culturally appropriate dress? Cook foods unique to their cultures (one of the main characters cooks throughout the play)? Or pepper their conversation with the language of their immigrant parents? The reviewer clearly wanted an "authentic" experience. Much like going to a Middle Eastern, Mexican, Vietnamese or any number of ethnic restaurants, she wanted the "real thing." But what exactly is the real thing?

Do I have to cater to her European–American curiosity about other cultures? A laudable thing, this curiosity, in so many other instances. But in this case, exactly how "authentic" do I have to be? How many hoops do I have to jump through exactly before the story I tell is regarded as legitimate?

Chapter 5

ReOrienting
A Middle Eastern American casting case study

Torange Yeghiazarian

Creating an artistic home

With support from friends and family, I founded Golden Thread Productions in 1996 as I was completing my Master of Arts degree in Theatre Arts from San Francisco State University. My intention was to establish a theater to produce my own plays and, in the process, to provide a home for other artists of Middle Eastern heritage. In my mind this identity included Iranians, Arabs, Turks, Armenians, Jews, and all the various tribes and ethnic minorities that make up the diversity of the region. We struggled with the imperialist baggage of the term "Middle East"; but after much consideration and months of debate, we were not able to find a better alternative. In an essay titled "Middle of What?," I explain the struggle and the way we made peace with it:

> In our vast imagination, the Middle East is defined not by geographical boundaries and political separations, but as the shared experience of the people who, throughout history, have been touched by its taste, melodies, and aromas. The Middle East lives inside us; as we redefine ourselves, we redefine the Middle East.

> (Yeghiazarian 2001, 48)

At the time, I did not realize that we had established the first theater company in the US devoted to the Middle East as a whole.[1] There were theater groups in the US working in Persian or Arabic, as well as those defining themselves as Jewish, Armenian, or Arab-American. These groups were doing important and necessary work but catering to isolated communities. I was interested in engaging the general theater audiences in the US. To accomplish this, I felt compelled to gather various segments of the Middle Eastern community under one umbrella—to amplify our voices and to build dialogue. With English as our common language, we could collaborate and engage in the US in a way that was not possible in the Middle East.

My inspiration came from two sources—the Asian American and the Latino Theater movements in the US. In terms of the former, springing from diverse communities that speak different languages and practice different religions, Asian Americans had found enough of a common ground to support a national theater movement. With the latter, political activism and the struggle for social justice had emboldened Chicano and Latino theater in the US. Like the Middle East, those communities had been plagued by wars and revolutions which the second and third hyphenated generations in the US were still processing. A few years later, much like Latino Americans in the 1980s and 1990s, Middle Eastern Americans would be vilified in the media and racially profiled by the government. Even in 1996, I felt a strong kinship with these communities and perceived a similar theatrical trajectory. I knew a larger umbrella would make our voices louder, expand our audience base, and increase our impact. There was power in numbers, especially as an immigrant.

As a playwright entering the workforce after graduate school, I was disappointed by regional theaters' lack of interest in plays dealing with the Middle East. The plays being produced in the 1990s offered a limited world view and were written mostly by white men, such as David Mamet, David Ives, and Tom Stoppard. Tony Kushner, Terence McNally, and Paula Vogel offered nuanced LGBTQ narratives, but still very much told from a Eurocentric perspective. I remember reading August Wilson and wondering why he was not being produced more in the US. I celebrated when David Henry Hwang's *M. Butterfly* and later Suzan-Lori Parks's *Topdog/Underdog* opened on Broadway. But more than ten years passed between those two events.

My plays often emerge from my experience of displacement in the aftermath of the revolution in Iran where I was born. My perspective is that of an immigrant woman. I am of Iranian and Armenian heritage and grew up both Muslim and Christian. I looked for narratives that reflected my experience and the many layers of my identity, but I did not find any. Not in the 1980s and 1990s. Where was my place in US theater? Was there a place for me and my stories? I recall an audition experience in 1989. I had applied to a professional actor training program in New York, which required the usual two-minute each classical and contemporary monologues. After I had finished, the auditor, a white man in his 50s, told me not to waste my time. He said that he liked my work but, because of my looks and my accent, I would never be cast in a leading role at a major theater. I recall feeling crushed. It had never occurred to me that, even if I were an excellent actor, there was no room for me in US theater. After licking my wounds for a few months, I decided to pursue theater anyway. I knew I would have to create my own opportunities, write my own material, and build interest in the stories I felt compelled to tell.

My Master's thesis at San Francisco State University became Golden Thread's inaugural production.[2] The company's founding mission was: "To celebrate Middle Eastern cultures and identities as represented across the globe."

Since our founding, Golden Thread Productions has premiered more than one hundred new plays from or about the Middle East, including seven original plays for young audiences based on Middle Eastern folktales. We have 22 resident artists and we have employed more than 1,000 artists. Golden Thread has served more than 50,000 audience members, with forty percent self-identifying as Middle Eastern and many from other underrepresented communities. A significant portion of our audience is made up of mainstream theater-goers, which tend to be predominantly older and white.[3]

ReOrient Festival of Short Plays

One of our goals at Golden Thread has always been to counter the monolithic perceptions of the Middle East in the US—the misconception that the Middle East is made up only of Muslims or Arabs, or that all Arabs are Muslim, or that Iranians are the same as Arabs, or that Israel is a European country. Representing the diversity of the Middle East was—and is—a defining core belief at Golden Thread. But, as a small company, we could only afford to produce one or two plays a year. And that seemed inadequate to represent the wide range of cultures and aesthetics that make up the Middle East. That is when we came up with the idea of producing a Festival of short plays. Each play would come from a different community and a different point of view. In this way our audience could experience truly varied representations of the Middle East in one evening, on one stage.

ReOrient Festival of Short Plays has become Golden Thread's signature offering. It has served as fertile ground for risk-taking artists and an inspiration for audiences seeking unconventional and provocative programming. Presented biennially in San Francisco, ReOrient Festival has served as a springboard for the careers of numerous Middle Eastern American playwrights such as Yussef El Guindi, Betty Shamieh, Novid Parsi, Mona Mansour, and Melis Aker (listed in chronological order of when they were first produced by the company). It has also introduced audiences to significant and rarely-produced dramatic works from the Middle East by authors such as Fatma Gallaire (Algeria), Tawfiq Al-Hakim (Egypt), and Sadegh Hedayat (Iran).

Today, ReOrient is comprised of: ReOrient Festival—an evening of short plays showcasing diverse aesthetics and perspectives; ReOrient Forum—in-depth conversations among artists, activists, and scholars in the form of panels or round-table discussions to contextualize and/or build upon themes explored in the Festival; and ReOrient Camp—a development retreat hosted by University of San Francisco months in advance of the Festival to offer the artists an opportunity for brainstorming and preparation without the pressures of an impending production. The Festival has a two-year production cycle. In the first year, we select the plays from an open call for submissions distributed nationally and internationally. The plays must be in English, ten to thirty minutes long, and written by a playwright of Middle Eastern heritage about any topic, or about the Middle East by a playwright of any heritage. The "from or about" criteria are meant to free Middle Eastern playwrights from the limitation of writing about their own experiences. It is also an invitation to playwrights not from the Middle East who want to write a play dealing with the region. All the submitted plays are read and about thirty are moved to round two. A selection committee made up of Golden Thread artists and other theater practitioners knowledgeable about theater of the Middle East recommend up to twelve plays to move forward. Considering the selection committee's ratings and recommendations, as Artistic Director I make the final decision about the lineup of the evening based on aesthetics, topicality, regional diversity, and production needs. To elicit dialogue, I often choose plays that present different perspectives on a particular conflict or political situation. Our goal is to offer a rich theatrical journey where the plays are in conversation with each other.

Once the plays are selected, I choose the directors and designers. Our production model for ReOrient is collaborative: directors share an ensemble cast and Festival designers design for the full Festival. We create a unit set and repertory lighting plot to house all the plays. We rely on props, costumes, and sound to differentiate time and space as well as to provide cultural specificity. We want the audience to be awed by the space seamlessly shifting from one play to the next, as well as the same actors transforming into different characters from different cultures.

Early in year two we start the casting process. Golden Thread operates under an Actors' Equity Association contract; about half the cast as well as the stage manager are members of Actors' Equity. To prepare for auditions, we create a casting matrix. We list all the characters in all the plays, specifying their gender, age, and ethnicity. Then, based on that information, we determine which characters can be played by the same actor. Each actor is cast in two to four plays. Age and gender are easier to define, but ethnicity is trickier. Because reflecting the diversity of the Middle East is a tenet of ReOrient, character backgrounds represent a wide range of national and cultural identities: Iranian, Armenian, Egyptian, Lebanese, Afghan, Palestinian, Moroccan, Turkish, Israeli, Syrian, Iraqi, as well as non–Middle Eastern characters. In a given year, we have produced as few as six and as many as eleven short plays in ReOrient. Depending on the number of characters in each play, the ensemble may include up to fourteen actors. Casting for ReOrient is challenging for several reasons: first, actors must be a good fit in multiple plays; second, directors must agree on sharing actors, which sometimes means compromising on their first choice. Also, casting is rarely a determining factor in play selection, which can lead to challenges later on.

Currently, we have a strong pool of actors of Middle Eastern heritage in the Bay Area from which to draw. But in the early years, our local Middle Eastern casting pool was predominantly Iranian, mainly because of Darvag Iranian theater company in Berkeley.[4] In those days, to drum up more Middle Eastern artistic participation, I would reach out to visual artists, dancers, and musicians of Middle Eastern heritage. Sometimes we would discover a new talent and nurture it; but, for the most part, our local professional acting pool was not of Middle Eastern heritage. Regardless, we forged ahead because, at Golden

Thread, producing the plays and putting Middle Eastern narratives on stage has always been the top priority. This is partly in response to the astonishing under-representation of Middle Eastern narratives in American theater, particularly disturbing considering that the US has been at war in the region for nearly thirty years. Even on the rare occasion that a Middle Eastern character is portrayed on stage or in film, they are either vilified or dehumanized. At Golden Thread we believe that, when the public has the opportunity to encounter a fully fleshed out character on stage and experience their reality, it would make waging war against them more difficult to justify. Telling our stories in the early 2000s was an act of resistance—and a matter of surviving the US policy in the Middle East. But how do we bring more Middle Eastern narratives to theater stages in the US when there are very few Middle Eastern actors?

I recall having a conversation with my graduate advisor about casting. It was 1998 and Golden Thread was producing an Iranian play, but we had only one Iranian actor in the cast of nine. I questioned if it made sense to produce the play with a non-Iranian cast. My advisor said that, by that measure, we should cast Brecht plays only with German actors and Chekhov plays only with Russian actors. He reminded me that the best plays are simultaneously specific and universal. He said theater is about becoming someone else and telling someone else's story. His comments helped me to worry less about the actors' ethnicities and focus more on their ability to embody the characters' experiences and tell the story.

We have continued this philosophy at Golden Thread with the added bonus now of having developed a significant pool of skilled Middle Eastern actors. But matching the casting needs of multiple plays is never easy. In the case of ReOrient Festival, we have the added challenge of actors needing to play multiple characters from a wide range of ethnicities. The ReOrient casting process often exposes preconceptions about how people from different countries actually look. In reality, the Middle East encompasses a wide range of physical appearances, from fair-skinned with red hair and green eyes to dark-skinned with black eyes and black hair. But in the US, popular media has drastically narrowed audiences' perceptions of Middle Eastern looks. For example, casting directors frequently opt for darker-skinned Latino and South Asian actors when casting a Middle Eastern character. In one instance, another theater company that was casting an Afghan character rejected the Asian actors whom I recommended because, to them, they did not look Afghan. But Afghanistan is in Central Asia! However, in the US, Asian mainly implies East Asian. Similarly, casting directors often use Caucasian or White to indicate non-Middle Eastern. This is odd because Caucasian refers to the Caucus Mountains, located north of Iran, the land where Armenia, Azerbaijan, and Turkey meet. At Golden Thread, we use the term "Anglo" to indicate a northern European character—but I'm sure someday someone will also unpack that term in an unexpected way for us.

Ultimately physical appearance is important insofar as the audience must buy into the dramatic conceit of the character. And, as my examples will demonstrate, often practical considerations such as comedic timing, nudity, language skills, and the number of Equity contracts will supersede considerations about an actor's physical appearance.

Case study: ReOrient 2009

It was ReOrient 2009, the festival's tenth anniversary and the last year we produced ReOrient annually. We selected eight plays from previous ReOrient festivals to remount and one new play to premiere (Table 5.1).

I led the casting process in collaboration with the directors and, when possible, in consultation with the playwrights. There were a total of twenty-six parts to cast—thirteen female, twelve male, and one flexible. Originally, we had budgeted for twelve actors including two Equity contracts; but once we created the casting grid, it became obvious that, because of age and language requirements, two parts—the elderly Armenian mother in *Abaga* and the elderly Egyptian father in *A Marriage Proposal*—had to be cast with one dedicated actor per part. We pulled

Table 5.1 ReOrient 2009 program.

Series 1	*No Such Cold Thing* by Naomi Wallace (2009): An American soldier has an unexpected encounter with two Afghan sisters who are ready to embark on a new life.
	Tamam by Betty Shamieh (2002): From one of the most highly praised Arab-American playwrights comes this story of a young Palestinian woman. Her name is Tamam; it means "enough"!
	Coming Home by Motti Lerner (2003): A compassionate inquiry into the fragility of the human spirit by one of Israel's most vocal voices against the occupation.
	Call Me Mehdi by Torange Yeghiazarian (2005): A cultural divide erupts in this bedroom comedy between an Iranian woman and her American husband.
Series 2	*I'm Not a Serial Killer* by Caveh Zahedi (1999): From the independent filmmaker responsible for *I Don't Hate Las Vegas Anymore*, comes a kooky comedy about a loveable loser's futile attempts at picking up the woman of his dreams.
	Abaga by Torange Yeghiazarian (2001): A lyrical tale of forbidden love between an Armenian man and a Turkish woman in Istanbul of 1915 repeats itself in Jerusalem of 1935 when their offspring falls for a Jewish immigrant.
	A Marriage Proposal by Yussef El Guindi (2001): Chekhov's classic comedy of class conflict and lemons adapted to an Egyptian family setting.
	Compression of a Casualty by Kevin Doyle (2004): Two CNN anchors find themselves stuck in the news report of an American soldier's death in Iraq.
	The Monologist Suffers Her Monologue by Yussef El Guindi (2007): A Palestinian-American explores her identity in this poignant and comedic monologue.

those two characters out of the matrix and focused on the other twenty-four parts. If we assigned two parts each to the rest of the actors, we could cast the Festival with thirteen actors: seven women and six men, ranging in age from twenty to sixty. The settings for the plays included Afghanistan, Armenia, Egypt, Iran, Iraq, Israel, Palestine, Turkey, and the US. There were two young US soldier parts, two Anglo male parts, and one young man of undefined ethnicity. In addition, there was a young Israeli soldier, a young Russian Jewish man, and a young Armenian man. In our casting matrix, we assumed that a non–Middle Eastern actor would play the US soldier parts and the Anglo male parts. We also allowed for the possibility of doubling one of the US/Anglo male parts with the Israeli soldier or the young Russian Jewish man, assuming they would be fair-skinned (yes, we actually thought this). The part of John in *Call Me Mehdi* and Yoni in *Coming Home* required nudity. We marked those as most likely assigned to the same actor. Similarly, some nudity was required in the parts of Ziba, the Iranian woman in *Call Me Mehdi*, and Talia, the young Israeli woman in *Coming Home*, which we also marked as most likely assigned to the same actress. Because the part of Ziba required Persian speaking, we assumed the Ziba/Talia track would be cast with an Iranian actress.

Could we find the right actors for all of these parts that were so specifically defined? After two weekends of auditions, our six Festival directors called back twenty-six actors from whom to cast their plays. We were able to maintain our Actors' Equity contract limit of two but had to increase the cast size to fourteen. There were many surprises in the final casting lineup. Many of our original assumptions were proven to be incorrect. We were reminded repeatedly that, at the end of the day, casting is about which actor can best embody the character and tell the story as envisioned by the playwright and the director. Not every actor can deliver comedic timing or understand stylistic choices. Not every actor is comfortable with nudity. And if the play has specific non-English language requirements, then the casting options are even more limited. Our one saving grace was Caveh Zahedi's *I'm Not a Serial Killer*, an abstract comedy with one man and two women of undefined ethnicity. That was a good holding place for any actor who needed a second part.

In *A Marriage Proposal*, Chekhov's comedy adapted to an Egyptian setting, the director intended to stage the play with slapstick and physical comedy. He wanted the class difference between Deenah and her suitor Nabil to be reflected in their physicality. The actors also needed to have impeccable comedic timing and natural chemistry. We found this combination in a highly versatile Iraqi actress and a tall Anglo actor with excellent clowning skills. An older Palestinian actor played the father. He and the young woman were fluent in Arabic and they picked up the Egyptian pronunciations easily. Their specificity helped our Anglo actor become convincing as an Egyptian character. This effect went beyond mannerisms and a few words of Arabic. The older character had a slight Arabic accent when speaking English. The young woman had none. This helped create a generational artifice in which the young man and

Table 5.2 ReOrient 2009 projected casting grid.

Gender	Age/Notes	Series 1: Thurs & Sat			Home	Series 2: Fri & Sun				
		Cold	Mehdi	Tamam	Home	Abaga	Serial	Proposal	Monologist	Compression
F	60s ME/Armenian					Mother	Host			
F	40s ME/Anglo				Ruth	Jeyran				
F	30s, ME/Cuban						Waitress			Soledad
F	30s Persian-speaking, nudity		Ziba		Talia					
F	30s ME					Zarin		Deenah	Hoda	
F	teen–20s ME	Meena								
F	20s ME	Alya		Nora and Maryam						
M	60s ME/Armenian/Egyptian					Hamper		Magdi		
M	40s Anglo				Daniel					Hemmer
M	30s, ME					Aram		Nabil		
M	20s Latino	Sergio					Man			
M	early 20s Anglo		John		Yoni					
M	early 20s ME/Anglo, nudity				David					Bertoldie

Table 5.3 ReOrient 2009 cast list by play.

Abaga		A Marriage Proposal	
Aram	Raffi	Magdi	Afif
Jeyran	Suraya	Nabil	Michael
Arama's Mother	Vida	Deenah	Dina
Hamper	Charles		
Zarin	Dina		
David	George		
Coming Home		No Such Cold Thing	
Yoni	Raffi	Meena	Nora
Daniel	Charles	Alya	Suraya
Ruth	Leah	Sergio	Basel
Talia	Maryam		
I Am Not a Serial Killer		Call Me Mehdi	
Host	Leah	Ziba	Ahou
Waitress	Sara	John	George
Man	Basel		
Compression of a Casualty		Tamam	
Bill Hemmer	Michael	Featuring Nora and Maryam	
Soledad O'Brien	Ahou		
Spc. Joel L. Bertoldie	George		
The Monologist Suffers			
Hoda	Sara		

the young woman seemed similar, more contemporary, compared to the older actor's old-worldliness. It was delightful to watch the same actor play Nabil in *A Marriage Proposal* one minute and television news personality Bill Hemmer in *Compression of a Casualty* the next minute.

In the case of *Coming Home*, an Israeli family's struggle with their son's PTSD after an incident at a checkpoint, the role of the young son Yoni was both emotionally demanding and required full nudity. We expected to have difficulty finding the right actor for this role and remained open to however it might be double cast. This track in the original casting matrix doubled with one of the US soldier roles or David, the Russian Jewish young man in *Abaga*. But the actor who rose to the challenge was an Armenian young man who was both sympathetic and vulnerable and possessed the intensity that the director was looking for in Yoni. The actor had recently visited Armenia and witnessed the effects of the conflict with Azerbaijan in Nagorno-Karabakh, an experience that most likely informed his acting choices in *Coming Home*. The rest of the cast consisted of two US Jewish actors, who played the parents, and an Iranian young woman performed the girlfriend. The play remains one of the most charged and provocative plays in ReOrient history. The actor who played Yoni was also cast as Aram, the Armenian young man in *Abaga*, the only "predictable" casting choice we made that year. The part of David, the young Russian Jewish man in *Abaga*, went to our Greek actor, who was triple-cast as Specialist Bertoldie in *Compression of a Casualty* and John in *Call Me Mehdi*, a character described in the play as Anglo. The Iranian actress who played the Iranian wife in *Call Me Mehdi* was also cast in *Compression of a Casualty* as Soledad O'Brien, the Cuban-Irish news anchorwoman.

One of the most satisfying aspects of experiencing ReOrient is to watch the actors transform from one play to the next, embodying contrasting characters and multitudes of cultures. This reflects our shared humanity in visceral and unspoken ways. It empowers Middle Eastern actors with the rare opportunity to portray Middle Eastern characters on stage that are every bit as layered and complicated as they are. ReOrient also offers them the opportunity to play parts for which they normally would not even be considered for. Casting unconventionally is one of the ways Golden Thread Productions helps counter dominant stereotypes of the Middle East. These casting decisions may largely be driven by necessity but, nonetheless, we make them thoughtfully and intentionally. The question of when and where it is appropriate and justified to push the audience's (and our own) expectations is one I ask myself and our artistic team on an ongoing basis.

Conclusion

Portraying multiple characters in ReOrient Festival gives an actor the opportunity to represent their own culture in one play, then to enter someone else's world in another play and represent a character from a completely different culture. These two possibilities cannot be mutually exclusive. I sometimes wonder if, in the fight for greater and more "authentic" representation of communities of color, we have lost sight of theater's intrinsic ability to help us connect by reaching beyond ourselves.

When does a play need that unspoken, indescribable cultural truth that only someone from the culture can bring; and when is there an opportunity to facilitate an actor's entry into a whole new cultural experience? The latter is more frequent at Golden Thread because most of our local actors are not of Middle Eastern heritage—in which case it becomes my job as the artistic director and the producer to provide access points to the context of the play, including bringing on board other knowledgeable artistic collaborators and decision-makers. In addition, when choosing actors, I look for cultural competence. By this I mean, in Golden Thread's case, the lived experience of otherness, of exclusion. Most immigrant communities in the US share similar experiences. Many were displaced as a result of political upheaval. Many lost resources, family ties, and/or social status when they resettled. These shared experiences provide a common vocabulary and an emotional toolbox from which to draw.

If activists and others who care about equity and representation demand that Middle Eastern characters only be performed by Middle Eastern actors, would they inadvertently make it impossible for Middle Eastern stories to be told on a wide scale in the US? If one of the goals of diversifying US theater is to see simultaneous productions of a Middle Eastern play across the country, then we must allow for leniency in casting. To help navigate this arduous terrain, Jamil Khoury of Silk Road Rising and I wrote an open letter to producers and artistic directors in the US, published in *American Theatre* magazine in 2017. There Jamil and I address the need for cultural competency in the rehearsal room by a creative decision-maker. Because we know that, even when Middle Eastern characters are represented, their portrayal is often laden with racism and bias. The most important consideration is to work with a producer, director, dramaturg—a creative decision-maker—who is knowledgeable about the region.

Having said that, theater-makers must also ask ourselves, "When does authenticity get in the way of creativity?" Human beings make discoveries through searching in the unknown. If we are expected only to begin from a place of knowing, will we stop being creative? Are we depriving ourselves of the opportunity to imagine? Of course we want more opportunities for Middle Eastern artists; but if we are limited to only writing about or playing characters from our own cultures, then we are creating a different kind of cultural ghetto where a community of color is only permitted to represent its own. We need to expand our definitions of community and artistic purview, not make them narrower.

At its core, ReOrient is about dialogue. Our goal is to stimulate greater understanding of the Middle East by sharing personal narratives that tackle some of the most complex issues of our times. ReOrient showcases varied aesthetic and alternative perspectives by producing a diverse collection of new short plays of the highest quality from or about the Middle East; and promotes deeper dialogues, risk-taking, and open expression among participants from diverse communities by building a supportive, honest, and inclusive framework for collaboration and exchange.

ReOrient has empowered members of a vilified community to tell our stories in our own words. The plays provide a context to examine who we are and our place in the world, in relation specifically to the Middle East and its vibrant global diaspora. At every stage of the program, the Festival provides opportunities for people of different cultural backgrounds to interact and build deeper connections with one another. ReOrient is at the core of Golden Thread's vision of creating a world where human connections made through the shared experience of live theater supersede political differences and promote a more just and vibrant society.

Notes

1 Today at Golden Thread we define the Middle East broadly and inclusively, embracing the multiplicity of ethnic and religious identities that span Southwest Asia, North Africa, Central Asia, the Caucasus, parts of Mediterranean Europe, and our diasporic communities.
2 *Operation No Penetration, Lysistrata 97!* (Next Stage, San Francisco, 1997), adapted and directed by Torange Yeghiazarian from Douglass Parker's English translation of the original by Aristophanes.
3 For more information about Golden Thread Productions, visit www.goldenthread.org.
4 Darvag Theater Group was founded in Berkeley in 1985 with the dual mission of exploring creative expression in theatre arts and maintaining a vital living connection with the group's Iranian heritage.

Bibliography

Khoury, Jamil, and Torange Yeghiazarian. 2017. "Middle Eastern American Theatre on Our Own Terms." *American Theatre Magazine*, September 29. www.americantheatre. org/2017/09/29/middle-eastern-american-theatre-on-our-terms
Yeghiazarian, Torange. 2001. "Middle of What?" *Callboard Magazine*, August, 48.

Chapter 6

Casting Middle Eastern American theater

Cultural, academic, and professional challenges

Michael Malek Najjar

The question asked by Torange Yeghiazarian—"Was there a place for me and my stories?"—is central to the casting issues facing Middle Eastern American/ North African American (MENA) performers today. Because MENA actors are relatively few in number, and because many other ethnicities can "pass" for being Middle Eastern, opportunities for MENA actors to play fully dimensional characters have been rare. When directors and producers strive for casting Middle Eastern character roles, they either cast actors who are not culturally specific (i.e. actors who can "pass"), or they cast actors based on look rather than cultural embodiment. "Passing" is defined here as casting actors who "look the part" despite not having any cultural affiliation with the race of the character. Also, actors are sometimes cast that may have cultural identification of some kind but lack the cultural embodiment of the character (linguistic ability, cultural acumen, etc.). With the rise of several Middle Eastern focused theater companies since the late 1990s—namely Golden Thread Productions in San Francisco, Silk Road Rising in Chicago, Noor Theatre in New York City, and New Arab American Works in Minneapolis—and with a growing interest in plays by and about Middle Easterners, the types and number of roles for MENA actors have improved. That said, the situation facing MENA performers today is not optimal since there are too few roles written for these performers, and the ones that are created are often stereotypical or minimal in number or prominence.

This situation has multiple causal factors that can be attributed to circumstances that come from both inside, and outside, the MENA community. The five issues I explore in this essay are: (1) cultural factors that contribute to the paucity of MENA actors in the field, (2) the challenges these actors face in academia and training, (3) the further challenges they face as they enter the professional field, (4) the state of a field that contains little to no opportunities for these actors, and (5) the profession now as it applies to these actors. What is clear is that MENA actors often find themselves relegated to playing stereotypical roles (terrorists, harem girls, Orientalized caricatures); "acceptable Middle Easterner roles" (the "good" agent, the funny sidekick, or the quiet immigrant); or they sublimate their identities altogether (changing their names, changing their appearances, or not playing any roles that have anything to do with Middle Easterners whatsoever). A few have found financial and critical success in the field of comedy, while others embrace their Middle Eastern identity after finding some artistic/financial achievement, while others still decide to forge a career (sometimes lucrative, most times not) writing and performing their own material. MENA actors are growing in number and opportunities are arising for them to play more dimensional, interesting, and complex characters. However, this process has taken a long time, and it will be even longer before there are enough prominent roles to satisfy the needs of these performers. In the meantime, I argue that it is necessary for these performers to embrace, rather than eschew, their cultural identities by deepening their connections to the languages and art forms that make their particular cultural backgrounds unique—and that there should be more MENA producing organizations whose mission is to tell these stories in a complex and multifaceted manner.

Issue 1: cultural factors

Middle Eastern Americans, many of whom were immigrants themselves, do not traditionally encourage their children to pursue a career in the arts. The circumstances that caused them to immigrate, such as war and poverty, made it necessary for these immigrants to work diligently to create a life in the United States. Because many of these immigrants were forced to work in difficult or less lucrative fields, the hope became that their children would pursue more lucrative careers such as medicine, law, or engineering. Pursuing an unstable career in the arts might seem counterintuitive in the minds of immigrants whose sole purpose was to provide a better life for their children. Palestinian American playwright and actor Betty Shamieh stated:

> I was told all my life in different ways by Palestinians and non-Palestinians that I would never make it as a Palestinian working in American theater, that it would be impossible for me to have an impact or a voice. Whatever small success I have achieved has been in spite of the constant messages of defeatism that are rife within the Arab-American community.
>
> (Bortot 2010)

Palestinian American journalist and stand-up comedian Ray Hanania put it this way:

> We as Muslims and Arabs are not represented in the news media. Part of the reason for this shortfall is our own fault. We all want our children to be doctors, lawyers, and engineers. No one wants their son or daughter to be a reporter, or a Hollywood movie producer. Yet while doctors, lawyers and engineers generate decent wages, the reporter and the Hollywood producer are the most effective professions in terms of influencing American society.
>
> (Hanania 2007, 227)

It is clear that the paucity of MENA actors is born, in part, from a lack of encouragement by families to pursue this career choice. Egyptian American comic Bassem Youssef quips that growing up in an Arab family one has three career choices: doctor, lawyer, or failure.[1] In her essay "A Quest for Identity: Racism and Acculturation among Immigrant Families," Arab American psychologist and professor Sandra Mattar writes that, during times of anxiety in a culture, immigrant parents tend to return to their roots, while their children may desire to cling to their "American" identity more strongly.

> How can you teach your children to be proud of their ethnicity when the message in the community around you is "you either assimilate or else you don't belong." There is no possibility of embracing one's culture unless mainstream society confronts its own fears around difference and is willing to embrace "the other" as he/she is.
>
> (Mattar 2004, 147)

The desire for parents to keep their children out of the fields of theater, film, and television is both born of economic insecurity and of a knowledge that mainstream American society is not very accepting of racial or cultural difference. These parents do not have to look far to see the prejudices they face. In his book, *Reel Bad Arabs: How Hollywood Vilifies a People*, Jack G. Shaheen writes that Arabs have been vilified in film since the very beginnings of the film industry. He calls this "The New Anti-Semitism," not because there is anything particularly new about it, but because "many of the anti-Semitic films directed against Arabs were released in the last third of the twentieth century, a time when Hollywood was steadily and increasingly eliminating stereotypical portraits of other groups" (Shaheen 2001, 6). Therefore, the desire to shield their children from a potentially hostile—and economically inviable—career is understandable. The difficulty, of course, is that if there are not enough Middle Eastern American actors entering the profession, there will be too few to make change in the industry. This creates a vicious cycle: there are poor representations of Middle Easterners in theater, film and television; but there are few Middle Easterners in positions of power to change these representations.

Issue 2: Middle Eastern Americans in academia and actor training

For those who do pursue acting as a career in theater, academia and actor training programs often provide their own difficulties. First, academic theater programs are either unable, or unwilling, to produce plays that are written by Middle Eastern Americans or contain Middle Eastern roles. If they do so, they often choose plays or musicals that contain stereotypical or inconsequential roles for MENA actors. Some of the few plays or musicals that contain Middle Easterners—such as *Oklahoma!* (Ali Hakim), *The Time of*

Your Life (The Arab), *Water by the Spoonful* (Professor Aman/Ghost), *Bengal Tiger in the Baghdad Zoo* (Musa/Iraqi Woman/Iraqi Man/Hadia), *The Happiest Song Plays Last* (Ali), and *Ruined* (Mr. Harari)—do contain roles meant to portray Middle Easterners, but they are often problematic because they represent this group as greedy, pernicious salesmen (*Oklahoma, Ruined*), the foil for American adventurism (*Water by the Spoonful, Bengal Tiger in the Baghdad Zoo, The Happiest Song Plays Last*), or ethnic bit players that add "character" to the plays (*The Time of Your Life*). Few university theaters produce plays by Middle Eastern Americans due to their inability to cast the roles with students of Middle Eastern backgrounds. The belief is that, if MENA students are not enrolled or available, it is better not to produce the plays at all rather than risk offending the MENA community. This leads to what I call "sins of omission," which is to say that a play is not chosen because the "right" actors cannot be found to play the roles. By doing this, however, theater programs do not expose their audiences to diasporic playwrights, do not pay royalties to those playwrights, and eliminate opportunities for those who identify as MENA to play fully dimensional and leading roles.

In my own work directing Middle Eastern American plays within the university system in a small city like Eugene, Oregon, I have rarely had any MENA actors audition and there were rarely any MENA actors within the department whatsoever.[2] That said, the non–MENA actors I have cast in plays such as Heather Raffo's *9 Parts of Desire*, Wajdi Mouawad's *Scorched*, Yussef El Guindi's *Pilgrims Musa and Sheri in the New World*, and Denmo Ibrahim's *Ecstasy: A Water Fable* have embraced the opportunity to "walk in the other's shoes" by learning Arabic songs, learning Muslim prayers, or embodying Arab dance forms such as the *dabke*. In this way, I have been able to direct MENA plays, expose audiences to MENA playwrights, and teach non–MENA students about the history, culture, and embodied practice of Middle Eastern forms. My hope is that these students will take this knowledge beyond their college experience and apply it to their personal and professional lives. I admit that, growing up in an Arab household, I have a deeper cultural knowledge than most directors. What this means is that either directors with cultural knowledge should be hired to direct these productions, or directors without such knowledge must strive to do everything they can (through research, interviews, study) to understand these cultures to the fullest extent. What I have avoided, of course, is any kind of literal "brownface"/"Arab face" (which would include having actors physically transform themselves with makeup, for instance). Thus far, audiences are willing to accept the conceit that non–MENA actors can play MENA roles. However, when MENA actors are available for casting, I believe it is a producer/director's responsibility to seek those actors first and to cast them, given that they too bring cultural embodiment to their roles.

Issue 3: problems in the industry (representation and casting)

The UCLA College of Social Sciences 2018 report "Hollywood Diversity: Five Years of Progress and Missed Opportunities" states that, although America's increasingly diverse audiences prefer diverse content in film and television, only 13.9 percent of the lead actors in "top films" are people of color, less than one out of ten film directors are female, and people of color were underrepresented among the directors of top films in 2016 where they accounted for only 11.3 percent of credited directors (Hunt et al. 2018, 45). What is also quite interesting is that there is a disparity between the depiction of Middle Easterners and Middle Eastern Americans. In their book *America on Film: Representing Race, Class, Gender, and Sexuality at the Movies*, Harry M. Benshoff and Sean Griffin write, "Intriguingly, one of the most significant things about Arab Americans onscreen in America is their relative scarcity: Hollywood has much more regularly depicted images of *Middle Eastern Arabs* while nearly ignoring the presence of *Arab Americans*" (Benshoff and Griffin 2011, 71). They state that Arabs on film are seen as those who cannot assimilate into Western society due to their allegiances to homeland or the Muslim faith. Films concentrate on "white American heroes battling Arabs in foreign lands" or Arab terrorists infiltrating the United States. Middle Eastern American actors are still regularly cast as terrorists or sheiks. Benshoff and Griffin write, "if they want to work, they are sometimes compelled to accept these roles. Also, many still feel compelled to alter or change their Arabic-sounding names in order to work in the business" (Benshoff and Griffin 2011, 75). Therefore, Arab Americans enter an industry that rarely accepts diversity and, among the few diverse individuals that work in the industry, Middle Eastern Americans are among the least employed or acknowledged.

Of course, Middle Eastern American actors can attempt to play roles of non-MENA characters. This is yet another passing strategy that allows actors to remain employed but does not provide the MENA community opportunities to hear MENA writers' voices. The African American community has always faced this problem. In his seminal essay "The Ground on Which I Stand," the late playwright August Wilson wrote, "We do not need colorblind casting; we need some theatres to develop our playwrights. We need those misguided financial resources to be put to better use. We cannot develop our playwrights with the meager resources at our disposal" (Wilson 1997, 499). Wilson argued that colorblind casting may lead to more acting opportunities for actors of color, but it denies playwrights the funding to develop plays from these communities, denying actors from those communities the opportunity to speak from their specific cultural backgrounds. Wilson's view on African American theater is a helpful guide for other minoritarian theater communities. MENA communities face similar challenges—how can the artistic production of these communities grow when they are not even listed as a recognized minority, therefore making them ineligible for funding through many governmental arts organizations?

These structural problems found in the entertainment industry have effects on MENA actors who wish to forge careers in theater, film, and television. In her one-woman play *I Heart Hamas*, Palestinian American writer and actress Jennifer Jajeh writes about this inability to be categorized and how she was constantly pressured to sublimate her Palestinian identity: "Maybe I shouldn't have done this show. Shit, is this show gonna ruin my career? Maybe I could try to be less political? Or maybe I could be less vocal about it? Or maybe I could be less Palestinian? Maybe that would make things easier" (Jajeh 2012). This casting issue is more than an intellectual exercise—it manifests itself in actors having employment or being stereotypically portrayed. Arab American actor James Asher addresses what he calls "archetypal casting" and the notion that Arab American identity seems to manifest itself particularly in physical appearance:

> I struggle with it to some degree because my look in the world of Hollywood or archetypal casting is pretty one dimensional and being a real human being I have so much more than this to offer. As an artist and generally as a human there is much greater breadth to those like myself that is simply not mirrored back to us in the field of our expertise. And this is precarious for a community of any identity or any individual for that matter—to not recognize oneself in the mirror of our shared culture. I assume the same is true for all archetypes and stereotypes that people find themselves cast in.
>
> (James Asher, email message to author, September 28, 2015)

For her part, Palestinian American writer, actor, and performer Najla Said recounts:

> This process would become further complicated as I ventured into the commercial world with the name Najla Said. I was repeatedly and constantly described by casting directors and agents as "ethnic" and then just as often rejected with, "No! You're like a Jewish Italian girl from New York. You're too white to be ethnic." I struggled to figure out which I was. I refused to change my name. I had no deep attachment to my culture, but I felt very strongly that I should not have to do something so arcane to be seen for all that I was. I felt that deep painful racist punch in my stomach every time I even considered the idea of becoming "Nancy Smith" so that I could get a job. I pressed on. My friends began to succeed.
>
> (Said 2013, 201)

Therefore, it seems that the actors who are of particular ethnicities are being overlooked for parts they may be qualified to play, while actors of other ethnicities are attempting to pass in order to play those roles as well. To counter these seemingly endemic problems, MENA theater producers have attempted to address the specific difficulties faced by this community by creating companies that focus solely upon MENA plays.

In "Middle Eastern American Theatre, on Our Terms", Khoury and Yeghiazarian (2017) discuss the casting issue for MENA actors. In it they state that there are MENA artists working in communities throughout the U.S. and that "You all should be working with more Middle Eastern American actors, directors, dramaturgs, and designers." They contend that, if MENA actors cannot be hired due to a lack of numbers or due to the cost of hiring actors from distant communities, "then it's okay to cast more widely in the interest of telling the story." The priority must be about telling MENA stories and discussing casting options with the playwrights to arrive at decisions that honor their intentions.

Issue 4: lack of material

Jack G. Shaheen also calls for more diversity in the writing rooms of Hollywood. The 2018 Hollywood Diversity Report reveals that the creators of television shows are 92–95 percent white while minority writers comprise 4.2–7.1 percent of the talent (Hunt et al. 2018, 34). This disparity leads to fewer stories about Middle Eastern Americans and more stereotypical portrayals of this group by those who have the power to create these images. Shaheen writes, "We can't wait around for the stereotype to fade into the sunset. That's not what stereotypes do. Instead, victims need to hunt the stereotypes down and eradicate them" (Shaheen 2008, 55). What is most troubling to MENA playwrights, directors, and actors is that the non-MENA plays that depict MENA characters (and often stereotype them) are usually the ones that garner the most awards and accolades. The dominant reasoning seems to be that, since this community cannot speak for itself, others must speak for it. While an entire cadre of MENA playwrights hailing from virtually every nation in the Middle East find themselves fighting for the one spot per season for the "ethnic play," or not getting produced whatsoever, MENA actors are relegated to playing roles by non-MENA playwrights where they find themselves in yet more stereotypical situations.

Noted Arab American scholar Evelyn Alsultany writes:

> If more and more Americans were to see more and more complex portrayals of Arabs, Muslims, Arab Americans, and Muslim Americans on television and film, who knows what the effect would be. Racism is endlessly flexible; resentment of the Other can be easily stoked; stereotyped assumptions are difficult to overcome. Perhaps the emergence of honest, and varied, and *human* portrayals of Arabs and Muslims would make little difference in a country, and a world, attuned to prejudice.
>
> (Alsultany 2012, 177)

It is my contention that, since it is clear that non-MENA playwrights have done a less-than-admirable job in portraying MENA characters, it is necessary for MENA authors to create the "honest, varied, and *human* portrayals" that Alsultany calls for. In a 2016 *New York Times* feature titled "Can Television Be Fair to Muslims?" several MENA actors, writers, and directors were asked about the depiction of Muslims on screen. Arab American screenwriter, director, and actress Cherien Dabis stated:

> I think we need real depictions. I was developing a show [in 2013–14] about a Muslim family in Dearborn, [Mich.], which is the largest community of Arabs outside the Middle East. I wanted to create an authentic family drama. When I took it to the marketplace, every suggestion was that I needed to have some kind of terrorist component. Ultimately I ended up incorporating it in a way that looked at false accusations of terrorism. But I lost interest in the show because I was like, we can't keep showing Muslims as terrorists, even if it's just a false accusation.
>
> (Quoted in Ryzik 2016)

Until this situation changes, MENA producers, directors, and writers must be in positions of power at major studios, theaters, and cultural institutions. Also, more MENA-based theaters must be founded, funded, and supported by their communities. We have seen success in San Francisco, Chicago, and New York. But other large, predominately MENA communities in Texas, Michigan, and Washington could also have companies with similar missions. This would generate even more writers, directors, actors, and designers who can bring these stories to the stage. Of course, it would be absolutely necessary that MENA communities support these theaters financially despite their misgivings about the arts. Otherwise, this movement will never achieve its fullest potential.

Issue 5: it's not just about DNA

In her essay, Yeghiazarian states that, when choosing actors, she looks for cultural competence. If MENA actors are going to find employment at this time, they should strive to acquire culturally specific knowledge and embodied practice necessary to play the roles for which they most likely will be cast more accurately. For instance, it does not matter that an actor "looks" Arab in a play where the character plays traditional Middle Eastern instruments such as the *oud*, but that the actor has the requisite knowledge of how to actually play the *oud*. If a play calls for a Persian *bandari* dance, it is vital that the performer contain the requisite embodied knowledge of that dance form. It would be of little use for actors of Middle Eastern descent to be cast in plays if they do not have this cultural knowledge and, in attempting to mimic such art forms, inadvertently create a mockery of those forms. If Middle Eastern American actors wish to be cast more frequently, they should embrace—and not eschew—their Middle Eastern heritages and learn as much as possible about Middle Eastern music, dance, song, and performance forms; doing so makes them both more castable and better representatives of the cultures they embody. Granted, it would be impossible for any actor to be expected to learn all MENA languages and cultures; but perhaps if they focus their attention on their own cultural embodied practices, they may find that they are drawn closer to their cultures personally and artistically. Tony Shalhoub won a Tony Award in 2018 for his portrayal of Tewfiq in *The Band's Visit* by not only bringing great humanity to the role, but also by speaking and singing in Arabic. Maz Jobrani and Aasif Mandvi, in Tony Kushner's *Homebody/Kabul*, played the roles of Dr. Qari Shah and Mullah Ali Aftar Durranni (respectively) by bringing their own cultural understandings to the characters and speaking in the various languages required in the play. Omar Metwally received strong reviews for his work in the Broadway production of *Sixteen Wounded*, which brought a necessary depth of character to the Palestinian character Mahmoud. These are only a few examples of how MENA actors have successfully merged their acting expertise with their cultural embodiment in Broadway-level productions.

Looking forward

MENA writers, directors, actors, and producers have a long way to go before they can bring their stories to mainstream American theater. Great inroads have been made by playwrights Yussef El Guindi, Betty Shamieh, and Heather Raffo (to name just a few). Filmmaker Cherien Dabis has created several personal films about her Arab American heritage and producer/directors Jamil Khoury and Torange Yeghiazarian have created theaters that focus their time, effort, and funds on telling MENA stories. It seems that, until the time comes when there are more MENA artists who are in positions of power, it is necessary that MENA artists also embrace their specific cultural heritages and capitalize on their unique histories, cultures, artistic practices, languages, and other skills. There is obviously a market for such plays, so why not tell these stories more authentically themselves, rather than relying on non-MENA artists doing so?

At a recent conference in Beirut, I made an open call to the gathered audience to encourage more of their young people to enter the entertainment industry. I was approached by several young MENA performing artists who grew up in the United States and who told me that they were dissuaded from becoming performers by their families. They also noted that, even when they did attempt to audition for plays and films, they found little success. This experience further demonstrated the difficult and frustrating terrain these artists must navigate both within their communities and the industry itself. What has become clear to me is that, until more MENA artists take initiatives to create theaters and films that are specifically devoted to telling MENA stories, change will be gradual at best. It is incumbent upon us in the MENA community to utilize whatever cultural capital we have accrued in order to better represent these communities in our films and on our stages. Casting this particular movement is not unlike the challenges faced by other minorities in the past. Although progress may take many generations, we can see that there is much promise for change.

Notes

1 Bassem Youssef said this during a stand-up performance I attended at the Hult Center for the Performing Arts in Eugene, Oregon on Friday, November 30, 2018.
2 Brian Herrera's article "'But Do We Have the Actors for That?': Some Principles of Practice for Staging Latinx Plays in a University Theatre Context" (Herrera 2017) explores the difficulties some university theatre faculty face when attempting to cast plays when actors of color are not available to portray roles meant for characters of color.

Bibliography

Alsultany, Evelyn. 2012. *Arabs and Muslims in the Media: Race and Representation after 9/11*. New York: New York University Press.

Benshoff, Harry M., and Sean Griffin. 2011. *America on Film: Representing Race, Class, Gender, and Sexuality at the Movies*. Malden, MA: Wiley-Blackwell.

Bortot, M. Scott. 2010. "Playwright Betty Shamieh Outlines Keys to Success for Arab-American Artists." 11 June. IIP Digital.

Hanania, Ray. 2007. *I'm Glad I Look Like a Terrorist: Growing Up Arab in America*. Tinley Park, IL: Urban Strategies Group.

Herrera, Brian Eugenio. 2017. "But Do We Have the Actors for That?: Some Principles of Practice for Staging Latinx Plays in a University Context." *Theatre Topics*, 27(1): 23–35.

Hunt, Darnell M., Ana-Christina Ramón, Michael Tran, Amberia Sargent, and Debanjan Roychoudhury. 2018. "Hollywood Diversity Report 2018: Five Years of Progress and Missed Opportunities." February 27. 2018. https://socialsciences.ucla.edu/wp-content/uploads/2018/02/UCLA-Hollywood-Diversity-Report-2018-2-27-18.pdf

Jajeh, Jennifer. 2012. *I Heart Hamas*. Unpublished manuscript held by chapter author.

Khoury, Jamil and Torange Yeghiazarian. 2017. "Middle Eastern American Theatre, on Our Terms." *American Theatre*, September 29. www.americantheatre.org/2017/09/29/middle-eastern-american-theatre-on-our-terms.

Mattar, Sandra. 2004. "A Quest for Identity: Racism and Acculturation among Immigrant Families." In *The Psychology of Prejudice and Discrimination*, edited by Jean Lau Chin, 137–159. Westport, CT: Praeger Perspectives.

Ryzik, Melena. 2016. "Can Television Be Fair to Muslims?" *The New York Times*, November 30. www.nytimes.com/2016/11/30/arts/television/can-television-be-fair-to-muslims.html

Said, Najla. 2013. *Looking for Palestine: Growing Up Confused in an Arab-American Family*. New York: Riverhead Books.

Shaheen, Jack G. 2008. *Guilty: Hollywood's Verdict on Arabs After 9/11*. Northampton, MA: Olive Branch Press.

___. 2001. *Reel Bad Arabs: How Hollywood Vilifies a People*. New York: Olive Branch Press.

Wilson, August. 1997. "The Ground on Which I Stand." *Callaloo*, 20(3): 493–503.

Part III

Casting and disability culture

Casting disabled actors

Taking our rightful place onstage?

Christine Bruno

From the recent outcry over Scarlet Johansson signing on to portray a transgender character in a feature film to a white actor cast as Martin Luther King, Jr., in a university production, examples of artists fighting for accurate representations of race, ethnicity, and gender identity are numerous and far-reaching.[1]

Where, then, does the appropriation of *disability* fall on the scale of outrage — or even consideration?

Disabled people are America's largest minority, representing twenty-five percent of the population (Centers for Disease Control and Prevention 2018)—an estimated 61 million—yet disabled *artists* remain grossly underrepresented on our stages. Of all characters on American television in 2016, just five percent were characters with disabilities. Of that five percent, fewer than two percent were played by disabled actors (Squire et al. 2017).

As a disability inclusion consultant, advocate, and proud union actor with a mobility disability, I breathe, eat, and sleep disability, equity, and inclusion in entertainment every day. From 2005 until the organization's closure in December 2017, I served as Disability Advocate for Inclusion in the Arts, then the nation's leading advocate for actors of color and performers with disabilities in American theater, film, and television. A direct liaison between disabled artists and decision makers, along with my colleague, David Harrell, I assisted the industry with all things disability (casting disabled actors, providing resources for accessible audition spaces, securing interpreters, script consulting to ensure accuracy, etc.). I facilitated workshops, delivered keynote addresses, spoke on panels, and gave interviews nationally and internationally. As an actor, my mere presence on stage is the embodiment of the "other"; as such, I am a constant advocate for inclusion. I share this with my colleagues from all underrepresented groups—from race and ethnicity to gender identification. Where, then, do we diverge?

As many of my disabled colleagues are fond of saying, disability is a "club" anyone can join at any time, whether through birth, age, illness or injury, and our numbers are increasing daily. Disability, unlike other underrepresented groups, also cuts across all lines—race, ethnicity, sexual orientation, gender identity, and age. It's no surprise, then, that disabled artists and advocacy organizations continue to ask why disability is still so often not included in conversations of equity, diversity, and inclusion, much less afforded an equal seat at the table, and what can we do to give disability the attention it deserves?

Within the disability community, we derisively call the appropriation of disability by a nondisabled actor "cripping up" or "cripface" (pretending to have a disability). Not only is this common practice universally accepted as a technical skill tucked away in an actor's bag of tricks, it is applauded and, more often than not, rewarded. Since the ceremony's inception in 1929, as of 2011, nineteen percent of Academy Award for Best Actor winners have received the coveted statue for playing a disabled character (Rodgers 2012); just two of those winners were, themselves, disabled actors.

Confronting these examples—and hundreds more like them—the argument seems an obvious one: disabled actors should, at the very least, be afforded the opportunity to play themselves. There are disabled artists who believe that nondisabled actors should *never* be allowed to play disabled characters (Harris 2014); that to do so implies, among other things, that we cannot speak for ourselves. The catch-22 then becomes, "Is this actor, inclusive of disability, the *best* actor for the role?"

Any disabled actor worth their salt will tell you that we are not interested in being cast simply because of our disability, but because we are the right actor for the role—any role, disability-specific or not—and if our lived experience brings to the character a nuance that illuminates the story and the director's vision, we will provide an authenticity and innate understanding that a nondisabled actor cannot. When an underrepresented artist is denied equitable professional opportunities—whether access to training, auditions, or work experience—the exclusion results in a serious loss to the cultural life of the nation, denies artists and audiences alike the artistic benefits of diversity, and denies the public an accurate reflection of the society in which we live.

How does this apply to you and the art you make? If your theater produces an annual production of *A Christmas Carol*, do you actively audition children with disabilities to play Tiny Tim? Consider the hundreds of productions of *The Glass Menagerie*. How many Lauras have been played by disabled actresses? Is your stage accessible to actors who use wheelchairs? Have you ever produced a show that required actors to play multiple roles, some of which included characters without disabilities, in effect, denying a disabled actor an opportunity? How often does your programming include work by disabled playwrights and/or directors? Has your artistic staff had a conversation about making an ongoing commitment to inclusive casting and proactively addressing issues of disability in your programming?

After decades of glacially slow movement, we have begun to make incremental but measurable progress, at least with respect to casting disabled actors in disability-specific roles, as evidenced by recent Broadway revivals of *The Glass Menagerie, Children of a Lesser God*, and DeafWest's *Spring Awakening*, as well as provocative new plays like Pulitzer Prize winner *Cost of Living* and

Teenage Dick, and regional productions of *The Curious Incident of the Dog in the Night-Time.* Organizations like the Casting Society of America (CSA) are stepping up efforts to audition and cast disabled actors in disability-specific and nondescript roles across all mediums. An increasing number of theater companies across the country are making commitments that highlight disability as an integral part of diversity. These examples, however, remain the exception. The full inclusion of disabled artists in the theater deserves our serious consideration; it makes economic sense, an understandable priority, particularly for for-profit theaters—Americans with disabilities reportedly have more than twenty-one billion dollars in discretionary spending (Yin et al. 2018)—but, more importantly, it gets to the heart of why we make art. How can *you* help bring disability in the American theater closer to the tipping point?

Note

1 An earlier version of this essay was originally published in *HowlRound* on April 7, 2014 with the title "Disability in American Theater: Where is the Tipping Point?"

Bibliography

Centers for Disease Control and Prevention. 2018. "1 in 4 US Adults Live With a Disability." August 16. www.cdc.gov/media/releases/2018/p0816-disability.html (accessed April 2, 2019).

Harris, Scott Jordan. 2014. "Able-Bodied Actors and Disability Drag: Why Disabled Roles Are Only for Disabled Performers." March 7. www.rogerebert.com/balder-and-dash/disabled-roles-disabled-performers (accessed April 2, 2019).

Rodgers, Lucy. 2012. "How to Win an Oscar." *BBC News*, February 27. www.bbc.com/news/entertainment-arts-16932374 (accessed April 2, 2019).

Squire, Tari Hartman, Kristina Kopić, and Daryl "Chill" Mitchell. 2017. "The Ruderman White Paper on the Challenge to Create More Authentic Disability Casting and Representation on TV." http://rudermanfoundation.org/white_papers/the-ruderman-white-paper-on-the-challenge-to-create-more-authentic-disability-casting-and-representation-on-tv (accessed April 2, 2019).

Yin, Michelle, Dahlia Shaewitz, Cynthia Overton, and Deeza-Mae Smith. 2018. "The Purchasing Power of Working-Age Adults with Disabilities." www.air.org/system/files/downloads/report/Hidden-Market-Spending-Power-of-People-with-Disabilities-April-2018.pdf (accessed April 2, 2019).

Chapter 8

The difference disability makes

Unique considerations in casting performers with disabilities

Carrie Sandahl

Introduction

The phone rings in my office at school. I do not recognize the number, but I answer anyway. On the other end of the phone is an earnest, slightly desperate-sounding casting director who needs help finding a disabled actor to audition. I receive such requests regularly and, each time, I celebrate the fact that the disability community's collective call for casting disabled actors in disabled roles has been heard. Yet I still find these long-in-coming phone conversations difficult because, despite advocates' demands for authentic casting, we in the field are still working to identify a substantial number of professionally trained disabled actors. There are simply not enough of them to meet demand. The casting director on the other end of the phone is disappointed that I cannot offer her a list of potential actors that meet her specifications—neither of us has the time for me to explain the reasons why trained disabled actors are so few and far between or what casting options the director might pursue should a suitable disabled actor not be found. I am grateful, then, to have the time and space in this essay to explore myriad issues around disability and casting—a conversation that is rife with contradictions, twists, and turns that take more than a brief phone call to unpack.

I speak from my experiences of having been a disabled theater student and now university faculty. I was also a Co-Project Investigator with Dr. Carol Gill on a three-year qualitative study funded by National Endowment of the Arts (NEA) on barriers and facilitators to arts careers for Americans with disabilities from childhood through adulthood (Gill and Sandahl 2009). I have participated in various research convenings, including one covering the state of physically integrated dance (AXIS Dance Company 2017) and others covering the intersection of art education and special education (Kennedy Center 2017). This range of research, mentoring, and creative work has given me opportunities to understand different forms of knowledge production—critical theory, qualitative research, arts-based research, and creative practice—that disabled theater artists face.

A scarcity mindset

Over the course of my education and career, I have heard stories from faculty, students, and professionals (both disabled and nondisabled) that actor training programs either outright reject or actively discourage disabled students from applying due to the assumption that there are too few disability-specific roles for disabled students to play when they graduate; and, therefore, the likelihood of being cast professionally is pretty much nil. This foundational assumption needs to be questioned: is it true that there are too few disability-specific roles in theater and related media? The answer is no ... and the answer is yes. Let me explain.

Foundational disability studies scholars explain that representation relies on disability's appearance and, paradoxically, on its *disappearance* over the course of a narrative arc. In his 1985 article, "Screening Stereotypes: Images of Disability in Television and Motion Pictures," the disabled historian Paul Longmore claims that not only do disabled characters exist, they are ubiquitous; however, we "usually screen them out of our consciousness even as we absorb" them (Longmore 2003, 131–132). He proposes that stereotypical portrayals (i.e. victims, villains, monsters, inspirational overcomers) function as "melodramatic devices" (133), representing and then purging an ostensibly nondisabled audience's social anxieties and fears around issues such as loss of bodily autonomy. Disabled characters function as a narrative's tools, rather than its subjects.

Disability studies literary scholars David T. Mitchell and Sharon L. Snyder further develop Longmore's insight in their 2000 book *Narrative Prosthesis and the Dependencies of Discourse*. They coin the term "narrative prosthesis" to describe a narrative's dependency on disability as an inciting incident, its arrival signaling "something out of place" (Mitchell and Snyder 2000, 10). A disabled character, they explain, is a "material metaphor," embodying a "problem to be solved" in the narrative. The problem of disability stands in for larger, more abstract social issues and is resolved by the narrative's end in one of four typical outcomes for the disabled character: cure, death, rescue from censure (saving the disabled character), or revaluation (changing disability's meaning) (53–54). Narratives relegate disabled characters to serving as catalysts for shoring up nondisabled characters' normalcy, ultimately rendering these disabled characters as forgettable.

I believe that when actual disabled actors inhabit disabled characters onstage, they are not so easily forgotten. These actors' appearance concretizes—and thereby closes uncomfortably—the distance between a metaphor's signifier and signified; their presence itself generates excess meaning, which is, supposedly, a negative distraction for the audience. The presence of disabled actors raises extra-textual questions about their impairment in real life, or what the disability community calls the spoken or unspoken "what happened to you?" question. It is difficult to turn disability into a metaphor when it is literally embodied. And when the actual disabled actor plays a role intended for a nondisabled actor, audiences supposedly become negatively distracted by waiting and wondering when the expected "problem" of disability will announce itself. I have heard it said that disability onstage is like Chekhov's gun—a play's promise to the audience. If disability appears in the opening act, it had better fire by the play's end.[1]

I pause here to summarize the contradictions I have laid out thus far. Fledgling disabled actors are told that the lack of roles for disabled actors precludes their entering the profession, while at the same time disabled characters are replete in representation. Disabled actors are told that their visible impairments must be explained by the narrative because audiences expect impairments to be significant to the plot—no explanation would be a detrimental distraction. Even though disabled characters' appearances in plays are so significant to the plot that audiences must not be distracted from them by actual disabled bodies, when asked, theater artists and audiences forget these characters exist at all and will struggle to name them. Narrative often relies on an instance of disability, but necessarily disposes of it one way or another by the play's end. But when disabled actors appear, these characters' disabilities are not as easily forgotten, generating excessive, distracting meaning.[2]

Cripping up

We now arrive at the twists and turns promised at the beginning of this essay. I have come to understand that the prognosis of "un-castable" is an especially insidious form of gaslighting that discourages disabled students from even trying to enter an actor training program, much less the profession. First, disabled students—who see disabled characters everywhere—are told there are no disabled roles—and that this lack of roles is a fact that cannot be overcome. Further confusion sets in when disabled students wonder why, if it is true that there are no disability-specific roles, they cannot overcome this *particular* obstacle by playing characters with no specified disability. Disabled people are conditioned by culture—and even by their own prior educational success—to believe that, if they are strong and determined, they overcome. They must have had enough tangible success in "overcoming" the obstacle of impairment (i.e. surgeries, rehabilitation, therapies) and stigma (i.e. educational discrimination, microaggressions, implicit bias) to even get to a place where they can aspire to a professional acting career. To make matters worse, they are given this prognosis as if it should have been obvious to them all along.

While disabled actors are told that their impairments are undesirable distractions, nondisabled actors routinely generate excess meaning when they play disabled characters. Instead of being excluded from playing these roles due to the distraction they cause, these nondisabled actors are amply rewarded with accolades for their portrayals of disabled characters. In the disability community, we have long joked that the best route to winning an Oscar is by "cripping up"—a term that UK playwright Kaite O'Reilly coined in 2002 and was subsequently taken up by disability activists to describe the practice of non-disabled actors mimicking impairments (Komporály 2005). Cripping up relies on its association with the shameful practice of white actors "blacking up" their faces with dark make-up to play African American characters in minstrel shows. Even after minstrelsy, the term "blacking up" has been used to describe white actors playing in "blackface" with or without the accompanying cosmetics. Asian Americans actors and advocates call out productions for casting white actors to perform in "yellowface." Similarly, the disability community accuses productions that cast nondisabled actors for disability-specific roles of "crip face." While the practice of yellowface and crip face are not precisely analogous to each other or to blackface, they draw on blackface's power in naming the violent erasure and displacement of oppressed people by such casting practices. While analogies are imperfect and their elements should not be conflated, it is important to consider that these types of performance can intersect, as in the case of white performers in blackface dancing as the "crippled" Jim Crow or the case of able-bodied actor Cuba Gooding, Jr., adopting the mannerisms of the black, intellectually disabled character Radio in the 2003 film by the same name. A full discussion of the specific, differing, and complex intersections of racism and ableism that inform both examples are beyond the scope of this essay. For now, I want to focus on how the issues of casting disabled actors for both disability-specific and non-specific roles are unique and their solutions may be different from what might be considered "authentic" casting in terms of race or ethnicity, for instance. Later in this essay, I return briefly to issues of intersectionality as they affect casting.

The disability community's eye-rolling about nondisabled actors getting Oscars for cripping up to play disabled characters is, unfortunately, no joke. Statistics have borne out our suspicions that Oscars are disproportionately awarded to nondisabled actors who have played characters with disabilities (Moyer 2015). In the Academy Awards' history, only two openly disabled actors have been awarded for playing these characters: Harold Russell for Best Supporting Actor in 1947 (*The Best Years of Our Lives*, 1946) and Marlee Matlin for Best Actress in 1987 (*Children of a Lesser God*, 1986).[3] Mimicking impairment is considered a consummate test of a nondisabled actor's technical skills. Media stories of actors' transformations into disabled characters proliferate to the point of becoming cliché. These stories delve into the actors' research for performing these roles: their engagement with medical professionals, their shadowing of actual disabled people, and their use of prosthetics. These nondisabled actors are praised for taking on the stigma of disability by temporarily deforming their Hollywood-beautiful bodies. And, as independent scholar and theater maker Eli Van Sickel (2015) points out, nondisabled actors garner even more praise by sacrificing their own physical health when they mimic impairments. By holding bodily postures—such as a spine curved by scoliosis or an armed contracted by cerebral palsy—nondisabled actors may inadvertently injure themselves or suffer from debilitating pain.

Because performing disability is considered a skill by nondisabled actors and not an identity, actual disabled actors are accused of not being "real" actors when they play disabled characters. Take Russell and Matlin, for example. Both won Oscars for their first movie roles; yet among the accolades lurked murmurs that they were undeserving, that they were not *really* acting, and that they were "just playing themselves." Matlin recounts how some critics said her "victory [was] the result of a pity vote and undeserved ('she's essentially a deaf person playing a deaf role')" (Matlin 2012). Critics generally praised Russell more for his sacrifice as an injured veteran than his acting and emphasized Russell's status as "untrained." Russell's obituary in *The Guardian* is typical: "Brave actor whose artificial hands helped him win two Oscars" (Bergan 2002). Assumptions contained within Roger Ebert's 2007 retrospective review of *The Best Years of Our Lives* suggest that, because Russell used his prostheses expertly in daily life, his use of them in the film did not entail acting choices. Ebert proclaims that when Homer, Russell's character, reveals to his fiancée Wilma that he is as "helpless as a baby" without his prosthetic arms, "We *know* Russell is speaking for himself, and the emotional power is overwhelming" (emphasis in the original). But do audiences truly "know" that Russell is as helpless as a baby without his prosthetic limbs? In actuality, the real-life Russell created make-shift prosthetics with his fellow amputees at Walter Reed Hospital in the weeks following his amputation so that he could hold a cigarette and perform other tasks (CriticsAtLarge 1981). Rather than helplessness, Russell's autobiographical account demonstrates resourcefulness, ingenuity, and the disability community in action rather than isolated, infantile helplessness.

The leaky pipeline

While uncommon, some disabled actors do get cast in disability-specific and non-specific roles in television, theater, and film, but the extent to which this happens is unclear. A handful of disability-centric theater companies dot the American landscape: Phamaly in Denver, National Theatre of the Deaf in Connecticut, The Apothetae in New York City, and the just-founded National Disability Theatre, among others. Disabled actors have appeared in high-profile productions, most notably Deaf West's Broadway productions of *Big River* (2003) and *Spring Awakening* (2015). *Spring Awakening* is also noteworthy for Broadway's first known appearance of a wheelchair-using actor, Ali Stroker, followed by the appearance of another wheelchair-using actor, Madison Ferris, cast as Laura in Broadway's 2017 revival of *The Glass Menagerie*. I could continue to name and count the actual number of disability-centric theater companies and disabled actors cast in mainstream productions; but the fact that it is even possible to do so is a testament to the practice's rarity. Will there be a substantial number of disabled actors to cast in theaters on Broadway and across the country in the foreseeable future? If so, when? How many Strokers and Ferrises are there in the actor-training pipeline? And how can counting and naming of specific instances mislead us into generalizations, thereby occluding the vastness of the problem?

The truth of the matter is that we cannot accurately count the number of professionally trained disabled actors or potential actors along the entire professional pipeline. For frustratingly concrete reasons, we do not have reliable numbers from the entertainment industry, from higher education, or even from the kindergarten through grade twelve system. In the 2016 white paper titled *Employment of Actors with Disabilities in Television*, funded by the Ruderman Family Foundation, researchers Danny Woodburn and Kristina Kopić explain that, while the demographics on age, race/ethnicity, and gender are collected on Casting Data Report Forms for big-budget television and film productions, disability demographics are not, which complicates our efforts to understand the nature and scope of the pipeline problem for mass media, let alone theater. The primary reason these numbers are not collected is because existing laws prohibit it. The researchers later turn to the Breakdown Services database for answers. Breakdown Services allows for actors seeking roles—including theatrical roles—to provide information about their disability status to those looking to cast them. Woodburn and Kopić report that, out of the service's 600,000 active users, "the total number of actors with disability equals a little over 4000" (2016, 14). As the researchers attempt to get more specific, it becomes clear just how small the talent pool is. For example, they explain that one casting director's search of the database revealed that only 1375 actors had input information about their specific impairments. The top categories included the following: 245 who are Deaf or hard of hearing, 230 with Down syndrome, 132 who are neurodiverse,[4] 113 little people, 135 wheelchair users, and 69 who are blind or low-vision. The data reveal the small overall number of actors who identify as disabled and how the numbers are smaller still when looking at specific impairment types. What this data does not reveal are these actors' type or level of training. So even in this data set, we cannot gather or even infer the number of trained disabled actors within it.[5]

Moving along the pipeline from the level of the profession to the level of higher education, we encounter the same lack of information due to laws preventing individual higher educational institutions from collecting disability demographics from the general student population, much less in specific departments (Raue and Lewis 2011). Individual colleges and universities may, though, collect the number of students seeking disability services; but these numbers are not representative, since not all disabled students seek services and, of the students who do seek services, we do not know how many of them are theater majors specializing in acting.

Disabled theater artist and scholar Victoria Ann Lewis has also expressed frustration at the difficulty in counting and locating disabled acting students. In her 2009 article "Disability and Access: A Manifesto for Actor Training," Lewis explains that students are denied entry into university training programs because they are assumed to be unemployable (another way of describing the "uncastable" argument) and because they are assumed to be incapable of mastering certain curricular standards in voice and movement training (Lewis 2009). She argues that university programs can, through imaginative collaboration with disabled students, adapt the curriculum and successfully train them. Lewis's article provides invaluable practical advice for university programs. And while Lewis's manifesto is a blueprint for the future, the small sample size of her research participants demonstrates just how rare it is for a disabled actor, especially one with a significant mobility impairment, to receive university actor training.

If we go further along the pipeline from higher education into the kindergarten-secondary education area, we can identify other leaks. In 2016, I participated in two research convenings conducted by the Kennedy Center's Office of VSA and Accessibility on the state of art education and special education for children with disabilities in the K-12 system. In addition to my own experience and the data we gathered in the 2010 NEA study I mentioned earlier, I brought to the conversation my experiences as a parent of two disabled children who receive special education services, including early intervention. During these convenings, I learned that most art education programs do not provide budding teachers the option to learn about disability accommodations and adaptations for artmaking. And neither do special education programs provide specific curricula in the arts. Despite federal law's mandate to include disabled children in public schools since the mid-1970s, arts education and special education have yet to join forces.

It became clear to me during my involvement in these convenings that our pipeline problem is not going to be resolved any time soon. At the convenings, researchers lamented the shrinking arts programming across the board in our K-12 public education system. Many disabled students need adaptations and accommodations to access the curriculum. Learning about the almost complete lack of formal teacher training in this area made me realize that expanding access to training for disabled artists is going to require efforts both inside and outside the K-12 system.

Interventions

Those of us working for both academic and professional theaters can share responsibility for improving opportunities for theater artists along the whole pipeline. Art education and special education are entrenched in medical model thinking, which considers disability to be primarily an individual pathology to be cured or ameliorated, rather than social model thinking, which considers people with disabilities a minority group whose oppression is caused by a mismatch between people and their environments. Students with disabilities have few opportunities to explore the arts in the same ways that their nondisabled peers do. In the K-12 system, not only do disabled students need to meet state-mandated outcomes, but they must also meet the goals in Individualized Education Plans (IEPs). These goals tend to focus on rehabilitation as much as they are in meeting curricular standards. I have seen IEPs that list improvement areas usually reserved for medicalized therapies: eye contact, attention, manual dexterity, and gross motor skills. I urged researchers to think carefully about how disabled children's primary access to the arts is through participation in therapies (art, dance/movement/drama) as well as in occupational therapy where art supplies are often used. Children do not understand the difference between using art supplies in therapy and using art supplies in art classes. While nondisabled students have arts experiences as a means of exploring creativity, disabled students are offered arts experiences as a means of enforcing normalization. It is no wonder that from early childhood disabled people are led to believe that they cannot be artists due to their impairments.[6]

If nondisabled theater artists are stuck in medical model thinking, believing they need to acquire specialized, therapy-like skills in order to interact with disabled people, then people with and without disabilities miss out on learning from one another outside a medicalized context. A medicalized context always privileges and enforces "normalcy," occluding the ways in which disabled ways of being might be generative and interesting. Theater artists have precisely the qualities necessary to engage with the ways in which disability might spark creativity—we have ample imagination. We create entire worlds for each production. We collaborate as producers, directors, designers, and technical practitioners as a rule. We are used to working with our bodies and the bodies of others. And disabled peoples' unique phenomenological and lived experience can inspire aesthetic innovation.

What follows is a list of additional ways we can address the pipeline problem and increase the participation of disabled artists as actors, designers, teachers, and directors:

1 Consider disabled ways of being an asset, not a burden. Seek out the work of professional artists with disabilities, both emerging and professional. Because this work may be difficult to find outside certain disability arts hubs, look online or take advantage of opportunities to see this work when you are visiting other cities nationally and internationally. Become familiar with aesthetic innovations in the field. I recommend exploring innovations in Deaf theater and integrated dance as I find them to be the most imaginative in creating new aesthetics.

2 While it is true that there are few trained disabled actors, they do exist. Find out who the trained disabled actors are in your area or who the promising disabled actors might be. When choosing a season, think about roles for these actors—both disability-specific and nonspecific. Choosing roles and plays for the disabled actors that you know will be more successful than trying to find a person to fill a very specific niche. Unless you have the budget for casting a wide net with your search, you will be hard pressed to locate a trained disabled actor who also fulfills other needs of the role. You may want to consider going beyond finding an actor whose impairment "matches" that called for by the script. For example, recent productions such as the 2016 collaboration between Chicago's The Gift

Theatre and Steppenwolf featured the disabled actor Michael Patrick Thornton, a wheelchair user, in the role of Richard III and without the requisite "hunchback."

3 Remember issues of intersectionality. The phone calls that I receive looking for very specific actors to cast are particularly difficult because one can be put in the difficult position of having to choose one kind of identity "authenticity" over another. Just in the past year I have been asked for assistance in finding actors who meet the following criteria: a young, Asian-American woman with a mobility impairment; a blind, gay, Latino in his twenties; and a middle-aged, Deaf Latino. How do age, gender, race, ethnicity, sexuality, and impairment-type work together to create meaning? How will these meanings impact your choices? Consult with and include people from the multiple identity groups represented by disabled characters in your play.

4 Audiences and critics will take note of whether a disabled actor plays a disabled or a nondisabled character. Prepare for how you might want to address the inevitable interest in a disabled actor's "what happened to you?" story. Involve the actor in these decisions. You may get backlash concerning the excess meaning generated when a disabled actor concretizes a metaphor, especially if the impairment called for in the script differs from the actor's impairment. Read the recent criticism, for instance, of Madison Ferris's portrayal of Laura in Broadway's *The Glass Menagerie*, which ranged from praise, to thoughtful reflection, to paternalism, to condemnation, to outrage. While Tennessee Williams calls for Laura to have a limp, Ferris uses a wheelchair. Accept that no matter what choice you make, you will get one or more of these reactions. Consider your willingness to be in solidarity with disabled people. Change will not happen unless more of us are willing to share in the praise, the outrage, and all the reactions in between that these casting choices elicit. These experiences have value.

5 When choosing a play, think about whether its disabled characters are stereotypes beyond rehabilitation. Question whether casting a disabled person in this role would lend authenticity to or naturalize a pernicious stereotype. In other words, would casting a disabled actor necessarily change the ableism of the role? Given the tendency to interpret disabled actors as "just playing themselves," might audiences and critics consider these stereotypes as real? If you feel uncomfortable with asking a disabled actor to give life to this stereotype, then consider whether this play overall warrants the sacrifice of disabled people's dignity.

6 Include guidelines on discussing disability in your press materials, such as preferred language and information on terms and tropes to be avoided (for example terms like "wheelchair-bound" and characterizing the actor as inspirational overcomer or suffering victim).

7 Offer in your seasons "relaxed performances," which make theater-going more accessible for people whose comportment is traditionally unwelcome in our theater spaces. In these performances, certain elements are "relaxed": lighting and sound may be adjusted to be less jarring for those with sensory issues; audience members are able to move about the space, including leaving and re-entering should they need or want to; house lights are kept at a glow; and behaviors—such as talking aloud during the show, making impairment-related noises, rocking, or "stimming"—are acceptable. In the US, these relaxed performances are typically called "sensory friendly" performances, they are mostly geared to those on the autism spectrum, and they tend to be "family friendly." The Museum of Contemporary Art Chicago offers relaxed performances in their regular season, including accommodations such as American Sign Language interpretation and audio description. In addition, these performances appeal to a wider segment of the disability population.

8 Seek involvement and mentorship of disabled artists in your area. These artists may be outside the theater, but their insights and talents can be put to use as consultants and collaborators. Bring these artists into your projects whether you are in the professional theater or academia.

9 Serve as a mentor yourself to disabled theater artists in your area.

10 Be aware that you may need to be flexible in ways you are not used to. You may, for example, run into issues with how you pay non-unionized disabled artists. These artists may rely on benefits such as Social Security Income, which limits how much one can make in a month. Consequences for exceeding these caps may result in losing benefits or paying them back. Be aware that disabled theater artists may have health-related issues affecting stamina. Have a clear plan for an understudy.

Conclusion

In this essay, I set out to discuss the unique differences disability makes when it comes to casting. You can find more information about the efforts organizations and individuals have taken to address the obstacles disabled actors face as well as concrete information on improving access and accommodations in your theaters and training programs. Until its recent closing, the Alliance for Inclusion in the Arts, for example, had long advocated for disabled actors, providing technical assistance and maintaining an extensive database of disabled actors. Though the organization has closed, their Facebook page[7] and website[8] remain valuable resources. Actors' Equity Association (AEA) and SAG-AFTRA (Screen Actors Guild-American Federation of Television and Radio Artists) ran a remarkable education and advocacy campaign called I AM PWD that promoted the casting of disabled actors, and they continue their efforts. Practical handbooks, such as Stephanie Barton Farcas's *Disability and Theatre: A Practical Manual for Inclusion in the Arts* (2018), are available. Some agents specialize in representing actors with disabilities and the company Breakdown Services allows actors to selectively disclose their disability status to casting directors searching for them. The organization Lights! Camera! Access! holds mentoring sessions for disabled people interested in working in the entertainment industry.[9] Even though those of us who are disability theater advocates cannot yet produce extensive lists of trained disabled actors, we are not being disingenuous when we call for authentic casting. Trained disabled actors do exist, even if they are not in the quantity needed to populate the theater and media landscapes. We need to think about the big picture and intervene at all levels, accepting responsibility for our roles in developing the pipeline in whatever way possible and using our imaginations to rethink how we make theater. We do what we can, where we can, when we can, and we can keep answering the phone.

Acknowledgment

This essay was written during a summer 2018 writer's residency at Ragdale in Lake Forest, IL, with support from a Creative Access Fellowship.

Notes

1 For additional writing on disability and casting as relates to theater, see Fox and Sandahl 2018 and Sandahl 2008.
2 See Sandahl 2018.
3 Arguably, other actors with disabilities have won, but at the time of their winning were not openly self-identified as having a disability or perceived as disabled at the time. Laura Dern and Robin Williams are two such examples.
4 I combined the numbers for those actors who self-identified as having autism or Asperger's.
5 I have also heard from industry insiders that these numbers may be inaccurate due to a misunderstanding by some nondisabled actors that they may enter themselves into this database if they believe that they can play disabled characters with these impairments. My analysis in this paper only critiques the data on the sample search done by Woodburn and Kopić (2016).
6 Most of the participants in our NEA study told Gill and me that they did not believe arts careers even a possibility for disabled people and that these beliefs were reinforced since their early childhood.
7 See www.facebook.com/InclusionInTheArts.
8 See http://inclusioninthearts.org.
9 See https://einsofcommunications.com/lights-camera-access-2-0.

Bibliography

AXIS Dance Company. 2017. "The Future of Physically Integrated Dance in the USA." https://static1.squarespace.com/static/53a9f1fbe4b08edefaf5367d/t/59a4840e6f4ca3313b 05c3fe/1503953949140/AxisDance-Report-DanceUSA2017-Final-AltTags%28lo-res% 29.pdf (accessed December 29, 2018).
Bergan, Ronald. 2002. "Obituary: Harold Russell." *The Guardian*, February 6. www. theguardian.com/news/2002/feb/06/guardianobituaries (accessed April 2, 2019).

CriticsAtLarge. 1981. "Interview with Harold Russell (1981)." https://www.mixcloud.com/CriticsAtLarge/interview-with-harold-russell-1981 (accessed December 29, 2018).

Ebert, Roger. 2007. "The Best Years of Our Lives Movie Review (1946) | Roger Ebert." December 29. www.rogerebert.com/reviews/the-best-years-of-our-lives-1946 (accessed April 2, 2019).

Fox, Ann M., and Carrie Sandahl. 2018. "Beyond 'Cripping Up' An Introduction." *Journal ofLiterary and Cultural Disability Studies*, 12(2): 121–127.

Gill, Carol, and Sandahl, Carrie. 2009. "Arts Career Outcomes and Opportunities for Americans with Disabilities: A Qualitative Study." http://artsedge.kennedy-center.org/2009NEASummit/papers.html (accessed November 25, 2017).

Kennedy Center. 2017. "The Arts and Special Education: A Map for Research." http://education.kennedy-center.org/pdf/educationresearch/3AERA_Paper-Abstract.pdf (accessed December 29, 2018).

Komporály, Jozefina. 2007. "'Cripping Up is the Twenty-first Century's Answer to Blacking Up': Conversation with Kaite O'Reilly on Theatre, Feminism, and Disability." *Gender Forum*, 12: 58–67.

Lewis, Victoria. 2009. "Disability and Access: A Manifesto for Actor Training." In *The Politics of American Actor Training*, edited by Ellen Margolis and Lisa Tyler Renaud, 177–197. New York: Routledge.

Longmore, Paul K. 2003. *Why I Burned My Book and Other Essays on Disability*. Philadelphia, PA: Temple University Press.

Matlin, Marlee. 2012. "Oscars: Marlee Matlin on Her Best Actress Win." https://ew.com/article/2012/02/21/oscars-marlee-matlin (accessed December 29, 2018).

Mitchell, David T., and Sharon L. Snyder. 2000. *Narrative Prosthesis: Disability and the Dependencies of Discourse*. Ann Arbor, MI: University of Michigan Press.

Moyer, Justin Wm. 2015. "Welcome, Eddie Redmayne: Since 'Rain Man,' Majority of Best Actor Oscar Winners Played Sick or Disabled." *The Washington Post*, February 23. www.washingtonpost.com/news/morning-mix/wp/2015/02/23/since-rain-man-majority-of-best-actor-winners-played-sick-or-disabled/?utm_term=.537a3d6cb509 (accessed December 29, 2018).

Raue, Kimberley, and Lewis, Laurie. 2011. *Students With Disabilities at Degree-Granting Postsecondary Institutions*. Statistical Analysis Report, 18. Washington, DC: National Center for Education Statistics, US Department of Education. https://nces.ed.gov/pubs2011/2011018.pdf (accessed April 2, 2019).

Sandahl, Carrie. 2008. "Why Disability Identity Matters: From Dramaturgy to Casting in John Belluso's Pyretown." *Text and Performance Quarterly*, 28(1–2): 225–241.

___. 2018. "Using Our Words: Exploring Representational Conundrums in Disability Drama and Performance." *Journal of Literary & Cultural Disability Studies*, 12(2): 129–144.

Van Sickel, Eli. 2015. "Bodies on the Line." https://howlround.com/bodies-line (accessed December 29, 2018).

Woodburn, Danny, and Kristina Kopić. 2016. *Employment of Actors with Disabilities in Television*. Boston, MA: Ruderman Family Foundation. http://rudermanfoundation.org/white_papers/employment-of-actors-with-disabilities-in-television (accessed December 29, 2018).

Chapter 9

A great and complicated thing

Reimagining disability

Victoria Lewis

Mike Ervin, Lynn Manning, Susan Nussbaum, and John Belluso are and were part of a wave of disabled playwrights writing plays in the 1990s from a new understanding of disability identity as socially constructed. They rejected the paternalistic dramaturgical devices embedded in both popular and elite entertainments, devices that generated an abundance of victims, villains, overcomers, super-crips, self-pitying malcontents, all to be physically or psychologically cured by the intervention of a benign nondisabled friend, doctor, lover, or assisted in a "heroic" suicide (see Longmore 2003, 131–146). It wasn't just that characters with disabilities had been added in lead roles—that was a longstanding convention: Brian Clark's *Whose Life Is It Anyway?*, *Richard III*, or theatrical adaptations of Steinbeck's *Of Mice and Men*. These new characters were aware of their rights. They were angry, funny, and at ease in a theatrical world where injustice was treated with Swiftian absurdity. These new depictions variously delighted, befuddled, or threatened literary departments in the regional theater, sometimes all three reactions in one room.

The fate of those plays by disabled playwrights is part of my subject here. Another is the resistance in the theater and the media to the new liberated model of disability now at least forty-five years old. As a disabled actor, director, and educator, I experienced this resistance in a variety of roles and settings as part of: first a Maoist People's Theater collective; followed by a feminist one; then as a member of the artistic staff of a progressive regional theater where I directed a workshop for disabled actors and writers. Along the way I was supporting cast for a major nighttime soap in which I was identified as a disabled legal secretary but never got a last name (the Latino valet to one of the show's rich power brokers also functioned for seven years without a surname); and, now, as an academic. In 2000, I joined the theater faculty of a small, southern California liberal arts college.

And everywhere there was resistance—a discomfort with a new concept of disability, accompanied by a sense of affront, as if one's emotional morality had been called into question. Or a lack of curiosity about disability as an aesthetic element and an aversion to such discussions as imposing political correctness on the artistic process. But such resistance by default creates a vacuum into which the dominant cultural imaginary, where the oldest stereotypes abide, steps in and supplies a readymade disabled character, one defined by inferiority, helplessness, gumption, powerlessness, evil—or at least a very bad attitude. I will investigate the possibility of plays by disabled writers countering these received stereotypes and, by extension, providing interesting, challenging roles for disabled actors.

Finally I will share a recent strategy that I have pursued in the academic setting to introduce this reconstituted disability identity into the campus's cultural imaginary by reaching outside of the theatre department for creative collaborations, including casting.

The cultural imaginary of disability

What are the cornerstones of disability in the dominant cultural imaginary? Taking a global view, disability activist and Marxist sociologist and theorist James Charlton concludes:

> Beliefs and attitudes about disability are individually experienced but socially constituted. They are, with few exceptions, pejorative. They are paternalistic and often sadistic and hypocritical. When complacently pejorative attitudes are not held, people with disabilities often experience a paradoxical set of "sympathetic" notions like the courageous or noble individual.
>
> (Charlton 1998, 51)

The norm in American public life and in the performing arts towards disability generally inclines towards the second option, that of sympathy, assigning the virtues of courage and nobility to the disabled individual. The dominant narrative of disability in Western drama reflects this sympathetic admiration: an *individual's* triumph over a *personal tragedy*. Unquestioned is disability as an inevitably tragic experience and missing is any social, historical, or collective context for the disability experience. This individualistic interpretation is one reason conservatives often appropriate the disabled figure, as it fulfills the "up by your bootstraps" ideology of individual exceptionalism.

The theatrical left and the disabled figure

The cultural left fails just as often to recognize the newly imagined civil rights model of disability. Progressive and radical theory and practice have traditionally assigned the disabled figure a negative role. When Emerson characterized conservatives as "effeminated by nature, born halt and blind" (in Thomson 1996, 42), he drew on a common trope of revolutionary rhetoric that equates aristocracy with effeminacy, weakness, and disability.

In twentieth-century People's Theater, the physically different body appears in service of guilt (the victim of capitalism, industrialization, war, etc.). This chorus from a mass recitation of the German troupe Red Megaphone is typical:

two million without work,

two million without bread.

Children, *pale hungry cripples*,

sickness, pain, filth and death.

(Bodek 1997, 107; italics added)

Contemporary liberal plots often celebrate the courageous disabled suicide who refuses a life of dependency without dignity and the nondisabled enabler who bravely assists the disabled character in achieving that noble goal.

Disability: A great and complicated thing

However, I found relief from the emotional sea of tears attached to disability in the popular media, whether reactionary or progressive, in the theoretical writings of leftist paragon Bertolt Brecht. In "Theatre for Pleasure or Instruction," Brecht confesses to the artistic crime of being a poet who needs the sciences, saying:

> Bad as it may sound, I have to admit I cannot get along as an artist without the use of one or two sciences.... [I]n my view *the great and complicated things that go on in the world* cannot be adequately recognized by people who do not use every possible aid to understanding.
>
> (Brecht 1964, 73; italics added)

I consider disability to be one of Brecht's "complicated things"—and not just complicated, but a *great* and complicated thing. Encountering, studying, researching the lived disability experience as well as the recent historical, legal, and theoretical reframing of disability identity is an essential element in the creation of disability theater.

In pursuit of that knowledge in the early 1990s in Los Angeles, as director of the Other Voices Project, I brought together a group of disabled writers to explore disability history through a collective writing process.[1] One was a sitdown comedian, several were actors eager to write good roles for themselves, one was a radio engineer, one was an art historian, and one signed up because Tuesday wasn't a good television night. I invited disability scholar Dr. Paul Longmore to the workshop. Longmore was mid-career at that point and already known for his witty, eloquent, and accessible lectures on disability history. He also had an interest in theater, so he accepted the invitation, presenting an overview of his course "The History of Human Difference: The Disability Minorities in America." All the writers received a copy of the recently published study of carnival freaks by sociologist Robert Bogdan, *Freak Show: Presenting Human Oddities for Amusement and Profit* (Bogdan 1998). Bogdan was one of the first scholars to position disability as a social construct.

In their previous writings, the disabled workshop members often found themselves repeating the disability tropes embedded in the dominant cultural imaginary. Listening to Longmore's challenge, the writers grappled with how to make effective drama if they had to abandon the convenient "narrative prosthesis" disability stereotypes provided (Mitchell and Snyder 2000, as discussed in Sandahl's case study), even though they knew those tropes to be harmful and distant from their own lived experiences. Longmore's lectures would provide the dramaturgical catalyst not only for the 1992 play *P.H.*reaks: The Hidden History of People with Disabilities* (2006) but, also, ten years later, for John Belluso's *The Body of Bourne* (2001).

The point is that, as Brecht notes, "great and complicated things"—such as the Disability Rights Movement (DRM) and the resulting international paradigm shift in the understanding of disability—cannot be accessed simply by looking within oneself and imagining the other's position. Given the persistent negative charge of disability in the dominant cultural imaginary, the likely result of such inner scrutiny will be a characterization of, at best, a noble, brave victim facing tragedy—i.e., a life with a permanent disability. Brecht continues his ironic confession, admitting the additional aesthetic error of bearing in mind "the findings of sociology ... economics and history" in his artistic practice (Brecht 1964, 74). Playwright John Belluso had something similar in mind with his pledge to create plays presenting disability as "a multifaceted network of social phenomenon" and, in the process, creating complex and challenging roles for disabled actors (Belluso 2006, 163).

Disabled playwrights: economics and history

In 1985, a few years before his consultancy with Other Voices, historian Paul Longmore issued a call for a new history of disabled people in a book review of several new biographies of the turn-of-the-last-century disabled essayist Randolph Bourne. In "The Life of Randolph Bourne and the Need for a History of Disabled People," Longmore effectively swept aside the individual triumph over personal tragedy narrative of personal, inspirational (auto)biographies of disabled overcomers. He proposed replacing these tired narratives with a new one stating: "When devaluation and discrimination happen to one person, it is biography, but when...similar experiences happen to millions it is social history" (Longmore 2003, 39). Applying Longmore's proposal to embedded economic inequities, activist Dr. Douglas Martin, speaking at the 1994 Contemporary Chautauqua: Performance and Disability, explained: "Most people don't know there is a link between poverty and disability ... Most people link disability with tragedy or bravery or gumption" (in Lewis 2000, 335).

One could argue that attention paid to "social history," specifically disability economics, is one identifier of contemporary disability drama. Certainly the economic given circumstances of disabled characters are dramaturgically central to these new plays: health care in John Belluso's "HMO romance," *Pyretown* (2006); organized charity in David Freeman's *Creeps* (2006) and Mike Ervin's *The History of Bowling* (2006); class (intertwined with race) in Susan Nussbaum's *No One as Nasty* (2006); and the economic argument for the elimination of disabled individuals as "useless eaters" under the Nazis in James MacDonald's *Unsex Me Here* (2017).

Hidden histories

Following historians Susan Burch's and Kim Nielsen's assertion that "historical scholarship is foundational to disability studies," recovering the hidden history of disability in the theater promises to disturb the roots, the foundation of stigma embedded in the cultural imaginary of disability (Burch and Nielsen 2015, 98). Two plays that explore hidden history include: a biographical epic exploring the life and legacy of disabled intellectual Randolph Bourne (1886–1918), John Belluso's *The Body of Bourne* (2001); and an investigation of the genocide of disabled people under the Third Reich, James MacDonald's *Unsex Me Here*.

Figure 9.1 The piano roll factory. Randolph Bourne (Clark Middleton) and Helen Clark Hummel (Ann Stocking) in John Belluso's *The Body of Bourne,* world premiere, Mark Taper Forum, 2000.
Photograph © 2019 Craig Schwartz Photography

Paul Longmore's ground-breaking essay on Randolph Bourne, discussed earlier, served as the foundation for Belluso's historical epic, as did the intellectual collaboration between Belluso and Longmore.[2] Reviewing recent biographies of Bourne, Longmore insisted that biographers had missed the ways in which Bourne's lived experience as a disabled man had "informed his approach to every subject and issue he addressed," a starting point for a "broad social critique" (Longmore 2003, 32). Belluso absorbed that argument and even used Bourne's writing of the extraordinary essay "On the Philosophy of Handicapped" (1911) as the through-line and climax of his play.

James MacDonald's *Unsex Me Here* (2017) is set in Hadamar, a small town in Germany, in the years 1933–1947. The Hadamar Euthanasia Centre was used by the Nazis for one of six T4 Euthanasia Programs, which performed mass sterilizations and mass murders of undesirable members of German society, specifically those with physical and mental disabilities. Approximately 14,000 disabled adults and children died at Hadamar. Two Hadamar Tribunals into wartime activities were held at the close of the war. The play is shaped around those tribunals with numerous flashbacks to life at Hadamar. But as the title suggests, quoting Lady Macbeth's prayer to the dark forces to ready her for regicide, the focus of the play is on the women involved in these mass murders, the female nurses.

Since the beginning of a self-identified disability drama, laughter has been the most common strategy used to attack the fear and pity embedded in the cultural imaginary. The sharpest and funniest pieces have come from those writers most deeply involved in changing the paradigm—for example, Mike Ervin is a longtime member of ADAPT, the radical arm of the DRM, responsible for countless protests across the country against the mass transit and nursing home industries. Ervin's *The History of Bowling* (2006) is a rom-com that, in ninety subversive minutes, takes on the dominant cultural imaginary of disability—the disabled person as asexual, shamed, and powerless—without getting anywhere near a tragic-but-brave or super-crip scenario.

These plays by disabled playwrights Belluso, Ervin, and MacDonald (and there are others) carry the "social energy" of the disability experience (Rokem 2000, 197). I encourage all theater studies and disability studies scholars and artists to seek out these plays and introduce them in course curriculum, readings, and productions to their campuses and town communities.

Higher education: changing spaces

Marxist sociologist James Charlton observes: "Historically, most people with disabilities live apart from the rest of society. Most people do not regularly interact with people with disabilities in the classroom, at work, at the movies, and so on" (Charlton 1998, 34). Educational policy-maker Carol Funckes echoes Charlton's observation:

Figure 9.2 Cast of John Belluso's *The Body of Bourne*, world premiere, Mark Taper
Forum, 2000.
Photograph © 2019 Craig Schwartz Photography

> If disabled artists are not represented in our higher education classrooms,
> they will not be a part of the social networking that occurs there and often
> propels a career in the arts. Equally important, if the next generation of arts
> leaders hasn't studied with and learned from disabled peers during their
> academic training, they will be less likely to view disability art as part of
> the arts agenda or to foster the professional employment and leadership of
> disabled artists.
>
> (Funckes 2009, 29)

Both observers agree: disabled people are missing in public life, though the
number of disabled people in the world today is conservatively estimated at one
billion. Charlton is concerned with basic survival for 80 percent of the world's
disabled population who live in abject poverty; and Funckes with careers in the
arts for young disabled Americans. Both single out one room—the classroom.

Charlton's and Funckes's analyses took on new meaning for me when I left
Other Voices in 2000 armed with a recently acquired doctorate in the history
of People's theater and the position of disability within that story. I took my
first academic position as a theater generalist at a small liberal arts college,
sixty miles east of downtown Los Angeles. There I found discussions of

disability issues limited to compliance (how wide doors should be) and housed in Disabled Student Services. Disability was missing from campus diversity initiatives and policies, and disability studies from classrooms and curricula.

These conditions are not unique to my campus, the University of Redlands—they are common in higher education across the United States. I found it difficult, mostly impossible, to cast plays by disabled playwrights with disabled actors. The same absence, to a lesser degree, applied to actors of color. Our department, like many small suburban schools, is predominantly white. The student body is more ethnically diverse, but those students tend not to major in theater. The focus of my artistic and advocacy work in community-based and professional theater for over twenty years seemed increasingly irrelevant. So I found myself well into the twenty-first century developing a project that, on first glance, was the opposite of all my previous advocacy and dramaturgical efforts in that actors would play across gender, ethnicity, class, sexual orientation, and ability.

One Day: On the Road to the ADA—a verbatim, documentary play

In some sense the catalyst for *One Day: On the Road to the ADA, a Reenactment of the Congressional Hearing of September 27, 1988* was the 25th anniversary of the passage of the Americans with Disabilities Act (ADA), which fell on July 26, 2015. I had a sabbatical during spring semester 2015 and an invitation to workshop the piece at UCLA via choreographer Victoria Marks, then chair of the Disability Studies minor. But I had begun work on the project in June 2012 and, at that point, I was only searching for a theatrical form that would fit the world I now inhabited—classrooms with no disabled students and, in theater, a demographic that did not reflect campus diversity.

Casting a reenactment

One Day's verbatim text is taken from the words of the twenty or so characters transcribed in the September 27, 1988, congressional record, the first joint hearing on what would become the ADA. The cast includes famous legislators, disabled leaders, one Navy admiral, and grassroots disabled activists from all over the country. Casting the hearing according to type would put a strain on all but the largest regional theaters. As the unpublished playscript advises:

> It is not expected that the play can be cast in a community setting according to ethnicity, gender, class, sexual orientation, impairment, or age of the historical characters. However every effort should be made to bring together as diverse a cast as possible, crossing all the aforementioned categories and with particular effort made to include disabled and deaf and hard of hearing participants.
>
> (Lewis 2018, 4)

In any case, the point wasn't to mimic, but to bear witness to this group of people who had forced an opening in the cultural imaginary, transforming not only disabled, but American identity. Emphasizing the actor as witness not character, a fifteen-foot by twenty-foot projection of a photo of the historical character was projected behind the actor/witness. In addition, the character photos were audio-described not just for blind and vision-impaired audience members, but for the whole audience. I was taking a cue from Irish disabled playwright Kaite O'Reilly who has incorporated access technologies into her surprising plays. These fissures in space and time allowed for a disjunction between the player and the historical figure. For example, thirty-year-old, blind, Latina-Native American Laura Hernandez played fourteen-year-old, blind, African-American Lakisha Griffin. The engine of the piece is the re-voicing of the words from the hearing, atten-tion paid to the rhythms and inflections implicit in those words and, argu-ably, the thoughts shaping the words. The actor's speech brings past events into the present, making the past matter again (for further discussion see Lewis and Wolf 2018).

Role preparation

At both schools, the play was attached to a specific class and curriculum—at UCLA, the project was incorporated into a "Perspectives on Disability Stu-dies" course, mostly populated by pre-health students. Students had studied foundational texts in the field and interacted with a number of leading dis-ability studies scholars. At Redlands, the majority of the cast came from a "Race and Social Protest" class, which included disability theory and history of the DRM. Thus both iterations of One Day… acknowledged the need for the mix of art and sciences to understand this "great and complicated thing," the emergence of the disability rights movement.

Both productions were open to university students, faculty, staff, disabled and nondisabled, all ages and ethnicities. But significantly, both sponsoring courses had large concentrations of students of color—at UCLA, 70 percent of the class; at Redlands, 40 percent. UCLA course instructor Sara Kishi Wolf analyzed the importance of that demographic to an increased understanding of disability observing that:

> a large percentage find their experience of systemic oppression reflected in that of disabled people and thus quickly understand how disability can be simultaneously a daily experience and a historically contingent concept that affects political and economic status.
>
> (Lewis and Wolf 2018, 190)

At Redlands, students exhibited a comparable level of receptivity to the social model of disability woven into in the congressional testimonies.

Figure 9.3 Laura Hernandez as Lakisha Griffin in *One Day on the Road to the ADA*, University of Redlands, 2018.
Photograph © Charles Convis

In both cases, recruiting d/Deaf, blind/vision-impaired, and physically disabled players from within the academic community was only minimally successful. It was necessary to reach out to the disability communities in Los Angeles and the Inland Empire.[3] These players, who were politicized and articulate, enhanced the conversation in the room. Importantly, at Redlands, thanks to a university grant, the disabled guest artists received modest honorariums and housing in acknowledgement of their expertise.

Conclusion

So, to return to Charlton (1998) and Funckes (2009) and those missing, crucial interactions in the education classroom, both noted in their discussions the isolation of disabled persons across time and place. For a few days there was a classroom where a horizontal relationship existed between all players: from an endowed Public Policy chair to those receiving public assistance; from those born after the bill had passed, to one cast member who was in the room on September 27, 1988; and from experienced disabled and nondisabled actors to many first-time players.

When the audience arrived, they were given roles as well (Republican or Democrat) and cheered their party's representatives, though the play also portrays the bi-partisanship necessary to pass a civil rights law. Everyone became a part of the event as if they were in that room that day demanding their rights. In an audience survey that we provided, many of the students in the audience indicated that *One Day...* was their first exposure to the ADA and to disability as a civil rights issue.

The play and performance hopefully made some room for a refashioning of disability in the cultural imaginary, moving out of the realm of folklore with its monsters and changelings, and closing the door on the codified world of melodrama past and present. What's next?

Notes

1 The Other Voices Project (1982–2006), founded by Victoria Lewis, was dedicated to the training of disabled actors and playwrights and housed in Los Angeles's Mark Taper Forum, a leading American regional theatre.
2 See Susan Schweik (2009, 207–8) for an insightful reading of the play and the relationship between playwright Belluso and scholar Paul Longmore.
3 The Inland Empire is a metropolitan area/region of Greater Los Angeles, including Riverside and San Bernardino counties.

Bibliography

Belluso, John. 2006. "Author's Statement." In *Beyond Victims and Villains: Contemporary Plays by Disabled Playwrights*, edited by Victoria Lewis, 163. New York: Theatre Communications Group.
Bodek, Richard. 1997. *Proletarian Performance in Weimar Berlin: Agitprop, Chorus, and Brecht*. London: Camden House.
Bogdan, Robert. 1998. *Freak Show: Presenting Human Oddities for Amusement and Profit*. Chicago, IL: University of Chicago Press.
Brecht, Bertolt. 1964. *Brecht on Theatre*. New York: Hill and Wang.
Burch, Susan, and Kim E. Nielsen. 2015. "History." In *Keywords for Disability Studies*, edited by Rachel Adams, Benjamin Reiss, and David Serlin, 95–97. New York: New York University Press.
Charlton, James I. 1998. *Nothing About Us Without Us: Disability Oppression and Empowerment*. Berkeley, CA: University of California Press.

Funckes, Carol. 2009. *The 2009 Summit: Careers in the Arts for People with Disabilities*. Issue Paper on Higher Education. Washington, DC: Kennedy Center.

Lewis, Victoria. 2000. "Other Voices, 1982–2000: Claiming Community, the Dillema of Disability and Difference in the People's Theater." PhD dissertation, University of California, Los Angeles, CA.

Lewis, Victoria, and Sara Kishi Wolf. 2018. "Activating the Past: Performing Disability Rights in the Classroom." *Journal of Literary & Cultural Disability Studies*, 12(2): 185–201.

Longmore, Paul K. 2003. *Why I Burned My Book and Other Essays on Disability*. Philadelphia, PA: Temple University Press.

Mitchell, David T., and Sharon L. Snyder. 2000. *Narrative Prosthesis: Disability and the Dependencies of Discourse*. Ann Arbor, MI: University of Michigan Press.

Rokem, Freddie. 2000. *Performing History: Theatrical representations of the past in contemporary theatre*. Iowa City, IA: University of Iowa Press.

Schweik, Susan. 2009. *The Ugly Laws: Disability in Public*. New York: New York University Press.

Thomson, Rosemarie Garland. 1996. *Extraordinary Bodies: Figuring Disability in American Studies*. New York: Columbia University Press.

Part IV

Casting and multilingual performance

Chapter 10

The sea will listen

Caridad Svich

Here we move
Across a variegated water-scape
Dramaturgy built on ebbs and tides
Rather than lines marked on the ground
Boundary-less
The Orphan Sea
Resists the boundaries placed
On humans and animals and nature
By forces seeking to own all
*
We are adrift in memory
Between and among invented passages
From the diaries of Penelope and Odysseus
We are she, he and they
And move across many maps
Seeking home
Here, the piece says
Could be one home
In the desert
Another here on ice
And another here on the dusty road of all roads
Paths of resistance and compromise
Negotiate the ebbs and tides
Of passage
With love
And face forces too of othering
City voices held/caught in the digital matrix of the corporate mine/d field
See too the beauty of Google Earth
The globe we cannot hold
But imagine that we can
With a mere click of a wireless mouse
Skittering past zones of want and plenty

Imagine who you could be
In fluid identities
In hybridity
In non-essentialized casting of selves
How will we be seen, then?
★
Today we mark this passage
Orphaned unto itself
Seeking new origins and re-birth
Which stories are ours?
Who will claim them?
Can stories be owned outright?
Remember Penelope as you see her in mind
As you see them
As you see him
Remember Odysseus as you see him
them/her
brother/sister/others are we all
If we let the tides give us strength to carry on
Hold close the whisper
Of the ancients
That knew a thing or two about drift
Before the word came into being
Seek solace
In the wide open spaces
That offer freedom to our hearts and minds
To dream a world anew
In this performance
We are who we could be
And also archival memories of who we were
On film, video, and YouTube
We are splintered whole
And in our whole-ness
Together
We find possible peace

Chapter 11

Setting a global table with multilingual theater

Eunice S. Ferreira

> "We want to do more diverse work but what can we do if actors of color do not audition?"
>
> "Our theater is in an area with Asian and Latino neighborhoods, but they just don't come see our shows."
>
> "Our campus is predominantly white and so are our majors. How can we diversify our season?"
>
> "I don't see color or anything. I just cast the best person for the role."
>
> "She has a strong accent and we're doing Shakespeare, not *West Side Story*."

From social media feeds to conversations on season planning, the above statements and questions may be familiar to theater artists from a variety of institutions and organizations. In the fall of 2016, I directed a multilingual premiere of *The Orphan Sea* by Caridad Svich at Skidmore College in Saratoga Springs, New York. Working on the multilingual production provided a rich opportunity to embody global and local intersections of art, community, and culture. Casting multilingual actors expands the representation of global stories on stage and more broadly reflects the diversity of our own campus, attracting new audiences and welcoming new students to the program. I suggest that the same can be true for other theater programs and companies that want to incorporate global perspectives in their research, training, and seasons.

Svich originally wrote *The Orphan Sea* in English and granted us permission to create a multilingual version. Our cast and creative team represented thirteen different languages and a breadth of cultural experiences that invigorated and guided our rehearsal process. The seventeen-member cast featured eight actors who were raised bilingually and/or were international students. Some actors were fluent in three languages while others varied in ability from basic conversation to near fluency. My colleagues claim it was the most racially, ethnically, and linguistically diverse cast in the history of the Skidmore Theater program.

The Orphan Sea serves as a case study for creating ensemble-based multilingual productions. Rehearsals and performances were sites to experiment with translation theory, multilingual performance strategies, and audience reception.

These practices build upon principles set forth in "The Welcome Table: Casting for an Integrated Society" by setting a *global* table for actors, creative team, staff, and audiences. This essay highlights the benefits of and strategies for creating multilingual productions, including: audience engagement and relationship building, casting, interdisciplinary and collaborative approaches, collective translation, and the use of multiple languages in rehearsal and performance.

Going multilingual

In my practice as a scholar artist, I advocate for plays that engage cultural and global issues and I strive to create opportunities to realize them through my teaching, research, and artistic endeavors. This mission shapes my view of classroom and rehearsal rooms as sites in which research, social justice, and the practice of community building inform artistic projects. This calling is central to my work and has become even more imperative in a political climate that increasingly nurtures xenophobic anxieties and policies.

The choice to direct a multilingual play is an invitation to engage in cross-cultural projects that celebrate different cultures, religions, identities, and perspectives. By specifically promoting auditions to people who speak several languages—a strategy that may be applied by all theater producers—we attracted new actors who otherwise may not have felt welcome to audition. International and bilingual actors often feel the sting of linguistic bias when it comes to casting. Some directors are not receptive to pronunciation or speech patterns that rattle their concept of realism or verisimilitude. However, the *reality* is that many actors and audience members live daily lives in more than one language. Multilingual performances reflect nation-wide linguistic diversity and the quotidian practices of local communities that challenge the hegemony of English—the *de facto* but not *official* language of the United States, in spite of various federal legislative attempts.[1]

"Going multilingual" is not a radical notion. Although multilingual productions are not prominently featured in the United States, playwrights throughout history have incorporated multiple languages. In *Speaking in Tongues: Languages at Play in the Theatre* (2006), Marvin Carlson extends Mikhail Bakhtin's literary concept of heteroglossia to theater and offers a critical study of this phenomenon. Carlson identifies multilingual examples dating from Greek antiquity to the present, for reasons ranging from playwrights' desires for verisimilitude to sociopolitical strategies often employed in postcolonial drama. For example, in my research on theater in the Cape Verde Islands, West Africa, I examine the ways in which the official language of Portuguese was used to suppress the Cape Verdean language and how the linguistic choices made by theater artists reinforce and/or subvert the neocolonial grip of Portuguese on the creole culture. As Carlson argues, "theatrical heteroglossia almost always involves a wide variety of social and cultural issues" (Carlson 2006, 14). In keeping with a sociolinguistic perspective, heteroglossia incorporates—but is not limited to—national languages. Our daily multi-layered and nuanced utterances reflect the ideologies of group affiliations such as class, gender, race, geographical origin, or age. By moving heteroglossia from the margins of theater practice to center stage, theater artists and audiences are invited to embody and witness diverse perspectives.

Collective translation was central to experimentations with theatrical heteroglossia in this case study. One of the functions of literary translation is to render the text of the source language into a second receptor language. In theater history classes, I foreground the importance of translation by reminding students that most of the semester's plays are only accessible to them in translation. Students in my "Translation and Performance" class, on the other hand, translate plays that have never before been published in English. Our task in translating *The Orphan Sea* deviated from standard methods in that we practiced translation as both a means and an end. Throughout the rehearsal process we explored how layering different languages might lead us to make new discoveries about:

rehearsal techniques
community
intertextuality
aesthetic possibilities
audience engagement

Translation is often viewed as a bridge between source and receptor cultures. Our collective approach expanded this metaphor by: building bridges from us to Svich's text; to each other; and ultimately to our audiences. In this way, we lived out what Edith Grossman, acclaimed translator of Spanish literature, describes as translation's

crucial capacity to ease and make more meaningful our relationships to those with whom we may not have had a connection before. Translation always helps us to know, to see from a different angle, to attribute new value to what once may have been unfamiliar. As nations and as individuals, we have a critical need for that kind of understanding and insight. The alternative is unthinkable.

(Grossman 2010, xi)

Finding a play to play with language

The pre-election vitriolic rhetoric against immigration was in full swing during the 2015/2016 academic year, fueling my commitment to direct a multilingual production the following season. My overall vision was to devise or find a play to intentionally welcome underrepresented students and allow us to create a production based on the ensemble's unique experiences, languages, and identities.

In order to reclaim visibility for the many immigrant populations that are integral parts of US history and culture, I considered adapting a "classic American drama" to challenge preconceived notions of who represents the nation by reinventing a canonical work through a feminist and global lens. This inclination led me to playwrights who share a similar perspective. The first person to come to mind was Caridad Svich, whose many roles include playwright, translator, lyricist, editor, and educator. A self-described child of immigrants, Svich has written over forty plays (including bilingual texts) and is the 2012 recipient of the OBIE for Lifetime Achievement.[2]

I have always been intrigued with Svich's dramaturgy and her impassioned writings on art and activism. José Zayas, frequent director of Svich's plays, identifies her as "One of the most intellectually rigorous and linguistically exciting playwrights working in America today. She sees art as provocation and her texts are blueprints for creative teams. There is no right way of doing her plays—there is only exploration and transformation" (Maxwell 2009, 33). Indeed, her dramaturgical style easily lends itself to multilingual versions, as do the topics at the heart of her writings, which she describes on her website as, "explorations of wanderlust, dispossession, biculturalism, bilingualism, construction of identity, and the many different emotional terrains that can be inhabited onstage."

I pitched my idea to direct a multilingual version of one of her plays as part of ongoing efforts to expand the global scope of our stages. Her encouraging email response was "I want to play!" We intuitively agreed that *The Orphan Sea* (Svich 2016a) resonated with this project's goals. The play was originally commissioned by the University of Missouri-Columbia Department of Theatre where Kevin Brown directed its 2014 premiere. Svich wrote the play in English, but had always wanted to include multiple languages. Skidmore would present the play's second production and its multilingual premiere. These two college productions model ways in which playwrights and programs can partner to develop new works, by providing production opportunities for playwrights and invaluable training for students.

The Orphan Sea is a metatheatrical play that weaves ancient tales with migration stories, bringing the global past, present, and future into collision. Inspired by the Greek myth of Odysseus and Penelope (the Trojan War's celebrated hero and his long-suffering wife who waits twenty years for his return), Svich riffs on the ancient trope of separation and reunion. As she describes, "This is a story of us, here, now, and also of who we were once. It is a story of those that cross rivers and seas and those that wait for them, of a lover who searches for one lost years ago, and of someone called Penelope, who may be waiting for someone called Odysseus" (Svich 2016a, 4). My vision was to bring her poetic musings in conversation with global migration stories through the medium of multiple languages, markers that would sonically reinforce numerous border crossings in the play and their real-life counterparts.

Figure 11.1 Promotional photo with the four Odysseus and Penelope couples. Clockwise from top center: Molly Burdick, David Gyampo, Ted Randell, Julianna Quiroz, Daniella Deutsch, Grant Landau-Williams, Bella Rinskaya, and Christopher Naughton. *The Orphan Sea* by Caridad Svich, multilingual premiere directed by Eunice S. Ferreira.
Photo by Sue Kessler, courtesy of Skidmore Theater

Svich also draws upon classical Greek dramaturgy by creating three choruses: an Odysseus chorus, a Penelope chorus, and a Chorus of the City. In keeping with the chorus's ancient civic function, our city chorus bore witness for and with the audience, often occupying audience seating areas. The metatheatricality of the text and our performance style acknowledged the play as a theatrical event with actors stepping out of role to directly address the audience in various languages. In rehearsal, we adopted the concept of the "tripartite actor," an acting theory developed by Gao Xingjian, experimental playwright and recipient of the 2000 Nobel Prize for Literature. In Gao's vision, influenced by Brecht's *Verfremdungseffekt*, the actor is simultaneously three subjects—actual self, self as actor, and actor as character (Conceison 2002). This notion compliments Svich's text, which ranges from intimate dialogue to poetic choral poems. The text demands a great deal from actors who may be constrained by training in realism. Instead, actors were invited to explore varied intersections with the text—as their actual selves (employing personal stories), the self as actor (applying Svich's metatheatrical references), and ultimately as a character.

I was nervous and excited to direct *The Orphan Sea* because of its drama-turgical structure—the very characteristic that makes this play receptive to multiple languages. The text is segmented into forty-two poetic "installations" or "spells" with few assigned lines. Settings include a memory garden, a raging river, a dusty road, a dry river bed, an ice floe and a rock in the middle of the ocean. Svich (2015) calls it a "waterscape play" whose form "is intentionally fluid, and designed to mimic, not in figurative fashion, the ebb and tide, cur-rents and flow of many oceans across the globe." Svich compliments the non-linear text with a dramaturgical musical structure of preludes, movements, and codas. Taking a leap of faith, we jumped into the unknown waters of *The Orphan Sea*. Swimming in this ancient myth of separation and reunion, we journeyed across time and geographies of space using installations of song, poetry, film, language, and dance. As we improvised with the openness of Svich's text, we asked ourselves:

- "How do we respond to global crises of displaced people and environ-mental threats on our Facebook news feed?"
- "What does it mean to cross digital, linguistic and physical borders?"

Casting a multilingual ensemble

With the playwright's approval to "play with her play," I now needed a cast with multilingual skills. The Skidmore Theater Department offers a Bachelor of Science degree, a pre-professional program within a liberal arts curriculum. Campus-wide undergraduate enrollment is approximately 2500 students with eleven percent international students and twenty-three percent identifying as domestic students of color. Theater majors and minors are predominantly white US citizens. Auditions are open to all students and non-majors can participate both on and off stage.

Theater seasons communicate the values of their producing organizations. Actors of color and actors for whom English is not the first language need to witness *intentionality and consistency* in casting and play selection to believe that they are welcome to audition and, moreover, to be cast. Contrary to what some may wish to believe, the success of the musical *Hamilton* has not paved a path of equitable access for underrepresented actors. Nor can institutions fulfill initiatives towards full cultural integration with one select play in any given season. Without *intentionality and consistency* in casting and hiring practices, theaters may unintentionally tokenize the actors and audiences they say they wish to attract.

The seventeen-member ensemble, with six international students and three bilingual US students, was a result of relationship-building with the Dean of Students Office, international advising, office of student diversity programs, world language faculty, and student club leaders in an effort to recruit and retain students who have been historically underrepresented on stage. These strategies are not unique to me. Almost every theater professor of color I know has fostered relationships with comparable programs and departments at their respective institutions. Student comments confirm that such outreach practices need to be *genuine and ongoing*, not only when a director has specific racial or ethnic casting needs. This is also true for theater companies in how they relate to various populations in their local communities and in the region.

In addition to the department's standard audition notices, I routinely distribute focused flyers to individuals and partnering programs. Students reported that the flyer's message—"*All* students, *All* Languages, *All* Experiences"—made them feel welcome. Auditions attracted more non-majors, students of color, and international students and several students auditioned in languages other than English. I was open to a variety of casting options, including characters who might be monolingual, bilingual, characters struggling with a new language, and characters who code shift (slip into another language) either as a character trait or as an overt theatrical device.

I invited thirty-two students to callbacks and encouraged them to share aspects of their unique identities through exercises drawing upon personal stories, languages, and intuitive modes of expression. I wanted the student who views her "accent" as a liability to know that her voice is an important part of who she is and she does not need to change it. Students created sound and movement compositions centered on themes of border crossing, migration, exile, separation, reunion, refugees, and environmental crises. They also made literal and metaphorical tableaux to which they added multilingual soundscapes and the student music director led them in call and response singing. It was one of the most rewarding callbacks and ultimately yielded six actors who were completely new to the department and an ensemble whose languages included Arabic, Asante Twi, English, French, German, Italian, Mandarin, Portuguese, Russian, and Spanish. I decided to assign parts after Svich's initial campus residency which, allowed me to include her feedback, ultimately casting four actors as Odysseus, four as Penelope, and ten as the city chorus.

Rehearsal as a laboratory for praxis, research, and performance

My approach to directing *The Orphan Sea* illustrates a model for multilingual theater as a laboratory for research, performance, and community building. Theater in an academic setting often provides an extended, exploratory rehearsal period and is a productive environment to nurture new works. Developing a translation in rehearsal was a new approach in my praxis and an extension of my work as a solo and collaborative translator. Thus, the entire process from rehearsal to performance offered sites of simultaneous learning as students and I experimented with various strategies including:

Figure 11.2 The ensemble performs the first choral movement "Crossings" in Arabic, Asante Twi, English, French, Mandarin, Portuguese, Russian and Spanish. *The Orphan Sea* by Caridad Svich, multilingual premiere directed by Eunice S. Ferreira.
Photo by Sue Kessler, courtesy of Skidmore Theater

> group translation
> layering languages
> instantaneous translation
> one character translating for another
> communicating with one another in different languages
> independent translation outside of rehearsal

Svich explained that the openness of the text, "where language and codes can shift and where that is part of the grammar of the play itself lends itself better to this kind of exploration because actors can bring who they are and the languages they have to the table—spoken, physical, and more" (email to author, June 14, 2016). Whereas a bilingual production usually requires actors with fluency in at least one of the performance languages, the multilingual flexibility afforded in a play like *The Orphan Sea* welcomes *all* linguistic and cultural expressions.

A ten-week rehearsal period provided the extended lab time needed to transform the text into a multilingual script and rehearse for performance. In order to create a more intimate experience, I requested our black box theater and the department inverted the production calendar to accommodate a lengthier rehearsal process for the project. I began rehearsals not knowing what we would translate from the original text. I introduced our production as a "research experiment," asking the cast and creative team to be collaborators and risk-takers. Whereas initial read-throughs often involve everyone sitting around a table with careful attention to the text *as it is written*, I invited the students to immediately initiate a linguistic playfulness with Svich's text using instantaneous and spontaneous translation.

In the ebb and flow of rehearsal, we embodied Svich's fluid dramaturgy, particularly in the first month as we investigated language, sound, movement and encouraged intuitive improvisational responses. Her poetic text demands choral work, which we explored with various patterns such as call-and-response and overlapping languages. We discovered a sonic performativity in using abstract vocalizations and various languages that not only served the choral passages but also added aural texture. The inherent musicality of Svich's text led us to experiment with live and recorded music to transform some of the poetic installations into mixtures of spoken and sung text. I frequently asked actors to select their own choral lines. These approaches were integral to our process and were beautifully supported by the creative team and the unique, imaginative contributions of a collaborative cast. Our fluid devising techniques were recorded by the stage manager while our dramaturg feverishly transcribed a complex, shifting multilingual text.

Figure 11.3 Julianna Quiroz, one of the four Penelopes, cries out in Spanish and English as she digs in the earth for the bones of Odysseus. *The Orphan Sea* by Caridad Svich, multilingual premiere directed by Eunice S. Ferreira. Photo by Sue Kessler, courtesy of Skidmore Theater

In addition to translating text, multiple languages also infused the rehearsal process from warm-ups to closing rituals. I often spoke to the cast in Portuguese or Cape Verdean Creole (Kriolu) while the student director practiced his French. The stage manager shared Persian family stories with an occasional Farsi exclamation while a student from China led a vocal warm-up with a Mandarin tongue twister. Students felt free to converse in other languages and teach each other new words. Everyone learned how to sing "Sodade," a nostalgic Cape Verdean ballad famously recorded by the late Cesária Évora.[3] "Sodade" became a cast favorite. Its melody was incorporated as hummed underscoring and recognized by my surprised Cape Verdean parents and other friends who drove two hundred miles to see the production.

During this extended rehearsal period, we lived out the intersections of community, culture, and art. One compelling instance took place during rehearsal on November 8, 2016, the evening of the US presidential election. As results streamed in, some cast members became distraught. In spite of possible political differences and varying degrees of investment in the US elections, students used our closing ritual as a demonstration of community. Drawing from the play's text, cast and production staff stood in a circle and shared "gifts of words" to one another while extending a companion gesture or movement phrase. Over the next few days, in both rehearsals and classes, I challenged students to critically consider the relationship between artists and civic engagement, questions we asked at the very start of our process. At the next rehearsal, I distributed an essay by Svich on art, ethics, and activism that was published just two weeks prior to elections (Svich 2016b). It was serendipitous to have such a timely essay from our playwright to bring into the rehearsal room, especially when one of the actors had recently questioned the efficacy of art to make social change. We interpreted Svich's essay as a choral reading and spent time in group reflection. At such a crucial point in rehearsal and in the students' lives, Svich's essay reminded them that what they do as artists *matters*.

Audience and community engagement

A liberal arts setting is an advantageous setting to support the interdisciplinary nature of theater-making. Colleagues from other departments enriched our research with seminars on US immigration policies, border activism, translation, environmental crises, and the myth of Odysseus and Penelope. Acting teachers offered workshops, colleagues from other departments assisted in translating projection titles, and a dance colleague created original choreography and shaped our previous rehearsal work. Thus, the entire process celebrated collaborations that extended beyond the department. "Going multilingual" means setting an ever-extending welcome table.

The multilingual version of *The Orphan Sea* premiered on November 30, 2016 and ran until December 6 in the Black Box of Skidmore's Janet Kinghorn

Bernhard Theater. Hesitancy about audience reception may steer some producers and directors away from staging multiple language productions; but I never
doubted that we would have a favorable response. In order to accommodate
our outreach efforts, we added an extra matinee for a total of eight performances. The production was well received with sold-out shows and many first-
time audience members.

As an invitation for the audience to adopt a global frame of mind, we
staged a student-curated interactive lobby experience. Music by international artists greeted patrons upon arriving and departing the theater.[4] A
display wall featured dramaturgical research, including images of migrant
crossings on the US/Mexico border to rafts of refugees on the shores of
Greek isles. A "Memory Wall" with a display heading from Svich's text—
"those who have crossed rivers and seas and those who have waited"—
invited audiences to memorialize names of family members with their own
migration stories. The projections designer created a digital lobby display for
audiences to record their names and countries of origin on an interactive
Google Map program. A nod to this interactive map was featured in large
scale during the performance in the installation "Thirty-one: the other day/
the waiting" in which Svich describes Penelope and Odysseus looking at a
digital map of the earth. The student designed a projection sequence that
began with an image of earth from space then slowly zoomed to an aerial
view of the theater building as a playful metatheatrical wink.

Audiences filed into the theater to the sounds of world music and then
listened to a multilingual pre-show announcement. For safety reasons, an
English language version preceded our special recording, in which each line
of instruction was spoken in a different language including Spanish, Arabic,
German, Asante Twi, and closing in French with a heartfelt "*merci.*" The set
designer transformed the intimate space into traverse staging in which
audiences sit on two sides facing one another. This arrangement highlighted
the audience's presence in the performance, reinforced multiplicity of perspectives, and intensified the last lines of the play as actors directly addressed
the audience, encouraging them to look at one another across the theater
space. The following lines were individually spoken in English, but the last
line, "Let us talk with each other," was repeated in unison layers of multiple languages as the lights slowly faded to black:

> Why don't you tell me, then, about what has happened to you in your
> stories of love,
> In your stories of crossing rivers and seas,
> Even the ones we may think of as orphaned?
> Tell me your stories.
> Let us talk with each other

(Svich 2016a, 203)

Hyperlinked dramaturgy in performance

In an early conversation, Svich exclaimed "We are constantly hyperlinking!" and introduced the term "hyperlinked dramaturgy" to describe ways in which theater can hyperlink us to other stories. The set design evoked elements of earth and water, providing creative possibilities for the ever-shifting landscapes of Svich's play with two large walls set at each end that served as surfaces for projections, staging and climbing. Projections on the opposing walls provided visual hyperlinking in tandem with lines spoken by the actors. Svich also assigns poetic titles to each of the scenes/installations/spells, which were too beautiful not to display in some way. We projected the titles in various languages as transition devices and as an aesthetic alternative to the ways in which most supertitles pragmatically provide linguistic translation. In our production, the series of beautifully sequenced multi-translations functioned as part of the visual world of the play.

In rehearsal, we discovered other ways in which gesture, movement, and sound could also provide this element of intertextuality or "hyperlinking." I offer two performance moments to exemplify how we interpreted Svich's term into performative codes.

The spell titled "in the silence" centers on an Odysseus believed to be dead and a Penelope who has been digging the earth in search of his bones. The reunited couple kneeled center stage in a sandbox while the cast sat in front of both sides of the audience. The repetition and rhythm of Svich's text begged for a musical interpretation. The emotional intensity of the sparse language reminded me of the song "De Nua" by Cape Verdean artist Sara Tavares. The song begins with the strong percussive pattern of Cape Verdean batuko music; but the first singing voice belongs to Ana Moura, a contemporary Portuguese fado singer. Tavares, singing in Kriolu, then joins Moura. The linguistic musical hybridity of the song served as a model for our interpretation. As Odysseus and Penelope embraced, the ensemble recreated a batuko rhythm to underscore their anticipated reunion. A chorus member, a Mexican international student, sang the text's opening and closing stanzas in a manner inspired by Portuguese fado, a style whose sentimental, soulful vibrato was well-suited to her rich, low voice. Odysseus and Penelope then sang their text while the cast continued to underscore with the batuko rhythm.

A second example, "Eight: letting go (migration)," featured the Chorus of the City who observed Odysseus while simultaneously commenting in English on his emotional state. Suddenly, Svich's text hyperlinks into a metatheatrical treatise on language itself and the chorus shifted into speaking in echoing layers of Arabic, English, French, Mandarin, and Spanish:

> and this has nothing to do with translation
> because there are many languages here
> and we have learned to speak some of them
> though there will always be others

we would rather not learn
too hard
and it is true, some languages are
our brains can only take so many vowels and consonants and symbols
it is much easier, far easier, yes, to let go

(Svich 2016a, 157)

The myth of the Tower of Babel inspired the physical and vocal work of the chorus in this installation. An oft-cited metaphor in translation theory, the story of Babel is a Biblical account that explains the creation of languages as a punishment for humanity's hubris in building "a tower that reaches to the heavens" (Gen. 11:1–9). As a visual and aural reference to this central translation metaphor, an actor perched high on a wall announced Svich's text in English, via a retractable drop-down microphone. Below him, the city chorus created a cacophony of language and sounds as they eventually made their way to the wall and formed a tower-like structure. Uttering distorted vowel and consonant sounds, they, too, like Babel, crumbled and fell to the ground.

Multilingual theater is local and global

Although the terms multilingual and global are not synonymous, they can be complimentary in helping theater artists imagine new possibilities for theater-making and audience engagement. In a post-production discussion, some audiences expressed that they wanted more languages in performance. Their feedback encourages me to take even greater risks in directing future multilingual productions.

If a theater program or company wants to represent more global and diverse stories on its stages, then this intent should consistently influence hiring practices, season selection, casting, training, classroom study, performance and audience development. For example:

- Acting teachers/directors could invite actors to perform monologues in languages of their own choice.
- Theaters could hire bilingual faculty and guest artists to teach, direct, and design.
- Teachers and dramaturgs could emphasize that many plays are only accessible through translation and encourage readings in the original language whenever possible.
- Artistic directors could start by producing staged readings of bilingual plays that include languages spoken in their immediate region.

Theater-making in multiple languages broadens representation on stage and fosters environments that value intersecting identities, perspectives, and cultural exchanges. Theater institutions that believe in creating theater that reflects varied experiences, are also required to nurture and train artists and organizational leaders. Casting multilingual actors and presenting multilingual productions is a means to nurture future artists who can dream and bring to fruition new theatrical possibilities.

Caridad Svich is such a dreamer. In her note for our production program, Svich describes the rare chance "to dream as big and wide as possible about what could be the future of theater," an opportunity granted to her with the play's original commission. She continues, "The chance to continue dreaming with this play occurred when Intellect published it in the UK this year, and continues now with this company here at Skidmore College—diving fearlessly and with love and multiple languages into its world. In a multiply broken world, let us dream of a better world."

Acknowledgment

I dedicate this essay to my family past and present—those who crossed rivers and seas and those who waited for them.

Notes

1 At the time of publication, the most recent bill is H.R. 997-English Language Unity Act of 2017 introduced by Rep. Steve King of Iowa (see www.congress.gov).
2 See www.caridadsvich.com.
3 Cesária Évora (1941–2011), affectionately called the "barefoot diva," was a cultural ambassador of the Cape Verde Islands. See a live performance of "Sodade" at www.youtube.com/watch?v=dNVrdYGiULM.
4 See https://euniceferreira.com/productions.

Bibliography

Banks, Daniel. 2013. "The Welcome Table: Casting for an Integrated Society." *Theatre Topics*, 23(1) (March): 1–18.
Carlson, Marvin A. 2006. *Speaking in Tongues: Language at Play in the Theatre*. Ann Arbor, MI: University of Michigan Press.
Conceison, Claire. 2002. "Fleshing out the Dramaturgy of Gao Xingjian." http://u.osu.edu/mclc/online-series/conceison (accessed April 2, 2019).
Grossman, Edith. 2010. *Why Translation Matters*. New Haven, CT: Yale University Press.
Maxwell, Justin. 2009. "Cartography Lessons with Caridad Svich: The Ancient and the Contemporary Collide in the Dreamscapes of Her Plays." *American Theatre*, July/August.
Svich, Caridad. 2015. "Archipelagos, Fragile shores, and Orphan Seas: A Reflection on Climate Change and Performance." *HowlRound*, September 23. http://howlround.com/archipelagos-fragile-shores-and-orphan-seas-a-reflection-on-climate-change-and-performance (accessed April 2, 2019).
___. 2016a. "The Orphan Sea." In *JARMAN (all this maddening beauty) and Other Plays*, edited by Caridad Svich, 143–204. Bristol: Intellect.
___. 2016b. "Six Hundred and Ninety-Two Million: On Art, Ethics and Activism." *HowlRound*, October 22. http://howlround.com/six-hundred-and-ninety-two-million-on-art-ethics-and-activism#disqus_thread (accessed April 2, 2019).

Chapter 12

Creating emergent spaces

Casting, community-building, and extended dramaturgy

Ann Elizabeth Armstrong

I began teaching "The Welcome Table" (Banks 2013) shortly after it was published in 2013. I asked graduate students to write an abstract of the essay, a productive task requiring them to articulate how theater works as a system of practices that engages audience assumptions. In particular, I appreciate how Banks operationalizes the problem of race, identity, and casting to move us to the edge of our discipline and see the power of theater to transform what Ayanna Thompson calls "sociologies of viewing" (in Banks 2013, 8). Banks questions the entire system, the foundation, or perhaps the very table we are setting. Systems theory, then, is a productive lens to consider opportunities for structural transformation at multiple sites. As a point of departure to consider the Skidmore production and "The Welcome Table's" project, systems theory helped me ponder important questions about change. Thinking beyond individual roles, plays, seasons, or methods, what strategies assist in leveraging multiple points in the system? Can production practices maintain an "open" rather than a "closed" system, allowing for divergent ways of thinking as well as welcoming a wide range of identities to the field? Why are networks resistant to change and what constitutes productive disruption? What are hubs that can restructure our system of values to generate diversity rather that discourage it? How can actors and students, transient participants in the system, contribute to lasting change in our disciplinary practices, moving towards emerging new forms?

By looking at theatrical production as a system, it becomes an extension of community-organizing, drawing from and influencing existing networks. In this light, new ways of thinking emerge that conceive of actors and audiences as participants in a shared community of practices. Established methods, such as community-based theater (Cohen-Cruz 2010), cultural community development (Woodson 2015), and applied theater (Nicholson 2014), already consider how performance arises from and contributes to community capacity. What if such community-based methods were applied to formulating our seasons, casting practices, and audience engagements?

Eunice Ferreira's production of Caridad Svich's *The Orphan Sea* builds a unique community by engaging multiple languages and cultures. Such community-building extends beyond the cast, through the production process and her audience engagements. Similar to Ferreira's work at Skidmore College, my own production practices at Miami University reflect the mission of a Bachelor of Arts degree. The liberal arts context encourages interdisciplinary and hybrid thinking, while a departmental production becomes a means for both practicing theater's craft and studying relationships between self and society. Unfortunately, however, liberal arts institutions have traditionally been inaccessible to large segments of society. How can community-engaged practices open up theater departments and liberal arts institutions as well as innovate new practices for the field of professional theater?

I borrow from psychologist R. Keith Sawyer's (2005) "emergence paradigm" and community-organizer adrienne maree brown's (2017) "emergent strategy" to consider how working at the boundaries of cultures, communities, or disciplines innovates new forms and practices. Inspired by the heterogeneous networks of communities as theorized by community-based artists, I am thinking about how to open up closed systems of making theater, creating new synergies. I wonder what structures allow for new hubs of cross-cultural exchange and create contact zones for dialogue? Ferreira's case study provides insight into constructing spaces for emerging forms and generating new relationships. I conclude by sharing audience engagement strategies inspired by community-based arts practices designed to include new artists and audiences at the table. By collapsing boundaries between dramaturgy, audience engagement, and performance, my own efforts blend strategies and production roles to create contact zones for dialogue. This "extended dramaturgy" invites participants into conversation while extending themes of the mainstage production into the community and creating new sites for performance. As Banks notes in "The Welcome Table," the project of changing our casting practices must happen in developing relationships with audiences and the community at large.

Emergent strategy and casting

In *Social Emergence: Societies as Complex Systems*, R. Keith Sawyer explains the phenomena of "emergence." Emergence is a process whereby the structure of a system changes due to the interaction of the agents within it (Sawyer 2005, 2). Such interactions at a lower level have the potential to reorganize the higher-level structures in order to reshape the entire system so that a new form emerges that was not implied by the sum of its parts. A classic example is a flock of birds, who form a "V" based on the interaction of pairs, not based upon a predetermined plan. A decentralized structure arises from the environmental feedback: the aerodynamic relationship of each pair reinforces the dynamic interplay, maintaining alignment in the structure. Sawyer's research examines how individual interactions in jazz ensembles and long-form theatrical improvisations innovate new forms. Through his study of communication and its effects on social organization, Sawyer details "metapragmatics" (Sawyer 2005, 182–187)—the complex communication between group members who must create an idiosyncratic language to coordinate their activities while negotiating obstacles. Like the flock of birds who receive aerodynamic feedback as they fly, the "metapragmatics" provide feedback that maintains alignment, a decentralized joint agreement within the group. Sawyer notes how individuals engage this complex interaction within a group context. Similarly, ensembles creating a devised work must create and sustain this meta-discourse that constrains and structures interactions. Thus, emergence is not merely a spontaneous and intuitive activity, but it arises amid particular contexts and must be developed and encouraged.

Social change facilitator and community organizer adrienne maree brown describes elements of an emergent process, calling it an "emergent strategy," a conscious effort to enact transformation through attention to process. In her book *Emergent Strategy: Shaping Change, Changing Worlds* (brown 2017), brown provides practical suggestions and tools that guide facilitation and a creative process. These tools are instructive for creating a space where emergence takes place. She lists six elements of an emergent strategy:

- Fractal: The Relationship between Small and Large
- Adaptative: How We Change
- Interdependence and Decentralization: Who We are and How We Share
- Non-linear and Iterative: The Pace and Pathways of Change
- Resilience and Transformative Justice: How We Recover and Transform
- Creating More Possibilities: How We Move Towards Life

(brown 2017, 50)

These six emergent elements can be found in Ferreira's case study of *The Orphan Sea* at Skidmore College. The *fractal* highlights how individual relationships reproduce to form a larger structure at multiple levels—the original impulse to produce the play stems from Svich's and Ferreira's prior relationship and their shared commitment to engaging cultural intersections that reflect their own lived experiences and aesthetics. Ferreira consciously builds upon her relationships with multiple university offices, allowing her to invite international students to the welcome table, seeking input outside the department. The relationship-building continues throughout the creative process and into audience engagements, making visible shared experiences and allowing multiple constituencies to see themselves on the stage.

In the casting process, Ferreira creates a situation where the international and multicultural student actors' language abilities and lived cultural experiences become assets, the necessary skills for this show. Then she casts an ensemble of actors much in the way that a devised project might be developed. Without specific roles, the ensemble takes time to create its own relationships and networks in response to the material, a strategy that allows for an emergent process that provides room for *adaptation*. Before sorting performers into three different choruses and then into different pairs within the scene structure, they explore synergies and resonances within their own skill sets and experiences, becoming *adaptive* in discovering how they complement each other. Ferreira crafts an emergent space where student actors direct creative decision making, thus leading to an ensemble that is *interdependent* and *decentralized* (as found in brown's emergent elements). Music, dance, and linguistic translations all serve as collaborative structures assisting with the metapragmatics that decentralize traditional self-contained roles like the director and playwright. The ensemble became translators, working between the text and their cultural experiences, devising their own metapragmatics by weaving in their unique talents and cultural languages. As Ferreira notes, Gao Xingjian's tripartite actor (composed of the self, actor as self, actor as character) facilitates this space of emergence where individual ensemble members can work at the intersection between text, ensemble, and self to innovate staging.

Being *adaptive, interdependent,* and *decentralized,* the ensemble grows its own unique network of relationships, but these must be sustained with a practice that allows the form to emerge. Company rituals serve as *iterative* practices that underscore and reiterate the values of intercultural exchange; they help to maintain alignment, especially when encountering obstacles. Ferreira describes the xenophobic tensions of the 2016 election and its effects upon the ensemble during rehearsal. Ferreira creates a space to consciously explore what is at stake in an intercultural creative process and the shifting politicized national context, emphasizing *resilience* and *transformative justice.* Putting the context in perspective and solidifying the ensemble's multifaceted relationship to that context, the artistic work takes on a deeper meaning. Finally, brown's last element emphasizes that the work leads to *more possibilities,* underscoring that the final result should multiply and extend the emerging form to others. Emergent strategy's *more possibilities* implies boundary crossing and hybrid forms that lead to unanticipated results. Ferreira's production, like some of my own described below, fostered a unique experience breaking boundaries and innovating new forms.

Emergent strategy and the open work

Svich's *The Orphan Sea* is an excellent example of what Umberto Eco calls an "open work" (Eco 1989, 4). Eco defines the "open work" as art designed to be open to interpretation, even incomplete until participants come along to "complete" it. An "open work" creates a structure for input and feedback, one that leads to dialogue. As Ferreira describes the "hyperlinked dramaturgy," she underscores how the intersection of actor and text becomes the focus. As a poetic text with implied actions and staging, Svich's *The Orphan Sea* resists a linear narrative. Because Svich uses three choruses with no differentiation of who is speaking each line, the production team must make significant choices in elaborating the blueprint that she's provided. This text becomes a fertile and playful open space for cultural encounter. The "open work" challenges the idea of a unified interpretation, allowing the ensemble to provide their own structure to the text that allows them to intersect stories, interpretations, and subjectivities. Whether devising, adapting a non-theatrical text, or staging an "open work," a director has the opportunity to consciously expand the networks of the ensemble and structure an emergent process that allows for different ways to configure characters and represent identities.

Ferreira's casting choices weave together various languages and cultures, and this richly layered ensemble creates the performance through a dialogic process with Svich's text. In order to cast a heterogeneous ensemble that reflects multiple dimensions beyond visible appearances, how can a director maintain a complex and nuanced creative framework? If a director is not casting a "character" per se, what elements might structure an ensemble that will expand the welcome table or lead to an emergent form? In her book *Theatre for Youth: Third Space*, Stephani Etheridge Woodson shares an adapted "diversity wheel" (Figure 12.1) that maps multilayered dimensions of an individual in relation to group affiliation. Building upon sociology and medical education, Woodson adapts her wheel to think about artistic and cultural issues (Woodson 2015, 98). With multiple dimensions, the casting process becomes even more complex when thinking through the dynamics of power. This is a multilayered process that relies on community context. For example, each dimension resonates with other members of the ensemble, as well as the play text being staged. Finally, each audience member will read the dimensions of the ensemble and the play text through their own lens, or "sociology of viewing," as well.

Woodson's wheel provides an excellent resource for thinking through these dimensions when casting. She uses this graphic as a lens to think through how devised performance fosters cultural community development, activating new dimensions of community identities and capacities through performance. The complex layers of power and context evoked by the wheel underscore the unstable and relational aspects of identity, a necessary perspective in employing an emergent strategy. Woodson's diversity wheel, along with Gao Xingjian's conceptualization of the tripartite actor, allows directors to think about weaving together an ensemble that explores individuals, group contexts, and the texts as well as the community/audience from which the performance arises. All these elements "contribute to the symbolic ecology of a place" and ensure an emergent strategy (Woodson 2015, 131). Though a director might not be devising or casting an ensemble explicitly for cultural community development, a resource like Woodson's diversity wheel, nevertheless, still helps a director make casting choices for any ensemble. Woodson's wheel is, then, a resource that articulates individual/group relations in order to become conscious of identities invited to the table and the assets they bring, a necessary step in developing the metapragmatics of an emergent strategy.

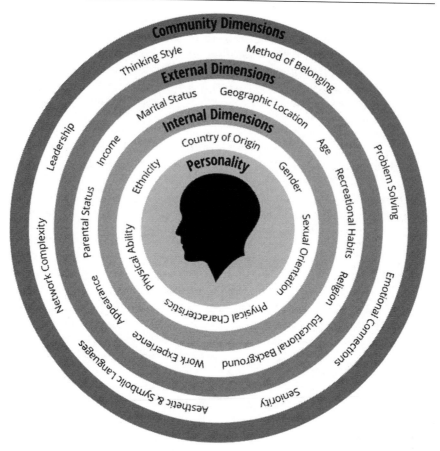

Figure 12.1 *Theatre for Youth* adapted diversity wheel.
Source: Woodson (2015). Reproduced with permission of the Licensor through PLSclear.

Emergent strategy for audience engagement: extended dramaturgy

Ferreira questioned the ensemble, "How do we respond to global crises of displaced people and environmental threats [...]? What does it mean to cross digital, linguistic, and physical borders?" (122). She then extended this question to the audience. Before the performances of *The Orphan Sea*, the dramaturgy/design team allowed audience members to "map" their origins and share memories of migration. Facilitating a schematic mapping of the community, they specifically aligned the world of the play with the world of the audience. Through interactive media before the show, as well as subsequent post-show discussions, the production team delivered the invitation, "Let us talk to each other"; they made visible community experiences of exile, diaspora, and border crossings, setting the stage for dialogue.

Individual productions, like *The Orphan Sea*, create deep engagements with particular audiences. Could the temporary communities built on a production-by-production basis be leveraged in order to sustain deeper engagements with our art form? Are there intermediary sites of participation that might help extend the welcome table, bringing new artists into our field? Ezra Lebank makes a provocative call:

> The profession our students are entering, whether or not it can be exclusively called theatre, requires a skill set that allows them to adapt to multimedia, hybrid, interactive, collaborative, physical, devised, site-specific, and/or community engaged performance opportunities. To prepare our students, these developments must become integral elements of our production seasons.
>
> (Lebank 2013)

Just as Ferreira makes language and culture key assets for her cast members, university productions have the opportunity to create emergent spaces for interdisciplinary innovation. I want to briefly discuss examples from my practice and think about the relationships between community-based, site-specific, interdisciplinary performance and the mainstage season. Can site-specific, community-based projects feed into an emergent strategy for educational theater? As audiences crave more opportunities for participation, can audience engagement strategies create a space for collaboration and dialogue that foster emergent strategy to build relationships and extend the field? Below I share two related examples illustrating how community-based strategies created new sites for performance that engaged multiple stakeholders and allowed for interdisciplinary innovation.

In 2004, I received a grant to create a theatrical performance about Freedom Summer 1964 and organize a reunion of Civil Rights Movement Veterans. Freedom Summer was a creative campaign in Mississippi that registered African American voters and provided support to rural communities struggling against Jim Crow segregation.[1] In June 1964, college students (mostly white volunteers) from all over the country convened in Oxford, Ohio, at Western College for Women to train for their activism.[2] Recruiting allies and challenging white privilege, activists confronted structural oppression and cultural differences in order to open up Mississippi's closed society. Most remember this historic event through the lynching of civil rights martyrs James Chaney, Andrew Goodman, and Mickey Schwerner shortly after leaving the first week of this orientation session.

Miami University (my institution) merged with Western College for Women in 1974, taking over the physical campus where the orientation took place. In 2004, speakers such as Bob Moses and Congressmen John Lewis were slated as reunion guest speakers and, for the first time since 1964, Civil Rights Movement veterans would return to the site of their training. Quickly, I had to confront the reality that few at my historically white Midwestern university had any context for this historic gathering. Yet, the site of Western College for Women, a pastoral campus with rolling hills and stone bridges, existed much as it did in 1964, haunted by the ghosts of those who were murdered shortly after leaving the campus. Given historical tensions (see note below), could I move forward to create a theatrical performance for our mainstage season about this history and engage a diverse group of stakeholders, including Western College Alumnae, Civil Rights Movement veterans, as well as current students? Could complex questions be explored through performance to help resolve rather than exacerbate difficult questions about ownership, authenticity, and identity politics that would come up in telling this story?[3]

In this moment, I needed to construct a contact zone where students could engage in—and even reconstruct—the cross-cultural dialogue that took place in 1964. Three weeks before the reunion, a multiethnic group of six multi-disciplinary students created a site-specific, immersive, community ritual—*Walk with Me: Freedom Summer Walking Tour*. Since then, more than one hundred different student pairs of tour guides have channeled voices from historic letters and archives as they walked small groups of visitors around the landscape, engaging trust exercises and replaying historic moments. These moments include the trainers reenacting nonviolent role-playing and staff announcing that three men were missing in Mississippi. This walking tour developed from a kind of emergent strategy, one that took on a life of its own. We had few precedents or models for the "tour" or ritual and, during the first year of leading the tour, we revised the work in response to our audiences.

Over the span of its ten-year life, the program trained theater majors and non-majors, who identified with Freedom Summer's history through their own concerns that ranged from, for example, LGBTQ marriage equality, immigration rights, racial equity, and disability rights. Students were not "cast" in the tour, but merely applied to serve with a short essay. Two scripted voices represented several different identities while portraying conflicts based on cultural misunderstandings. Moving between third person narration and first person role playing, tour guides did not mimetically become their characters but instead illustrated the story of training participants to volunteer for the summer. The tour relied upon the audience participants' physical participation in simple actions affirming their commitment to join in the struggle for freedom. Elsewhere, I have written about the tour as a pedagogy of embodiment engaging white privilege (Armstrong 2007, 201–222).

Walk with Me: Freedom Summer Walking Tour was not a fully staged, mimetic performance; instead it was led by performers reading from note cards, focusing on the telling of a community's story, animating the site and its historic ghosts. Like a processional cycle play, the tour embedded this narrative from our community's memory into the landscape, and, in the process, raised the profile of the theater department beyond its majors. Many of the tour guides from this program went on to audition and perform in mainstage performances, minor in theater, or take theater classes as non-majors. In some cases, students from other disciplines went on to pursue performance within their own fields of museum studies or education.

Then, in 2009, I led the commissioning of a play about Freedom Summer for our department's mainstage season. *Down in Mississippi* by Carlyle Brown featured a leading role for a black man and a chorus of black women as well as two white college student characters. Despite the on-going Freedom Summer walking tours, the casting pool was not a multiethnic group. The *Walk with Me* tour had built many institutional relationships, but students are a transient population. After hiring a professional actor to play the male lead and convening a community church choir for the chorus, we were disappointed that the premiere production would not engage more student actors. However, as evidenced by the tour, many students across the university were willing to engage deeply with this history. The history contained a strong performative question: "If you were a college student in 1964, would you go to Mississippi?" How could we continue to leverage this question to expand sites for participation?

In collaboration with Dr. Katie Johnson, a professor in English and the production dramaturg, we launched the "Freedom Summer Ambassadors," a team of dramaturgs who co-curated a lobby display featuring interactive media and performers playing "in-role" as characters, such as a black mother who lost her son and a Student Nonviolent Coordinating Committee trainer coaching others in nonviolent strategy. For audience members who arrived early, they had a chance to apply to be a Freedom Summer volunteer or to attempt to fill out a voter registration form like those used at the time in Mississippi. Inspired by the local connections to the historic orientation, the Freedom Summer Ambassadors created an immersive environment, bringing many of the participatory insights from the walking tour into the theater's lobby. Freedom Summer Ambassadors came from a variety of departments, including an interdisciplinary studies program in which Dr. Johnson and I taught. Several Ambassadors developed an interest in theater, later minoring, auditioning, or taking classes, bringing multiple forms of diversity into our department community. These not only included race but also different disciplinary interests and ways of thinking. Several also became *Walk with Me* tour guides. Community members, university students, and Civil Rights Movement veterans who all came to see *Down in Mississippi* engaged the world of the play in this contact zone created before the performance and through post-show and curricular programming.

I share these two examples—the *Walk with Me* tour and the Freedom Summer Ambassadors—to mark emergent strategy experiments that complemented standard mainstage productions, providing entry points for students from a variety of disciplines, identities, and interests. The projects increased our sense of place and sense of self as a university community. Like the fractal, the projects encouraged new relationships between individuals and between different units on campus; they were projects led by students who worked in an interdependent and decentralized structure, while adapting to one another's unique talents, interests, and community connections. The *Walk with Me* tour was, in particular, nonlinear and iterative, contributing to sustaining the narrative of Freedom Summer at Miami University. The Freedom Summer Ambassadors' engagement with *Down in Mississippi* demonstrated how the performative lobby display created more possibilities, including outcomes that we did not anticipate. Both of these performances contributed to resilience and transformative justice, creating spaces for reflecting upon the present and the past and drawing the community into understanding their potential to engage and extend this civil rights legacy. Like Ferreira's *The Orphan Sea* production, these projects brought new participants to the table by recognizing the assets they contributed. Furthermore, they aligned the world of the play with the world of the community to explore resonances there. Both of these projects opened up a space for dialogue and exploration. Their success might lie in the pedagogical role of a theater department in an educational setting and the ability to borrow from applied theater forms and community-organizing. How can such work be replicated in the professional theater to continue extending the "welcome table" to make more possibilities?

Notes

1 For more information about this history, see Wisconsin Historical Society (n.d.).
2 The Western College for Women rented their campus for two one-week orientation sessions that were led by activists from Student Nonviolent Coordinating Committee (SNCC), lawyers from the NAACP, Mississippi activists, and national civil rights leaders. It was attended by approximately 800 of the 1000 volunteers. The first week focused on voter registration strategies and the second on freedom schools. Both sessions trained participants in community organizing and nonviolent resistance. As a decentralized and emergent strategy, the staff coordinated volunteers at this orientation in order to set up projects in approximately forty different Mississippi communities.
3 The Western College for Women was the host for the orientation and defended this controversial choice. In 2004, many felt that Miami University was appropriating the history of the women's college. Though individual Miami University students and faculty participated in Freedom Summer, the university as an organization had no relationship to the historic events, actively distancing themselves from the event at different points in history. Hence, in 2004, it was critical to move past superficial representations and instead create spaces of dialogue between current students, Western College Alumnae, and Civil Rights Movement veterans.

Bibliography

Armstrong, Ann Elizabeth. 2007. "In Search of the Beloved Community: Engaging Agents of Change through Freedom Summer 1964." In *Radical Acts: Theatre and Feminist Pedagogies of Change*, edited by Ann Elizabeth Armstrong and Kathleen Juhl, 201–222. San Francisco, CA: Aunt Lute Press.
Banks, Daniel. 2013. "The Welcome Table: Casting for an Integrated Society." *Theatre Topics*, 23(1) (March): 1–18.

brown, adrienne maree. 2017. *Emergent Strategy: Shaping Change, Changing Worlds.* Chico, CA: AK Press.

Cohen-Cruz, Jan. 2010. *Engaged Performance: Theatre as Call and Response.* New York: Routledge.

Eco, Umberto. 1989. *The Open Work.* Translated by Anna Cancogni. Cambridge, MA: Harvard University Press.

Lebank, Ezra. 2013. "Little Lemon: A Case for Reimagining the University Season." *Howlround*, December 15, 2013. https://howlround.com/little-lemon (accessed April 2, 2019).

Nicholson, Helen. 2014. *Applied Drama: The Gift of Theatre.* New York: Palgrave Macmillan.

Sawyer, R. Keith. 2005. *Social Emergence: Societies as Complex Systems.* New York: Cambridge University Press.

Wisconsin Historical Society. n.d. "What was 1964 Freedom Summer Project?" www.wisconsinhistory.org/Records/Article/CS3707 (accessed April 2, 2019).

Woodson, Stephani Etheridge. 2015. *Theatre for Youth Third Space: Performance, Democracy, and Community Cultural Development.* Bristol: Intellect.

Part V

Casting contemporary Native American theater

Chapter 13

Journey

Ty Defoe (Giizhig)

When I left my reservation from the northern part of Turtle Island this is what I knew…

I am Anishinaabe.

I canoe on the lake with torches, and know the process to prepare wild rice.

I am Oneida.

I play Lacrosse made from hickory sticks and listen to stories about Sky Woman falling from the sky.

I can speak my mother language.

I can sing hand drum songs.

I can play flute.

I know stories about birch bark, about jumping mouse shape-shifting into an eagle.

I know my long hair has medicine in it.

I know I'm two-spirit and prefer not to operate on a binary.

I know, one day I will transition using what my mother calls "the white man's medicine."

I go to Los Angeles.

Uncle Milton told me there would be a large community of Indigenous Peoples

out west, who are making art, doing things like making theater.

I want to be maker of stories.

Time passes.

Surfing happens.

Getting lost happens.

I met an elder woman.

She is a nurse, she says people expect me to show up "on time."

We adopt one another.

She is Black and dying of cancer.

Every day I make her carrot juice.

We pray together just like back home.

I burn sage for her.

Her children are from the Shawnee Nation and are Black.

We make ceremony.

We make ritual.
We talk blood memory.
I tell them stories.
They said, I should get into acting.
I go to auditions.
I travel from place to place,
office to office wearing my ribbon shirt,
sometimes the beaded medallion my father gave me when I left home,
sometimes I use the gift of looking people in the eye
my mother gave to me, to ensure people were telling the truth.

BREAKDOWN:
American Indian girl. Any age. Dark hair.
I show up.
Would you be willing to cut your hair?
Can you speak the Indian language?
Can you pop out of the bushes and scream and then run?
Can I shake your hand? I never met a Native American person before.
Do you know there is something very spiritual about you?
How long have you lived here in the States?
I never told anyone this before but my grandmother had some Indian in her.
Wait, you are Indian, like feather Indian?
Time passes.
Surfing happens.
A near-death experience happens.
In the undertow
with the sky above
In slow motion
I think, I don't "play"
American Indian
Native American
Princess Creamy Corn
or Squaw #12.
I make it to shore
Untangled from seaweed
I look out, take a breath, give thanks.
I am me.

Chapter 14

Native Voices at the Autry

Casting the room

Jean Bruce Scott and Randy Reinholz (Choctaw)

Native Voices at the Autry (NVA) puts Native narratives at the center of the American story to facilitate a more inclusive dialogue about what it means to be "American."[1] By supporting Native theater productions and theater artists, NVA creates space and resources to tell Native stories. We partner with a wide range of arts and educational institutions, Native communities and service organizations, theater, film, television, and new media professionals to make Native theater available to broader audiences.

There are scores of elders, Native American, First Nations, Alaska Native, and Native Hawaiian theater artists both with us and those whose spirits continue to guide the path of self-representation in the American theater.[2] While there are too many to name, we recognize that we stand on the shoulders of giants. We are deeply grateful for their leadership, artistry, and courageous contributions to the field. There are also many valued allies in this work and we are deeply grateful for their support and recognition of Native theater artists as professional colleagues in this collaborative art.

For the purposes of this chapter we use the term "Native" to describe this group of playwrights and theater artists. While focusing on first-hand experiences of NVA, we realize that self-representation and the community of Native theater artists has grown exponentially, especially over the past ten years, due to the hard work and talent of these artists.

Creating space

The twenty-five-year evolution of NVA and its hard-won stature in the American theater yields critical insights into casting a movement one room at a time. Our play selection process, casting practices, rigorous new play development strategies, and productions inform our theater making practices.

We are fortunate to have partnered with the Autry Museum of the American West since 1999. The Autry's mission is to "bring together the stories of all peoples of the American West, connecting the past with the present to inspire our shared future" (Autry Museum 2018). As the resident theater company at the Autry, we are currently the only Actors' Equity Association (a.

k.a. Equity) theater company in the United States dedicated solely to developing and producing new works for the stage by Native playwrights. Through our association with Equity, Native actors who are cast in our productions can join the union allowing them to be considered for a larger range of roles in Los Angeles, across the country, and on Broadway.

We have worked with playwrights from over a hundred distinct Native nations from across North America to develop and produce critically acclaimed productions, including:

- 26 unique Equity productions (including 23 world premieres).
- 15 playwright retreats.
- 25 national and international touring shows and performances.
- 15 radio plays.
- 25 new play festivals.
- 9 short play festivals.
- 200 unique titles developed.
- over 230 workshops of plays and 275 public staged readings.[3]

Scripts and papers containing NVA history are archived at the Autry.[4]

Humble beginnings

Native Voices began as a gathering place for Native playwrights to develop and present work in 1993 at Illinois State University. The impulse for the work was to see how Randy Reinholz's cultural background—as an enrolled member of the Choctaw Nation of Oklahoma—and his experience in the LORT (League of Resident Theaters) system might inform directing Native plays in a university setting with theater students, staff, and faculty in lead artistic roles. Jean Bruce Scott, the co-founder of Native Voices, brought twenty years of experience working on new scripts in theater, television, and film to the process.

> We thought it would be an easy task to find a contemporary Native play to produce on a college campus.

Little did we know that by sending out our first call for scripts and contacting literary managers and departments of theater to ask for recommendations of contemporary Native plays to produce, we were doing something that had not been done before. After calling The Old Globe, Oregon Shakespeare Festival, Indiana Rep, New World Theatre, The Public Theatre, the Mark Taper Forum, South Coast Rep, and other mainstream theaters across the country, the resounding response was: "We don't know of any Native plays, but if you find one let us know."

There were few published scripts. Some playwrights' names bubbled up: Gerald Visnor, Hanay Geiogamah, and Tomson Highway. We contacted them and the circle widened to include researching who was doing work on Native

American narratives academically and in community. Native playwrights William A. Lang, Judy Lee Oliva, and Diane Glancy taught at universities; William S. Yellow Robe, Jr. and Bruce King taught at the Institute of American Indian Arts in Santa Fe, New Mexico; Daniel David Moses and Drew Hayden Taylor were actively developing and producing new work at Native Earth in Toronto; and Spider-woman Theater, which had developed and presented work at La MaMa, was still creating new work and performing. Ann Haugo,[5] then a graduate student at the University of Illinois, and William Wortman,[6] a librarian at Miami University, Ohio, provided recommendations of plays to read and playwrights to contact.

Between 1994 and 1996, Native Voices facilitated script development and the production of two plays written by Native playwrights.[7] We produced three festivals—two at Illinois State University and one in New York at the American Indian Community House—featuring twelve Native plays. Each play was given a weeklong workshop followed by public readings and talkbacks. Nine plays workshopped at Illinois State University included casts of students and faculty. In the process we discovered we had two Native students in the theater department. Visiting artists were billeted in faculty homes; we had community meals and invited participants to sit in on workshops other than their own. The festival produced at the American Indian Community House in New York featured local all-Native casts in three Native plays.

With the playwrights' permission, both Native and non-Native actors (students, local actors, staff, or faculty) were cast in Native roles, essentially giving Illinois State University the confidence to present Native plays. There were also two important productions during this time. In 1995, Reinholz directed Marie Clements's *Now Look What You Made Me Do* at Illinois State University with an all-student, non-Native cast. Then in 1996, Betsy Theobald directed an Equity production of *The Baby Blues* by Drew Hayden Taylor at PENN State Center Stage with professional Native actors from across the US and Canada cast in all Native roles.

Native Voices devised a strategy for bringing in literary managers from LORT stages to dramaturg and direct during our new play festivals, thereby putting Native playwrights in rooms with the people who were looking for them. New World Theatre, The Public Theatre, the Mark Taper Forum, Oregon Shakespeare Festival, Indiana Rep, Playwrights Center, and others sent dramaturgs to the festival. They heard every play during the festival week and worked on at least one of them.

> *Something else interesting happened, we were putting Native playwrights in a room together where they could talk and swap story, comment on one another's work and tell us what they wanted.*

Complicated issues

NVA advocates casting all Native roles in Equity productions with Native actors. Casting Native actors who are from the tribe identified in the text is not necessary unless a playwright specifically requests it. Other productions should be cast with the Native playwright's preference and Native actor availability. To continue to expand the field and grow the Native actor talent pool, NVA encourages theaters and universities to identify and work with local Native theater artists and actors whenever possible. We also encourage theaters and universities to identify Native theater artists and invite them into their institutions as visiting artists and colleagues.

For a long time, Native people and stories were portrayed as pan-Indian. While pan-Indian may denote a cultural perspective or set of practices employed by all American Indian people, it also implies that all Indians are alike. There are some people in academia and the American theater who may not be aware that there are over 573 federally recognized tribes and over 250 additional tribes seeking federal recognition, which can take decades to achieve (National Conference of State Legislatures 2018).[8]

The US Department of the Interior (2018) states that "tribal constitutions, articles of incorporation or ordinances" determine an individual's tribal enrollment. Two common requirements for membership are lineal descent from someone named on the tribe's base roll or relationship to a tribal member who descended from someone named on the base roll.[9] Other conditions such as blood quantum, tribal residency, or continued contact with the tribe are common.

Our theater sits on the traditional homelands of the Gabrielino-Tongva people. This information has widespread agreement. Yet the question of who are the enrolled members of the Gabrielino-Tongva people is still disputed. There is no federal recognition for Gabrielino-Tongva people. Can anyone imagine a Native organization that claims to be a home for Native stories that would deny the rights of self-representation to the traditional caretakers of their land?

We know that artists associated with Native Voices often speak with each other about what it means to be Native American. How does a person authenticate their identity? In Los Angeles, where the status of California Indians is complex, NVA has adopted a self-identification policy.[10] We know a large number of artists belong to unrecognized tribes and face legal issues that are often in court for decades. This should not stop artists from claiming their Native culture and traditions. Artists take responsibility for their own status. We make it clear that Native artists will be engaged in dialogue about their heritage. This allows artists to participate while examining their family narratives. Many have located family members and been able to document their family history. Some have found out they cannot document family ties and choose to work as an ally with NVA, but not claim Native heritage.

Native theater artists are here to stay

A long-standing, self-fulfilling prophecy that the American theater uses when dismissing Native people who want to participate in theater goes something like this: "We can't produce Native plays, because there are no professional

Native actors." What has been said over and over again by Eurocentric professional theater artists is that they just do not know professional Native American theater artists, therefore they assume those artists do not exist. NVA disproves this through twenty-five years of productions that demonstrate and document the talent of Native theater artists and introduces theater professionals to the field.

Ignoring Native theater reflects an obvious disregard for current information. In April 2018 *American Theatre* magazine dedicated its cover and several articles to "Staging Our Native Nation." There have been similar articles in *American Theatre* over the years. NVA productions have been regularly reviewed in the Los Angeles region and prominent theater journals since 1999. OSF, Arena Stage, Kansas City Rep, Portland Center Stage all produced Native plays featuring Native actors in 2017–2018. There is ample evidence that there is a large talent pool of Native artists.

Since this volume is about casting, we will focus on the continued growth of the acting talent pool at NVA and our work to expand opportunities for them. A central need has been to bridge the gap between what was known about Native theater and the myths commonly repeated in professional and academic theater. Native theater and performance have always existed in communities and urban centers throughout the US whether or not it has been acknowledged by the American theater or academics. Those sentiments have not matched our experience of a growing professional talent pool of Native theater artists.

Native actors have had to confront an industry that has historically offered few opportunities for them. Native characters were stereotypical, marginalized, or non-speaking roles that were constructed within the context of a Eurocentric worldview. Or worse, if there was a lead role, it was played by a non-Native actor in redface. Too often Native characters are subservient to the major characters and seldom a driving force in the narrative. Of course, Native artists made work during this period, but the academy and industry often disregarded the importance of it and their talent. They certainly weren't developing it.

As NVA and scripts by Native playwrights have evolved over the past few decades, we see fully developed Native characters that determine the action in the story, employing Native American knowledge and attributes that resonate with community members as truthful. Scripts by Native writers normally situate Native characters in lead roles, which positions Native actors to develop the skills necessary to compete in all genres of theater, film, television, and new media. This process of training is closely aligned with the way Native actors have traditionally developed skills—preparing them to interpret both Native and non-Native lead roles in all arenas. NVA invests in artist development (playwright, actor, director) and focuses attention on the talent our community has to offer while telling important stories through a Native lens.

Casting the room

Beyond casting actors, NVA dedicates time and resources to "casting the room." We are very conscious of who we bring in as actors and how those artists work with Native playwrights. We are simultaneously intentional with regard to the selection of dramaturgs and other creative collaborators who must first serve the script and the playwright, while facilitating a process that embraces the knowledge in the room.

In this section, we discuss some of the unique opportunities and needs of casting two recent plays at NVA. These case studies outline casting and production considerations for *Off the Rails* by Randy Reinholz (Choctaw) and *They Don't Talk Back* by Frank Henry Kassh Katasse (Tlingit). Both plays have roles that require traditional Native dance, language, song, and theatricalized ritual. We will address casting issues and include our common practices when working with Native artists. For instance, at NVA it is common to include tribal identity when Native artists are listed in writing, by stating the name of the artist, followed by tribal affiliations in parenthesis.

In addition to casting specific roles, we always consider the makeup and cultural knowledge of the room. Besides the playwright's cultural knowledge, we need culture bearers present in the room to bring information that may extend beyond the knowledge of the director, the actors cast in the production, or those hired as designers. *Off The Rails* and *They Don't Talk Back* are two recent examples of scripts that required cultural consultants during their conception and development, as well as many aspects of production.

Off the Rails

Off the Rails grew out of Reinholz's desire to use the Bard's words for Native American actors to revisit US history and put Native American characters in charge. Shakespeare's *Measure for Measure*, a favorite of Reinholz's, gave him the perfect set up for reworking the play. He placed his characters in 1880s Genoa, Nebraska, home to the fourth American Indian Boarding School in the United States. The play gives agency to Native Americans onstage—especially Native women. Mistress Overdone who disappears in Shakespeare's play becomes Madame Overdone who drives the action in Reinholz's muscular reworking of the plot.

Madame Overdone (Lakota and French), owner of The Stewed Prunes Saloon, steps in when General Gatt, the mayor of Genoa, leaves town to further personal business interests. James MacDonald, a Choctaw lawyer and Gatt's right-hand man, investigates the newly arrived boarding school superintendent's books and discovers Captain Angelo's long history of impropriety. Isabel, once a boarding school student, is preparing to become a teacher. She returns to Genoa to argue for her brother's life when the stern and seemingly immovable Captain Angelo demands that he hang for

Figure 14.1 2017 Oregon Shakespeare Festival production of *Off the Rails* by Randy Reinholz (Choctaw). Madame Overdone, played by Sheila Tousey (Menominee, Stockbridge Munsee) hatches a plan to free Isabel, played by Lily Gladstone (Blackfeet, Nez Perce) and Momaday, played by Shaun Taylor-Corbett (Blackfeet) from Angelo's treachery.
Photo by Jenny Graham, Oregon Shakespeare Festival

the offense of loving (and marrying in the Pawnee way) the Irish orphan Caitlin. Each of these actions demonstrates the resilience of Native people and their ability to use the government's forced education to upend proposed outcomes to their advantage. Reinholz's decision to use Shakespeare and comedy to tell this story speaks to Native American humor, collapses history in upon itself, and shines a light on what remains a shameful half-century of US history.

We made two trips to the Genoa American Indian Boarding School in Nebraska, which had students from a wide range of nations. Purposefully, *Off the Rails* has characters of Paiute, Kiowa, Lakota, Pawnee, and Choctaw heritages represented on stage. Those roles had many demands for cultural competencies. Each tribal identity needed to be distinct. Casting sessions followed traditional professional protocols, with the caveat that actors who identified as Native play the Native characters. Audition sides, requiring actors to use Native languages, came with phonetic pronunciations or websites containing pronunciations for the required language.

NVA prepared for the Autry's production of *Off the Rails* by offering workshops for Native theater artists in playing Shakespeare. We had also recently offered musical theater workshops to facilitate the development process of *Distant Thunder,* a musical by Lynne Taylor-Corbett and Shaun Taylor-Corbett (Blackfeet). *Off the Rails* contains ten songs in a variety of styles and languages. Those skill-building efforts informed casting *Off the Rails* during its development in 2014 at NVA in Los Angeles and La Jolla Playhouse in San Diego, as well as the 2015 production at the Autry, directed by Chris Anthony. The text required seven Native actors in a cast of seventeen. We cast eleven Native actors to play all of the Native roles and four non-Native roles.

Soon after the Los Angeles production, the Oregon Shakespeare Festival (OSF) selected *Off the Rails* for its 2017 season, making it the first play by a Native American playwright to be produced by the theater during its eighty-two-year history. The process of casting both the NVA production and OSF production provides insights into aspects of NVA's efforts.

When OSF made the commitment to produce *Off the Rails,* Native Voices was asked to assist in the casting and production processes. OSF's Artistic Director Bill Rauch directed and purposefully filled key creative leadership roles with people of Native heritage. We requested that costume designer E. B. Brooks (Sami, Algonquin) costume the production and Duane Minard (Yurok) serve as the movement coordinator; Native musician Ty Defoe (*Giizhig*) served as music advisor to the OSF workshops. Waylon Lenk (Karuk) was one of the dramaturgs. These artists have long-standing relationships with NVA and brought significant research and cultural knowledge to the production.

As we worked with OSF's casting director Joy Dickson to cast the seven Native roles in *Off the Rails,* she mentioned that, when she contacted Equity in 2016, there were very few Native American members in the union. Clearly, we had to work with the union, as well as theater companies working with Native actors, to ensure that we considered the largest talent pool possible. Joy made casting trips to Minneapolis, New York, and Los Angeles, where NVA hosted casting sessions. NVA provided our database of Native artists and additional actors auditioned on tape.[11]

Beyond casting Native actors in *Off the Rails,* OSF cast Native actors in the season's acting company. This breakthrough has paved the way for OSF to consider other Native plays for production and to ask why or how a Native character might exist in any of the plays they produce. The result is a growing presence of Native actors on the OSF stage.

They Don't Talk Back

NVA thoroughly engaged "casting the room" for our production of *They Don't Talk Back* by Frank Henry Kaash Katasse (Tlingit) in association with La Jolla Playhouse and Perseverance Theatre. Frank's play draws from his life experience and the script grew tremendously when he suggested we bring highly-gifted musician and Tlingit culture bearer Edward Littlefield into the process. Edward speaks Tlingit language, knows traditional performance styles, and is also an accomplished contemporary musician and composer. While developing the play it became clear that the performers needed to have first-hand knowledge of the place where the script was set, which the playwright describes as follows:

> It's a small undisclosed Southeast Alaskan fishing town. Population is less than a 1000 year-round residents. There aren't any roads in or out of the town. Everything comes in by floatplane or a weekly ferry. There are roads within the town, but everything is within walking distance.
> (Frank Henry Kaash Katasse, personal communication, summer 2015)

With this description in mind, NVA considered the difficulty that the actors might have relying on imagination alone to portray this unique setting accurately. We raised the funds to take the cast to Juneau, Alaska, where we met the playwright and worked with language speakers, cultural consultants, and Tlingit artists. We also visited Tlingit fishing villages in rural Southeast Alaska. We had many contributors to this cultural exchange who were vital to the success of the show.

The opening of *They Don't Talk Back* is a three-page poem in Tlingit language. There are not many Tlingit speakers and even fewer actors, so that is part of the reason we took the cast of the show to Alaska. While in Juneau, the cast studied language and movement, camped, went on a five-hour ferry ride to visit the towns of Haynes and Klukwan where Jones P. Hotch Jr., Chilkat Indian Village Tribal Council President, hosted us. The investment of this research supported all of the actors, especially Duane Minard a gifted Yurok actor who speaks several languages. For the role of Paul, Sr., Minard learned and performed the Tlingit sections of the play as if he were a native speaker. Minard's amazing ability, in tandem with the director's and cast's Alaska research, aided language acquisition and cultural competencies developed during rehearsals. In turn, these processes informed and enhanced the production team and the Autry and La Jolla Playhouse productions.

The play was then produced at Perseverance Theatre in Juneau, Alaska, and the Performing Arts Center in Anchorage, Alaska, with a cast that included two of the Los Angeles actors and three local actors, including two who spoke Tlingit. Reinholz directed the production in all four locations.

Closing thoughts

NVA is fortunate to be based in Los Angeles where many Native actors come to further their careers. However, one of the challenges of working in Los Angeles is that actors are often cast in higher-paying roles in which case NVA, according to the rules for a signatory theater of Equity, loses them to other projects. Recently, core NVA actors have landed long-running jobs in regional theater, on and off Broadway, and in film or television roles. While it is difficult to cast around these projects or recast any of this talented group of actors, we believe that work begets work and our goal has always been to have Native

Figure 14.2 2016 Native Voices at the Autry production of *They Don't Talk Back* by
Frank Henry Kaash Katasse (Tlingit). Grandfather teaches Paul, Sr. why
"they don't talk back." Young Paul, played by Kholan Studi (Cherokee) in
mask; Grandfather, played by Brian Wescott (Athabascan, Yup'ik) in mask;
and Paul, Sr. played by Duane Minard (Yurok) in back.
Photo by Craig Schwartz, Native Voices at the Autry

voices on the American stage. So, we keep casting established and emerging
artists in our new play development workshops and productions, and we continue to train more artists to augment the thriving Native talent pool.

We invite some of these artists into the Native Voices Artists Ensemble to
teach or polish skills demanded of professional theater artists, as well as those
required of traditional performance or language styles dictated by tribal nations.
In development and production, where Native characters speak tribal languages, perform traditional dance, sing, or drum in specific styles, NVA relies
on the playwright and, when needed, brings in traditional culture bearers or
language speakers for workshops and artist training.

NVA continues to grow the Native talent pool through utilizing the apprentice system. We ask NVA actors to play lead and supporting roles. Actors often begin as understudies or are cast in staged readings with more established actors. This apprenticeship happens between accomplished, emerging, and new actors, in a wide array of events and production. Actors are always learning from and being challenged by each other in rehearsal and onstage.

We have recently employed a new strategy to broaden the range of the artists in the Native Voices Artists Ensemble—the collective creation of new work by ensemble members. The ensemble created *Stories from the Indian Boarding School*—a production that employs a touring company of four actors and a stage manager—to present the show at arts institutions, theaters, colleges, and universities. *Stories from the Indian Boarding School* was conceived with all actors playing across gender and age constraints. Growing out of a year-long process, actors read and researched the Indian Boarding School system, which allowed them to write and create the stories they wanted to tell, while gaining the confidence needed to lead post-show talkbacks.

Expanding the kind of theater we do is as important as Native artists confronting the past practices of a society that systematically erased or excluded Native stories. For too long Native stories and images have been appropriated to whitewash US history. NVA's work is to disrupt those processes, while creating a supportive atmosphere for making art. NVA's processes are evaluated, revised, and modified regularly; and with each project new ways of working are utilized.[12] While we are proud of our production history, we recognize that there is work to be done in both process and production. We value the feedback provided by elders, community members, stakeholders, and allies and strive for continued improvement.

Including Native artists and voices in the American theater requires a broader set of actions than those utilized in the LORT theater system or taught in drama schools in the twentieth century or before. As we work to expand theater produced in the US in the twenty-first century, Native and non-Native theater artists must be more intentional and expand the narrative of our shared history. NVA is purposeful in its commitment to putting Native voices and stories on the American stage. Moving forward, there are no excuses for theaters to exclude the descendants of the first nations of this land—they are, and always have been, here.

Notes

1 We realize there are many Americas, but we use the term "American" intentionally. For us, American specifically relates to, or is characteristic of, the United States population today, as well as this land's first inhabitants. In this way, we seek to demonstrate the presence of indigenous peoples who are native to this land and its "American" narratives.

2 We use the term "American theater" to refer to theater produced in the United States.

3 This information is correct as of June 2019.

4 The Autry Museum of the American West's Research Center and Archives is scheduled to open in 2020. For more information contact rroom@theautry.org.

5 Ann Haugo's efforts were critical; she created one of the first annotated bibliographies of the field, which led to more connections and collaborations between Native artists.

6 William Wortman's efforts were also deeply important; he founded the Native American Women Playwrights Archive at Miami University, Ohio. http://spec.lib. miamioh.edu/home/nawpa.

7 For a more detailed history of NVA during this period see our chapter, "Native Voices: New Directions in New Play Development" (Reinholz and Scott 2000).

8 It took the Shinnecock Indian Nation thirty-two years for approval.

9 According to the Department of the Interior (2018), "A 'base roll' is the original list of members as designated in a tribal constitution or other document specifying enrollment criteria."

10 As discussed further by Courtney Elkin Mohler (Santa Barbara Chumash) in the epilogue that follows this chapter.

11 Native actors are invited to submit their headshot and resume at http://bit.ly/Form NVActorSubmission.

12 For more detail about considerations for working in communities when making theater founded in reciprocity see Reinholz (forthcoming).

Bibliography

American Theatre Magazine. 2018. "Staging Our Native Nation." *American Theatre Magazine*, April.

Autry Museum. 2018. "What is the Autry?" https://theautry.org/about-us (accessed April 3, 2019).

National Conference of State Legislatures. 2018. "Federal and State Recognized Tribes." www.ncsl.org/research/state-tribal-institute/list-of-federal-and-state-recognized-tribes. aspx (accessed April 3, 2019).

Reinholz, Randy, and Jean Bruce Scott. 2000. "Native Voices: New Directions in New Play Development." In *American Indian Theater in Performance: A Reader*, edited by Hanay Geiogamah and Jaye T. Darby, 265–282. Los Angeles, CA: UCLA American Indian Studies Center.

Reinholz, Randy. Forthcoming. "Global Citizenry and Community Outreach: Strategies to Enact Community Engagement Practices That Create Good Neighbors, Support Global Understanding, and Lead to Intentional Actions." In *Cultivating Leadership: A Primer for Academic Theatre Programs*, edited by Mark A. Heckler and Barbara O. Korner. St. Paul, MN: Association for Theatre in Higher Education.

US Department of the Interior. 2018. "Tribal Enrollment Process." www.doi.gov/ tribes/enrollment (accessed April 3, 2019).

Chapter 15

Decolonial practices for contemporary Native Theater

Courtney Elkin Mohler (Santa Barbara Chumash)

I am the real Hollywood Indian,
the one who left and remained the same
who emerged from dark desert canyons and minds of frightened girls,
who lived to tell the tale and keeps telling,
shouting out blood to all who will listen
spitting red on a page to all who will hear
and I am still here
——Carolyn Dunn (Muscogee/Cherokee/
Choctaw)[1]

Gifted the opportunity to respond to the decades long work of my elders, Jean Bruce Scott and Randy Reinholz (Choctaw), I smile with gratitude. As a young director and scholar, Native Voices at the Autry (NVA) invited me to its table, both figuratively and literally. I began as Reinholz's directing assistant as we workshopped *Carbon Black* by Terry Gomez (Comanche) in 2009 and received training at NVA in professional directing that was a radical departure from my doctoral program in Critical Studies in Theatre at UCLA. The unique, egalitarian process in which I participated profoundly altered my understanding of how theater can and should be made in order to honor all our relations through creative work.

I grew up making theater of the school auditorium, Eurocentric fairy tale and white-washed musical variety. Though aware of my mixed California Indian, white and Spanish-Californian cultural roots, it was not until I encountered Hanay Geiogamah (Kiowa Delaware) at UCLA that I had any sense that Native American theater existed. Professor Geiogamah's mentorship was instrumental throughout my studies, wherein I served as a teaching and research assistant in the American Indian Studies Center that Geiogamah directed at the time. Even in that capacity, my experience as an actor and burgeoning theater scholar did not allow me to participate in making Native Theater. I read scripts, taught history, wrote and theorized about representation, omission, colonial desire, cultural imperialism, and performance as resistance. But unfortunately my doctoral course of study did not include Indigenous ways of knowing and took me away from co-creating practical theater. I felt pressure to conform to the kinds of institutional knowledge production that are recognized within the colonial space of the academy.

Time and space between those graduate years and my current life-role as a mother and scholar-director now offer me perspective—I recognize the distance that can exist between the pursuit of critical theory and the meaning and process of making Native American theater. I completed a dissertation that explored the ebb and flow of identity transformation in my ancestral homeland, Santa Barbara, California. My work looked at the social and political changes in this coastal southern California city as it rehearsed and created belonging through the annual celebrations of the "Old Spanish Days" Fiestas, which have been in practice since 1919.[2] Despite its rigorous focus on othering, erasure, and instances of resistance, my project left little room to dive deeply into the creative practices of contemporary Native dramatists.

Craving the joy of making theater, I introduced myself to Reinholz and Scott as an aspiring director, a Native Californian, and a doctoral student in 2009. The two invited me to attend a rehearsal and then encouraged me to apply as a directing apprentice for their annual Festival of Native Plays. When I arrived at the NVA playwriting workshop that year, I was overwhelmed to finally be in a room full of Native artists from across North America. This was a spirited place, full of contemporary ideas about Native, First Nations, United States, and Canadian life, centered by a diversity of spiritual, storytelling, and art making traditions that we shared in the service of the plays.

Native Voices at the Autry provides a space dedicated to lifting Native stories through the art of polished, professional theater. As a scholar of critical studies besot by theory, I was greatly impacted by the potential of practical theater-making to transform material and artistic conditions for contemporary Native people. The convergence of completing my dissertation and beginning to work at NVA showed me that my practical theater skills as a stage actor and emerging director could be a source of empowerment for me and the Native people with whom I worked. I began to stitch my fragmented self back to a place of balance by rejecting the colonial binary between intellectual and creative pursuit; and I began to witness, document, and participate in what I call "Indigenous theatrical praxis."

The ways in which this kind of a production is realized—the processes of creative decision-making, as well as the spiritual and political reverberations of the work itself—are instrumental to Indigenous theatrical praxis. The collaborative genesis and development of a play—how it works in performance to lift up Indigenous stories and beauty—illustrate how Indigenous theatrical praxis works towards decolonization (Mohler 2009, 245). This praxis by definition *decolonizes*; therefore, Indigenous theatrical praxis should be seen as a revolutionary force in contemporary theater and within the settler colonial context beyond the stage doors.

Over the past few decades I have witnessed and participated in making theater that respects Indigenous knowledge and perspectives; with this experience I offer four goals for practitioners who wish to advance decolonization through theater. All four of these themes connect meaningfully with casting and have the potential to transform the status quo for theater making broadly. The simple graphic shown in Figure 15.1 references a medicine wheel, with four corners and four directions represented. Medicine wheels, which are circular spaces delineated with lines radiating out from the circle's center to create four equal quadrants, are physical manifestations of traditional Indigenous cosmologies. Today tribal communities throughout North America confer each of the four quadrants with key psychic, physical, emotional, and spiritual qualities, and associate these spaces with the natural phenomena, flora, and fauna that connect with their tribal experiences of balance within their homeland (Mohler 2015, 13). I employ this symbol to imply that none of these four goals should be prioritized over another; each attribute is necessary to achieve Indigenous theatrical praxis.

The reclamation of (theatrical) space

Most representations of Native people have little to do with their subjects, but can reveal a great deal about the non-native artists who have created them. From Disney's Tiger Lily to Johnny Depp's recent film portrayal of Tonto, from the mascot controversy over Cleveland's Chief Wahoo to the litany of "last" Indians that entertained white audiences of the nineteenth and twentieth centuries with rollicking adventures of a bygone time, Indians have appeared

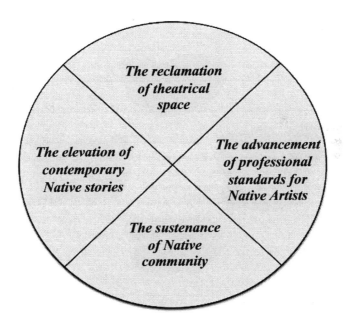

Figure 15.1 A medicine wheel of Indigenous theatrical praxis.

according to white fantasies, often in service of white ideals, land theft, and imperialist spirits. As Devon A. Mihesuah points out, "in the entertainment field, producers make enormous profit from portraying Indians in the way the (majority) public wants to see them ... Stereotyping also allows those who do it to feel superior to the group being stereotyped" (Mihesuah 1996, 115). The extent of such myths about the vanished or historically frozen Native person was buoyed up by casting practices that allowed non-Native actors, sometimes even white actors in red face, to play these roles.

The stage and screen have not historically provided equitable opportunities for Native peoples to produce meaningful creative work. It is only with the telling of our Native stories—from the perspectives of our writers, and with the acting interpretations, culturally attuned design, production, and directing choices—that we can contest, reshape, reimagine: reclaim the theatrical space. The work that a group of artists can create with people from dozens of tribal backgrounds extends far beyond reactionary or corrective and is not only about the final product. As an example, when Native Voices at the Autry gathers a community of artists together to break bread and tell stories, we collectively create, we lift each other up, we tell the stories that have chosen our playwrights, and we tell those stories in ways that make good sense to us as Native artists. Critical success from theater professionals and praise from multi-ethnic audiences are added benefits to putting our people, traditions, styles, and stories first. A remedy to the centuries of representational violence is doing what Native peoples have been doing all along: getting together, making choices, telling stories about—and from—the way we see the world around us.

The elevation of contemporary Indigenous stories

In her path-breaking book *Decolonizing Methodologies: Research and Indigenous Peoples*, theorist Linda Tuhiwai Smith (Māori) writes, "The story and the story teller both serve to connect the past with the future, one generation with the other, the land with the people and the people with the story" (Smith 1999, 145). Some of these stories that Indigenous playwrights tell have been tragic, painful meditations on loss, violence, and the injustice of being Indigenous in a settler colonial world. Some have been knee-slapping, uproarious comedies featuring beloved tricksters, cranky grandmas, and angst-ridden teenagers. And many contemporary Native plays do not neatly fit into any dramatic genre, or even straddle "normal" dramatic modes. The boundaries between creative genres are often blurred in Native art: a Native play might include elements of storying, music, poetry, and dance in order to capture the holistic and inter-connected experience of Indigenous lives. Just as Native lives can be complex, funny, painful, twisty, spiritual, political, rewarding, and hard, so must be the stories we write and perform. This was the wisdom I had been deprived of during my years away from theater practice while pursuing the doctorate of philosophy.

To share Native stories—whether through film, literature, poetry, dance, or visual art—is a powerful and political act in the settler colonial context of the US, and theater is a perfect medium to honor Native traditions because, like oral narratives, theater requires community. Christopher B. Teuton (Cherokee Nation) writes, "The oral communicative context is communal, while writing 'isolates' the reader; the oral communicative event is, at the very least, dialectic, but the readers' text never responds; the oral event exists in the present, writing exists as a record of past thought" (Teuton 2008, 195). Perhaps one of the most exciting aspects of creating Native Theater is the homecoming effect of actors embodying the stories set forth in the scripts. Whereas Western theatrical tradition "begins" with the text and performances are often measured by the artistry and acumen of the writer, Native playwrights generally utilize the form of scriptwriting to structure a story that must be embodied, experienced by the performers and audiences together in a communicative context. The dramatic structure and elements of any given play are important, but only in so far as they invite the audience to witness, feel, and participate in the lifting up of an Indigenous story.

The creative process for Indigenous artists can also be quite different from that of non-Native folks. Anishinaabe writer Louise Erdrich describes the holistic genesis of Native creativity as she closes her novel *The Master Butchers Singing Club*:

> Our songs travel the earth. We sing to one another. Not a single note is ever lost and no song is original. They all come from the same place and go back to a time when only the stones howled.
>
> (Erdrich 2003, 288)

Creativity, inspiration, the labor behind practice, as well as the end "goal" for a work of Native art, interconnect on a continuum with the spirit and experience of life forces far beyond the individual artist, ensemble, or production. In my work as a dramaturg and director, I have had numerous discussions with Native playwrights about what has motivated their writing of a scene, character, or entire play. The illustration below (Figure 15.2) gestures at the creative continuum experienced by Native artists, by which a story chooses them to tell.

I set these hypothetical incitements in the shape of the sun to remind us of the generative energy that touches the entire earth and all of our relations; the sun, which gives life force to plants, sets our water systems in motion, warms our bodies, and grows our food, humbles us with its timelessness. Like the sun, our stories existed before we were born and will exist after our death. Such creative forces are not exclusive to Native playwrights. But it is rare that a Native play will materialize without the writer experiencing a spiritual nudge.

Lakota visionary, poet, and scholar Paula Gunn Allen described vividly the ritual of creation for Indigenous people. She wrote that traditions of ceremonial creativity were modeled by the goddesses, gods, and gender-fluid deities who shared their creative energies, gifts, and powers with women, men, and two-spirited people:

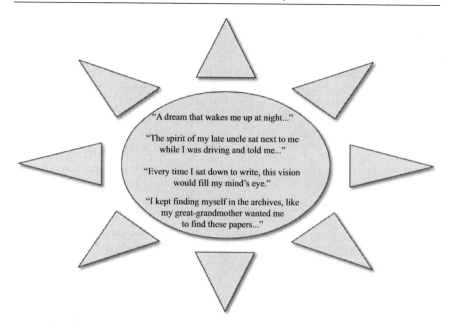

"A dream that wakes me up at night..."

"The spirit of my late uncle sat next to me while I was driving and told me..."

"Every time I sat down to write, this vision would fill my mind's eye."

"I kept finding myself in the archives, like my great-grandmother wanted me to find these papers..."

Figure 15.2 **Creative continuum.**

There is a spirit that pervades everything, that is capable of powerful song and radiant movement, and that moves in and out of the mind ... This spirit, this power of intelligence, has many names and many emblems. ... Her variety and multiplicity testify to her complexity: she is the true creatrix for she is thought itself, from which all else was born ... She is the only creator of thought, and thought precedes creation.

(Allen 1992, 13–15)

Thought Woman for the Laguna Pueblo, Spiderwoman for the Hopi, and countless other spiritual Beings teach the people how to seek balance through creation and destruction. This force is timeless and dynamic, connecting the writer/performer/artist with inspiration so that they can tell the story that will restore balance. The violence and injustice of colonization have thrown the world into a chaotic storm of imbalance, as one group of powerful people dominates, not only the culture, but also the land, resources, and all other forms of life on Earth. Indigenous storytelling and art making, Indigenous *creation* restores balance because, as Gloria Bird (Nez Perce) writes, telling our stories as witnesses to colonization "undoes those processes that attempt to keep us in the grips of the colonizer's mental bondage" (Bird 2000, 29). As Native playwrights write contemporary stories, always linked to the past and future, holes are poked in the darkness of colonial oppression. Both Audre Lorde and

Joy Harjo (Creek) have separately written, "we were never meant to survive" (in Bird 2000, 29). Centering our stories disrupts the monolithic imperial power structures that yearn for total domination.

The advancement of professional standards for Native Theater artists

Opinions about casting Native roles vary significantly throughout the field. On one end of the spectrum is the history of redface, violent representations of howling, wigged studio "savages." On the other end of the spectrum are countless Native scripts trapped in anthologies because well-meaning artistic directors fear the casting process. For these reasons, there has been an under-standable tension with casting Native characters and stories "authentically" with Native actors. Geiogamah, among many other key Native Theater makers from his generation into the present, feels strongly that a play should not be produced in any capacity without Native actors playing Native roles (Geiogamah 1980, 4). Some directors and playwrights feel strongly that an actor from the same tribal background as the character she is to play should be cast over a Native actor from a different tribe. This type of particularity and concern over the "optics of authenticity," while perhaps ideal in some circumstances, makes casting incred-ibly challenging, even in cities like New York or Los Angeles that have relatively large pools of Native talent. Over the past fifty years, this identity-based view would render casting a Native show nearly impossible for many regions throughout the US and in university settings.

The development of Native Theater remained stymied without dedicated theatrical spaces to develop and promote Native artists, combined with the fear that producers and programs held of "doing it wrong." The impression had been, "Well we'd love to do a Native play, but we don't know any Native directors. And even if we could find a great director, we would never be able to cast it!" As Scott and Reinholz discuss in their case study, Native American, First Nations, and Hawaiian and Alaskan Natives have incredible stories to tell; in 2019 there is no shortage of vital, important, entertaining Native plays to produce, despite casting concerns (excuses?) used by many professional theaters.

I have frequently heard talk of the "problem of the pipeline" for Native actors. With so few roles for Native actors in mainstream theater, television, and film, the same handful of Indigenous screen actors are the most likely to be cast; the so-called pipeline problem ponders what will happen when well-known actors are too old to play all of the Indian roles or are no longer with us. NVA offers one model to address this issue by sustaining a community of Native artists who teach and learn from one another, modeling professional treatment of Native artists, and acting as a conduit for regional artistic directors and film and television industry professionals to connect with Native talent. This community-oriented approach offers Native artists an "incubator" or cul-turally immersive space, which gives young artists resources to develop their artistic energies within a company system that intentionally uses and resists the industry's dominant culture. While there is more work to be done to educate the non-native power brokers of professional theater, attention to the pipeline problem can transform the conversation around inclusion in professional and academic theater. There is a role for performance scholars and critics to play here as well; critical analysis too often concentrates on the aesthetics, themes, audience size, and reception when assessing "niche" shows or productions, with little or no attention to the company or production's ability to positively alter material factors for Indigenous people. Actively advancing the professional standards, networking ability, and frequency of paid jobs for Indigenous artists is revolutionary beyond matters of representation and inclusion.

Additionally, NVA's approach to casting has widened the perception of what an Indian actor might look like by casting people who are members of federally recognized tribes, as well as self-identified and mixed Native people. This radically inclusive practice opens up opportunities for Indigenous artists like myself, whose Native identity may not be immediately recognizable, people who could pass as non-Native because of mixed heritage, and those—like me—whose tribe or clan are not federally recognized because of colonial land theft and termination policies. I advocate for theater companies to consider the land base their company inhabits and consider adopting a policy to work with self-identified Native artists as opposed to only those who have federal recognition. As only one treacherous example, the US Federal government does not formally recognize any tribes whose ancestral home included the coastal areas of Southern California; in other words, the peoples indigenous to the lands that now occupied by the cities of Los Angeles, Santa Barbara, San Jose, and San Francisco are landless tribes, without federal recognition. Companies, whose missions include relationship-building and artistic practice, that engage within their local communities should research which tribal groups stewarded the land their company now occupies and should consult with local Native groups regarding recognition and citizenship. Due to the relocation policies of the 1950s and 1960s, major cities—in which many regional and LORT theaters operate—are home to Native people from across the country, many with mixed heritage, many who are not federally recognized. Casting self-identified Native actors lifts the voices of as many artists as possible and creates emotional and physical space for artists to discuss potential challenges and solutions to casting Native works in a variety of performance contexts. When this inclusive Indigenous community gathers and reflects together, individual artists feel supported to take risks in order to further Native Theater in their own communities.

The sustenance of Native artistic community

Nourished by the empowering experience of making Native art together, community emerges. Chickasaw poet and novelist Linda Hogan explains the nefarious goal of Western dominated education and cultural arts, "They want us to believe that we don't exist. I realize now that the stories are eternal. They will go on as long as there are people to speak them. And the people will always be there. The people will listen to the world and translate it into a human tongue" (Hogan 1990, 72). When artists reclaim theatrical space, opportunities to give testimony and to bear witness arise. This can happen formally in community meals, during the extended introductions of participants, the blessings of workshops, and concluding ensemble reflections, as well as informally during rehearsal breaks, carpool rides, or in an after-rehearsal or workshop social gathering. Indeed, many Native plays shared with audiences contain deeply personal testimonies of the authors, or personal stories passed on to the authors to be used as source material in script development.

Although Native Theater is neither exclusively nor explicitly dedicated to solving social, economic, and political issues for Indigenous communities, some of the best of productions do just that. Recent productions have explored the current threat of pipeline spills in sacred water systems, alcoholism, addiction, poverty in reservation communities, and domestic and sexual violence endured by Native women. These are not the issues that mainstream theater, film, or television has told about Native people. These complex stories and nuanced characters belie the vanishing Indian narrative on which settler colonization relies to continue to hold its death grip on Indigenous peoples and resources.

A call to action

Theater professionals in the United States habitually lament the field's supposed impending decline. Competition with film and television, high operating costs, and an aging white audience are favorite explanations for this doomsday prognosis. Yet the Broadway League reports that, between the 2013/2014 and 2017/2018 seasons, non-white ticket buyers rose from 20 to 25 percent (Broadway League 2014; Broadway League 2018). This demographic shift corresponds with the most diverse Broadway season on record, which employed an array of "diverse" actors, directors, and playwrights. This change correlates with the ways in which the American public consumes other forms of narrative entertainment, such as television and film. Ana-Cristina Ramón, the principle author of the "UCLA Hollywood Diversity Report," shares the key take-away from the five-year comprehensive study:

> Our reports have continually shown that diversity sells, but the TV and film product continues to fall short. So audiences are left wanting more representation on screen that reflects the world they see in their daily lives.
> (In Wolf 2018)

The report finds that films with casts composed of 21–30 percent non-white actors earned the highest median return on investment and enjoyed the highest median global box office ticket sales. Conversely, "Films with the most racially homogenous casts were the poorest financial performers" (Wolf 2018). US audiences are realizing the wealth of rich narratives and perspectives that they have been denied. Despite majority white audience demographics, professional theater companies that produce works centered on non-white perspectives are selling out shows and receiving rave reviews.[3]

The primary goals for productive, meaningful Indigenous theatrical praxis are neither easy nor impossible for the industry to employ. The growth of Native Theater over the past twenty years has been hard fought but undeniable. By advancing professional standards for Native artists, thereby sustaining a thriving artistic community that respects traditions and generational experience, and by centering Indigenous stories and perspectives, the US theater industry could awaken diverse audiences to the wisdom of the land's original caretakers. By prioritizing Indigenous knowledge and bearing witness to collectively created contemporary Native stories, theater companies and audiences alike would participate in nothing less than decolonization.

Notes

1 See Dunn (2002, 88).
2 The story of the coastal bands of the Chumash includes much shape-shifting for survival: many of my ancestors converted (or pretended to convert) to Catholicism and intermarried with immigrants from Spain, as well as with Indigenous and mixed-blood peoples from throughout the territories of New Spain. In the Booster era of the late 1910s and 1920s, many of the remaining Barbareños survived by working for or intermarrying with wealthy, white Americans. Each generation adapted and resisted variously to the changing power structures. The annually held "Fiestas" provided a fertile ground upon which to rehearse, perform, and transform the community and space of the region in ways that reflected the changing tides of identification over time.
3 Following the Oregon Shakespeare Festival's (OSF) 2017 production of *Off the Rails* by Randy Reinholz, three plays by Native women were produced professionally in Oregon in the spring of 2018: *The Thanksgiving Play* by Larissa Fasthorse (Sincagu Lakota) at Artists Repertory Theatre; DeLanna Studi's (Cherokee) one-woman show *And So We Walked* at Portland Center Stage at the Armory (PSC); and Mary Kathryn Nagle's (Cherokee) *Manahatta* at OSF. Nagle's commissioned work *Crossing Mnisose* will premiere at PSC in 2019.

Bibliography

Allen, Paula G. 1992. *The Sacred Hoop: Recovering the Feminine in American Indian Traditions*. Boston, MA: Beacon Press.
Bird, Gloria. 2000. "Breaking the Silence." In *Speaking for the Generations: Native Writers on Writing*, edited by Simon J. Ortiz, 26–49. Tucson, AZ: University of Arizona Press.
Broadway League. 2014. "Demographics of the Broadway Audience 2013–2014." www.broadwayleague.com/research/research-reports (accessed December 7, 2018).
Broadway League. 2018. "Demographics of the Broadway Audience 2017–2018." www.broadwayleague.com/research/research-reports (accessed December 7, 2018).
Dunn, Carolyn. 2002. "I am the Real Hollywood Indian." In Carolyn Dunn, *Outfoxing Coyote: Poems*. Los Angeles, CA: That Painted Horse Press.

Erdrich, Louise. 2003. *The Master Butchers Singing Club*. 1st ed. New York: HarperCollins Publishers.

Geiogamah, Hanay, and Jeffrey Huntsman, eds. 1980. *New Native American Drama: Three Plays*. Norman, OK: University of Oklahoma Press.

Hogan, Linda. 1990. "Linda Hogan." In *Winged Words: American Indian Writers Speak*, edited by Laura Coltelli, 71–88. Lincoln, NE: University of Nebraska Press.

Mihesuah, Devon A. 1996. *American Indians: Stereotypes & Realities*. Atlanta, GA: Clarity Press.

Mohler, Courtney Elkin. 2009. "'We Are Not Guilty!': The Creation of an Indigenous Theatrical Praxis." In *American Indian Performing Arts: Critical Directions*, edited by Hanay Geiogamah and Jaye T. Darby, 243–274. Los Angeles, CA: Regents of University of California.

___. 2015. "A Burning Vision of Decolonization: Marie Clements, Ecological Drama, and Indigenous Theatrical Praxis." *Ecumenica*, 8(2): 9–26.

Smith, Linda T. 1999. *Decolonizing Methodologies: Research and Indigenous Peoples*. London: Zed Books.

Teuton, Christopher B. 2008. "Theorizing American Indian Literature: Applying Oral Concepts to Written Traditions." In *Reasoning Together: The Native Critics Collective*, edited by Craig S. Womack, Daniel Heath Justice, and Christopher B. Teuton, 193–233. Norman, OK: University of Oklahoma Press.

Wolf, Jessica. 2018. "'Black Panther' success amplifies findings of UCLA's Hollywood Diversity Report." February 27. http://newsroom.ucla.edu/releases/hollywood-diversity-report-2018-ucla (accessed December 28, 2018).

Part VI

Subverting stereotypes

Chapter 16

Whose story is this to tell?

Mei Ann Teo

We are living in a sea change in which a multiplicity of our Asian American and Asian heritage stories are finally being told in the mainstream. Movements are happening around the country, calling out occurrences of blackface, brownface, redface, yellowface, and cripface. Stories from the margins of society are confronting and disrupting the grand narrative of white supremacy and patriarchy, reclaiming narratives in ways that are visible, undeniable, and even, as *Black Panther* and *Crazy Rich Asians* proved, finding a wide audience.

And yet?

As an artistic director, I still come across problematic narratives that are traced to the cultural makeup of the production teams not aligning with the content of the show, and white directors disproportionately being hired to direct works by people of color.

As a dramaturg, I still find myself as the only person of Asian descent and heritage in rooms with all white creative teams for a show set in Ancient China. Rule: if you need a cultural consultant—who happens to be the only person on the creative team who is of that cultural heritage—in order to impart all the knowledge for a piece set in that culture, it's a clear indication that you have a problem.

As an educator, I still witness the furious battles of "whose story is this to tell?", and the deep pain and frustration of the queer, trans, poc students and the subsequent paralysis or knee jerk reactions of cisgender heteronormative, white students and, yes, even faculty and staff.

Nayyiah Waheed describes these tensions so powerfully:

> some people
> when they hear
> your story.
> contract.
> others
> upon hearing
> your story.
> expand.

and
this is how
you
know.

(Waheed 2013, 158)

These are complex issues arising from cycles of violence and silencing in history, and there is no one-size-fits-all solution. The pertinent question is, in the midst of reactionary contracting: *How we can expand together?* As a professor, I developed a framework to analyze each situation by examining *context, intent,* and *impact,* in the hope that, together, they would provide more clarity for artistic choices towards justice. *Context* requires a thorough understanding of history and identifying the parameters and realities of the situation. *Intent* examines the intentions of the makers in producing the work, while necessarily taking into account underlying assumptions and implicit bias. This leads ultimately to *impact*—what is the harm caused and how do we hold ourselves and each other accountable to move towards collective liberation? Does one person from a community speak for everyone else? How do we measure impact? While this framework served as a launching pad for discussion, I found that it was not a foolproof method against racism and sexism—it still contained loopholes to circumvent justice. Ultimately, when I became an artistic director, I found that it came down to these two questions: What are we perpetuating? What are we dismantling?

Theater makers work in the realm of the imagination; but, for too long, Asians have only been the imagined or the invisible. How can we as Asian artists gain creative control over the expansion of how we are considered and seen? There are fundamentally problematic assumptions when the burden of authentic experience is placed in dramaturgy and not creation. As Edward Said writes, "because of Orientalism the Orient was not (and is not) a free subject of thought or action" (Said 1978, 3). The dominant culture tells stories of marginalized peoples in limited paradigms, castrating complexity by casting them as exotic, created to serve, to be dominated. I have learned my own culture through the lens of those who are imagining me. I have also been reduced to sameness because they have imagined me in their own image.

Walidah Imarisha writes in her introduction to *Octavia's Brood: Science Fiction Stories from Social Justice Movements,* "decolonization of the imagination is the most dangerous and subversive form there is: for it is where all other forms of decolonization are born. Once the imagination is unshackled, liberation is limitless" (Imarisha 2015, 1).

This chapter examines the ways in which Asian American theater makers, grounded by authentic experience, have unshackled their imaginations. Though it is certain that our stories have made others contract, by continuing to tell our stories, we will ourselves expand.

Bibliography

Imarisha, Walidah. 2015. "Introduction." In *Octavia's Brood: Science Fiction Stories from Social Justice Movements*, edited by Walidah Imarisha and adrienne maree brown. Oakland, CA: AK Press.

Said, Edward. 1978. *Orientalism*. New York: Pantheon Books.

Waheed, Nayyirah. 2013. *salt*. Portsmouth, NH: CreateSpace Independent Publishing Platform.

Chapter 17

Casting, cross-racial performance, and the work of creativity

Dorinne Kondo

Casting is one of a complex of practices that can reproduce/contest conventional definitions of race[1] and multiple structures of power in the theater industry (Kondo 2018). For Asian Americans, the 1990–1991 *Miss Saigon* casting controversy marks a milestone in our history, when art, politics, and community engagement coalesced in political protests against the casting of Jonathan Pryce as the mixed-race character The Engineer. Activists, including playwright David Henry Hwang, advocated for equal opportunity, referencing histories of exclusion that had marginalized actors of color. The *Miss Saigon* protests centered on one crucial aspect of what is at stake at the casting table: *creative labor*. Minoritarian actors should be able to "play themselves," given historical erasure and appropriation, continuing practices of blackface, brownface, yellowface, redface, and the still prevalent strategy of whitewashing, in which originally Asian or Asian American characters become white in their cinematic incarnations.[2]

What the *Miss Saigon* protests elided, however, is the other, equally crucial, aspect of casting: *creative vision*. Whose imaginations and whose ways of being in the world are realized onstage? What are the politics of representation of these stagings? *Miss Saigon* has fostered multiple generations of Asian American actors who boast Broadway experience. Yet they have honed their acting, singing, and dancing chops while playing hypersexual, sleazy pimps and prostitutes, lotus blossoms who sacrifice themselves for white men, asexual cadres, and Oriental hordes submissive to Oriental despots (Kondo 1997). This heartwrenching contradiction underscores the point that *creative labor*—hiring artists of color to play ourselves and/or color-conscious casting—must be paired with *creative vision*.

Social transformation—what I call worldmaking—can occur in the theater world and reverberate beyond. In theater, pressure points for remaking power relations exist at multiple levels. Casting, writing, directing, design—the creative team—are of course crucial. So are crew and support staff, without whom a production would be impossible. Producers, artistic and managerial leadership, granting agencies, foundations, and corporate donors constitute critically important players, who can both perpetuate and challenge structural inequalities in the theater industry. More broadly, ideologies about "art" as the transcendental sublime ensure its dismissal as merely decorative and feminine (see Kondo 2018, ch. 2). Neoliberal capitalism shapes the racialized, gendered economies of theater: finance capital reigns, multinational media conglomerates enter Broadway, and state support for the arts dwindles in favor of corporate sponsorship and private funding. The discourse of individual entrepreneurship compels artists to become "artrepreneurs" (Harvie 2013, 62), powerfully shaping the possibilities for aesthetic/political intervention at this historical moment.

Here I spotlight the works of Anna Deavere Smith and David Henry Hwang, two prominent artists of color, as acts of what I call *reparative creativity*: redressing histories of exclusion in the theater industry and in our society generally. Inflected through the work of psychoanalyst Melanie Klein (1984) and building on queer theory and performance studies (Sedgwick 2003; Muñoz 2006; Eng 2011; Chambers-Letson 2006), reparative creativity engages strategies to reassemble the fragments of psyches and bodies shattered by structural violence. The reparative contests notions of linear progress and radical rupture; the process of repair is never accomplished once and for all. Kleinian approaches thus echo Foucault's conceptions of power as both creative and coercive. We can never transcend power, though we can rearrange always shifting power relations in their multiplicity, contradiction, and complexity, in order to enact consequential change. Progressive *creative visions* and *creative labor* can foster acts of *reparative creativity* that help us to remake the theater world, our inner psychic worlds, and the larger social world.

I launch this essay with the politics of multiracial collaboration and cross-racial casting in Anna Deavere Smith's work. I served as a dramaturg for three of her productions: *Twilight: Los Angeles, 1992, House Arrest* (1997), and *Let Me Down Easy* (2009). I analyze the 1993 world premiere of *Twilight: Los Angeles, 1992*, for its ambitious creative reach and its creative process that worked through artistic/political conflict. Though I write more than twenty-five years after the Los Angeles uprisings, *Twilight* has, alas, rarely been equaled since, for both its *creative vision* that foregrounds issues of racism and inequality, and for its power-sensitive attention to *creative labor*: racial, gender, and sexual difference in the production team.

My second analytic node spotlights the politics of cross-racial casting in three of David Henry Hwang's plays: *Yellow Face* (2007–2008), *Kung Fu* (2014), and *Soft Power* (2018). All three integrate progressive creative visions that thematize structural barriers to the *creative labor* of playing "ourselves" and engage cross-racial performance to contest the marginalization of artists of color. While I did not serve as dramaturg for these productions, for *Yellow Face* I shared extensive dramaturgical notes with Hwang and dramaturg/producer Oskar Eustis (Kondo 2018). I analyze the problems and the promise of cross-racial casting and performance through these works, gesturing toward possibilities for *reparative creativity* in the theater world.

Cross-racial performance and the work of creativity in Anna Deavere Smith's *Twilight: Los Angeles, 1992*

Anna Deavere Smith's career as a solo performance artist traces its origins to casting practices and the lack of satisfying roles for actors of color. As a light-skinned African American woman, Smith found herself labelled by casting directors as "too black" or "not black enough." Like many artists of color who face similar barriers, Smith decided to create her own work; for her, this assumed the genre-bending form of documentary theater, using her interviews with everyday people as dialogue for her one-woman shows. Here at last, she was not limited by being "too black" or "too white"; indeed, Smith herself has claimed that her racial ambiguity helped her cross racial lines in her performances.

Smith's work enacts racialized and gendered multiplicity as more than an array of power-evasive differences; that is, liberal multiculturalism figures race in terms of a substance-attribute metaphysics in which race as skin color merely modifies the "substance" of consciousness and the Human. I argue that "race," "gender" and other power-laden, structural forces both index and produce the boundaries of the Human. Which groups count as more Human than others? What histories of racism and colonialism produce those structural inequalities? Smith's work invokes and intervenes into those histories. We see an African American woman taking center stage—a vision that remains too rare in US theater—performing everyday people of various races, genders, and national-ities, many of whom have never been seen on the stages of mainstream US theater. Smith's disruptions of structural racism combine her gendered, raced body on stage with the gendered, racialized multiplicity of characters she embodies and her thematic invocation of the histories of structural forces that position her characters differently and unequally.

Smith's *creative vision* foregrounds urgent social issues: racial conflict and urban violence (*Fires in the Mirror, Twilight: Los Angeles, 1992*); the press, prisons, and the presidency, including the Founding Fathers' enmeshment in slavery (*House Arrest*); mortality, health care inequality, death (*Let Me Down Easy*); and the school-to-prison pipeline (*Notes from the Field*). Her plays underline the political significance of racialized, gendered, power-laden difference in the characters she portrays and the multiracial teams she assembles.

Smith's *creative process—the work of creativity*—underscores her commitment to progressive creative visions and to a multiracial artistic team. She welcomed multiple points of view into the rehearsal room, allowing our passionate back-stage conflicts of interpretation to emerge. My knowledge of Smith's rehearsal process, as much as the final productions, fosters my fierce loyalty to her work. I served as one of four dramaturgs on the world premiere of *Twilight: Los Angeles, 1992* at the Mark Taper Forum in Los Angeles (for a more extensive theorization, see Kondo 2018, ch. 4). Scholarly analyses of *Twilight* focus on the finished product, most often the film made many years later. My experience with the backstage creative process allows me a unique analytic perspective on Smith's work, especially with *Twilight*.[3]

Triangulating *creative vision, creative labor,* and *creative process (the work of creativity)* offers ways to remake structures of power in the theater and to promote a progressive politics through acts of *reparative creativity*. Smith enacts one approach to the *how* at a granular level, when we assemble our creative teams, sit in the rehearsal room, or face the laptop screen. Her innovations begin with a vision that foregrounds attention to the political: theorizing acting as a "broad jump to the other" (Wong 2016); honoring difference yet attempting to make (inevitably partial) connections across those differences; welcoming multiple, discrepant perspectives—even if painful and challenging—into the rehearsal room.

Smith has declared repeatedly that she does not trust theater to attend to issues of race and structural inequality: "It just doesn't. It still sticks in these other hierarchical forms" (Smith, discussion with the author, 2012). Her intent in inviting people with well-established careers outside the theater to collaborate was to "shake up" theatrical hierarchy (Smith 1994). Her *work of creativity* insists that transforming theater's Eurocentric assumptions, challenging whiteness more generally, requires welcoming other people into the room who may push us in more progressive directions, forcing us to see our own implications in larger systems of power. My impassioned loyalty to Smith derives from her openness to challenges to her own assumptions. Smith told me, "I ... want to be in a position ... as painful as it is ... to have my own prejudices assaulted" (Smith, discussion with the author, April 26, 2012). How many among us would do the same?

Twilight: creative process

Gordon Davidson, then Artistic Director of Center Theatre Group, commissioned Smith to create a one-person show about the Los Angeles uprisings of 1992, when the police beating of African American motorist Rodney King resulted in a trial that initially exonerated the officers. Their acquittal set off five days of fiery protests that consumed the city.

The uprisings affected the entire multiracial city, though its most dramatic manifestations erupted in the Black, Brown, Asian—and less affluent— South and East sides of Los Angeles. To address this complexity, Smith first met with racially specific "focus groups"; I participated in the Asian American discussion.[4] Smith asked me to collaborate as dramaturg, along with *Los Angeles Times* reporter (later, Pulitzer Prize-winning novelist) Héctor Tobar, poet Elizabeth Alexander (then at the University of Chicago, now President of the Mellon Foundation), and Associate Artistic Director at the Taper, Oskar Eustis (now Artistic Director at The Public Theater). We met for a workshop in the late winter of 1993 and went into rehearsal in May of that year.

Smith's rehearsal process centered on enacting excerpts from the day's interviews. She performed as she listened to the tapes on her Walkman (yes, it was that long ago!); the people in the room offered notes about characters' performability, thematics, the politics of racial representation, sequencing. While recognizing the disproportionate damage that Korean American business owners suffered, I tried mightily to advocate for the inclusion of various Asian American perspectives that would complicate the black-white binary—no mean feat at that time, when "communities" were essentialized in the media and Asian American multiplicity was subsumed under the rubric of "Korean."

On occasion our discussions became heated, given the urgency of that moment, when racial tensions still bristled. The dramaturgs and our notes became a "drama behind the drama," as we gave notes while the rest of the creative team witnessed our discussions and sometimes interjected their own comments. When Smith constructed a segment in which Latinx and Asian American characters spoke in ways that for me paradoxically reinscribed the Black/white binary, I said so, both in writing and in the rehearsal room. At one point I stated that "if this is the way Asian Americans are represented, I (and in theory other Asian Americans in the audience) would walk out." Smith looked understandably disturbed. I felt that Smith should hear these comments in the rehearsal room so that she might preempt similar reactions from Asian Americans once the production moved into the theater. My remarks were infused with the searing political urgency that many racialized communities felt at that moment. Perhaps because I already knew Smith and was in an outspoken phase of my career, I was, as Smith later called me, "blunt." She has said publicly that, rather than apologizing for my remarks, I would follow my critical comments with faxes that said, essentially, "and furthermore…" "She's tough…she made me cry," Smith recently said of me (Smith 2018).

One night our backstage drama during previews assumed a particularly spectacular form. Héctor and I argued for the inclusion of the characters Rudy Salas, a Chicanx artist, and Dan Kuramoto, a Japanese American jazz musician who grew up in East Los Angeles, a mostly Latinx community. I wanted Dan's monologue to end the play. His words about Los Angeles as "a new racial frontier" resonated strongly in the wake of the uprisings in our multiracial city. I advocated for more Asian American and Latinx characters, because "our asses are on the line with our communities." Smith countered that she was responsible to the theater community, a comment that in the moment felt acutely painful. Had I poured my passion into the production for naught? I raced home and cried for two hours; the very next day, I came to rehearsal to find that Smith had reincorporated both Dan and Rudy. Within 24 hours, I had gone from sobbing to beaming, indexing the emotional volatility of our *work of creativity*. Because Smith listened and took our perspectives seriously, we were able to work through painful conflict.

Twilight had its world premiere at the Mark Taper Forum in Los Angeles a year after the "riots"/uprisings/rebellion/civil unrest. Not only did *Twilight*

Figure 17.1 Anna Deavere Smith as Mrs. Young Soon Han in *Twilight: Los Angeles, 1992*, world premiere at the Mark Taper Forum, Los Angeles, 1993. Photograph © Jay Thompson Archives/Craig Schwartz

claim the stage for underrepresented people of color, Smith's own body intervened into the theater world's Eurocentricity. Rather than standing on the margins relegated to roles supporting white protagonists, an African American woman assumed center stage and played all the parts.[5] Equally important, Smith's play was notable for its attention to racial and gender equity among the crew and the creative team. Backstage labor, including designers, stage managers, hair stylists, makeup artists, prop masters, costume designers, marketing staff, can transform the ethnic/racial significance of a production. Our *Twilight* team was an impressively multiracial group and, alas, remains impressive these many years later.

Perhaps my greatest takeaway from working with Smith is her openness to others, both in her acting theory/practice and her creative process. The *work of creativity* is inevitably fraught with power relations; to open oneself to power-laden difference can be painful and demanding. Not many among us confront our sites of privilege, our "zones of sanctioned ignorance" (Spivak 2003). *Twilight*, in its world premiere, enacted a commitment to cross-racial coalition, to the porosity and relationality of identities, to the painful hard work required to transform conventional aesthetic practice. Our goal, then, need not be a "safe," power-free notion of community. Rather, we should seek to enact coalitions and collaborations that are ultimately generative, even if painful, difficult, challenging.

Cross-racial casting as theme and practice: the work of David Henry Hwang

David Henry Hwang's *Yellow Face* (a comic, semi-autobiographical play), *Kung Fu* (a "dance-ical"), and *Soft Power* ("a play with a musical") are genre-bending works that thematize the politics of Asian/Asian American identity and the lived effects of globally circulating Orientalisms. These plays address casting as a central element of both thematics (*creative vision*) and production (*creative labor*, hiring actors of color to play across race and gender). I have known Hwang since the late 1980s, when the first version of *M. Butterfly* appeared on Broadway and have written about his work ever since.[6] I consider myself to be a colleague and a partner in struggle. In this essay I concentrate on thematics and on production: *creative vision* and *creative labor*.

Yellow Face

David Henry Hwang's *Yellow Face* explores the implications of casting controversies for ideologies of the post-racial, the assumption that race no longer matters. Premiering in 2007, anticipating the 2008 Obama victory that some imagined to be the inauguration of a postracial era for the United States, *Yellow Face* asks: What is race? Who can play whom at this moment in history? *Yellow Face* engages both the apparent expansion of racial possibilities and the continuing structural, racial inequalities that shape the lives of Asian Americans. Hwang's work stages racism as "vulnerability to premature death" (Gilmore 2007, 28), even for people of color who seem to possess wealth and privilege.

Thematically, *Yellow Face* directly addresses the legacy of *Miss Saigon* and the vexed issues of race and casting, often with a farcical tone that spotlights racial ambiguity. The play opens with the *Miss Saigon* protests, in which protagonist DHH (is he David Henry Hwang? To what extent?) becomes involved. Partially in response, he writes a play called *Face Value* (as did Hwang), a farce of mistaken racial identity in which Asian actors play in whiteface and white actors assume yellowface. Searching for the right actor to play the lead Asian role, the casting director discovers Marcus Dahlman, who received excellent reviews in a Japanese American play—but Marcus doesn't "look Asian." Presuming that Marcus is mixed race, the team hires him, and he becomes a theatrical sensation—until DHH discovers that Marcus is "a white guy." Marcus is fired, though DHH cannot reveal why. How do we cast "authentically" at a historical moment when "race" as a construct is coming undone?

Hwang's works trace Orientalisms that shape both Asian and Asian American lives. The tonally serious second act of *Yellow Face* stages enduring Orientalisms that animate geopolitics (US–China relations) and come home to beleaguer DHH's family via the campaign finance scandals of the 1990s. The bank founded by DHH's father, HYH (Henry Y. Hwang), was among the Chinese American financial institutions linked by government and media to illegal donations to the Gore presidential campaign. HYH is accused of money laundering for China, but the accusations are never proved.

Hoary stereotypes—the "sneaky Oriental" and the "Oriental despot bent on world domination"—thus circulate in oppressive new ways. The harassment robs HYH of his American Dream and his will to live as he battles cancer. Here, racism signifies vulnerability to premature death as depression, the loss of will, and the leaching of life energy that racism engenders. Hwang connects his father's persecution by government authorities to the case of Los Alamos physicist Wen Ho Lee, who was held in solitary confinement for 278 days on espionage charges. Lee was eventually pardoned and received an apology from the US government. The *New York Times* reporter who broke the campaign finance scandals wrote the Wen Ho Lee stories; protagonist DHH confronts the reporter in a pivotal scene in the play.

Yellow Face ends on a Pirandellian note. We find that Marcus is the playwright's creation, not a "real" character. The play ends with Marcus in China, where people accept him and "give him face"—i.e., show him respect. DHH closes the play by embarking on his own uncertain, ongoing quest for his own face. At first glance, that DHH's doppelganger is a "white guy" seems highly problematic. Nuancing his decision, Hwang explained to me that, when he was asked to be spokesperson for the Asian American community, he felt unprepared. Nonetheless, he did the best he could—as though he were a white guy in yellowface (D. Hwang, in discussion with author, June 20, 2007).

The initial productions of *Yellow Face* (world premiere at the Taper, then production at The Public, both 2007) included striking cross-racial, cross-gender performances.[7] The principal characters were played by the same actor (DHH by Hoon Lee; Marcus Dahlman by Peter Scanavino at the Taper and Noah Bean at the Public; NWOAOC—name withheld on advice of official counsel—by white actor Tony Torn). The ensemble included a Eurasian woman (Julienne Hanzelka Kim), a middle-aged Asian American man (Tzi Ma at the Taper, Francis Jue at the Public), a white woman (Kathryn Layng), and a white man (Lucas Caleb Rooney).

Apart from Hoon Lee, actors of color played freely across race and gender, as did white women, while white men, with the one exception of Rooney, played only white men. These casting choices created amusingly effective results. Petite, slender Kim played Don Mihail, a robust Russian banker, who broke the news that actor Marcus had become a resounding success as the King in *The King and I*. Her performance defamiliarizes "masculinity," demonstrating its performative construction. She also played Asian American characters including Marcus's girlfriend Leah and a young Asian American fan who flirts with DHH online. Blonde actress Layng—Hwang's spouse in "real life"—played male casting director Miles Newman, actress Jane Krakowski (who was in *Face Value*), and her own mother-in-law, Dorothy Hwang. The cross-gender casting wittily parodied the ways men stereotypically take up space; it was equally amusing to see Layng perform her mother-in-law.

Should white women play Asian Americans or other people of color? Does gender "make it all right?" In this case, the fact that Kathryn Layng embodied her mother-in-law adds complexities that would not exist if another white actress had played the role. For example, a production of *Twilight* at USC's School of Dramatic Arts cast a white actress as Mrs. Young-soon Han, whose store had burned in the "riots," in a performance that used "the accent." If no Asian American actors were available (cross-gender casting would be a possibility) I would have been more comfortable with an actress of color as Han. Still, even in Layng's case, do the ironic resonances of casting her as her mother-in-law justify the use of white women to enact women of color?

Yellow Face, then, raises critical questions in its *creative vision* and its *creative labor* that spotlight a multiracial cast who plays across race and gender. What are the political implications for casting when conventional racial categories are destabilized and an actor's "identity" becomes increasingly difficult to ascertain? How do we stage racism as circulating Orientalisms and "vulnerability to premature death?"

Kung Fu

Transnational Asian/American identity and the racialized existential consequences of casting shape Hwang's "dance-ical" *Kung Fu*, which premiered at the Signature Theatre in 2014. The play centers on Bruce Lee's struggles to find success before he became an international film star. Lee builds his martial arts studio, courts his white wife, and seems on the brink of career breakthrough with his television role as Kato, sidekick to the Green Hornet. The climactic pivot of the play is a devastating case of whitewashing. Studio executives greenlight Lee's proposed series *Kung Fu*, but they give the lead role to white actor David Carradine, who will play the protagonist Caine in yellowface, complete with taped eyelids. The play ends as Lee goes back to Hong Kong, seemingly in defeat—yet the audience knows that dazzling international success awaits him.

The only role requiring a white actor was that of Bruce Lee's wife. Importantly, actors of color played across the lines of ethnicity and race (not gender) *within* peoples of color. A Korean American man played a Japanese American man recently returned from the internment camps; he performs an abject Asian American masculinity that is timid and athletically inept, the foil to Bruce Lee's confident Chinese male prowess. Here we find layered contradictions and complexities. Chinese masculinity is dominant. What are the politics of that move, given intra-Asian imperial rivalries and histories of domination/

subordination? Further, what are the politics of casting a Korean American as Japanese American, given that Japan brutally colonized Korea—even if Japanese Americans had been incarcerated in the US during World War II?

Actors of color playing across race produced complicated effects. Male actors of color played white men, notably the racist studio executives, adding an edge of ironic critique to the characters' racist dialogue. Even more fascinating were the political complexities of actors of color playing other people of color. One telling example involved Bruce Lee's travels to India to scout locations (for a film that will never be made) with white actor James Coburn, who is played by an African American actor. Their South Asian driver, complete with "the accent" and servile demeanor, is played by another African American actor. At one performance, I sat next to a young South Asian American couple, who exclaimed, "Oh no!" when they heard "the accent." While it was satisfying to see an African American actor disrupt whiteness by playing Coburn, the acting choices in the portrayal of the South Asian driver give one pause. Is it better if an African American actor rather than a white actor plays a South Asian role? Would it have made a difference had he not used "the accent" or had behaved in a less servile manner? Stereotypical accents and gestures are not stripped of their oppressive power, even if other people of color enact them. Our own subject positions and that of our characters are never neutral; we perform each other across and within historically specific matrices of power.

Soft Power

Soft Power, "a play with a musical," had its world premiere at the Ahmanson Theatre in Los Angeles in June 2018, produced by Center Theatre Group as part of its fiftieth anniversary season and co-produced by East West Players, the longest continuously running theater of color in the US, established in 1960. *Soft Power* moved to the Curran (another co-producer) in San Francisco in late June 2018. Hwang generated the initial concept, wrote the book and the framing play, and collaborated with Jeanine Tesori, renowned composer of many Broadway musicals (*Fun Home; Caroline, or Change*).

Soft Power extends themes in Hwang's body of work on two fronts. First, it explores the racialization of Asia and Asian Americans, a leitmotif of his creative vision. In his last four works (*Yellow Face, Chinglish, Kung Fu, Soft Power*), Hwang demonstrates a growing interest in China and geopolitical relations. Second, Hwang pursues his longstanding mission to deconstruct a racially problematic dramatic canon, literally rewriting classic operas, plays, and musicals. *M. Butterfly* is a deconstructive reversal/reconfiguration of gendered, sexualized and racial power relations in *Madama Butterfly*; Hwang rewrote the book for the *Flower Drum Song* revival; *Soft Power* reverses the power relations in *The King and I*. This time, Chinese film executive Xue Xing "tutors" both Hillary Clinton and the white male senators, vice president, and supreme court justices, persuading them to lay down their guns and to dedicate themselves to a new, cosmopolitan vision that traces its origins to the Silk Road.

Figure 17.2 Left–right: Jon Hoche; Daniel May (facing away); Kendyl Ito; Kristen Faith Oei; Maria-Christina Oliveras (obscured); Raymond J. Lee; Jaygee Macapugay and Geena Quintos in the world premiere of David Henry Hwang and Jeanine Tesori's *Soft Power* at Center Theatre Group/Ahmanson Theatre. Directed by Leigh Silverman and choreographed by Sam Pinkleton for CTG Ahmanson Theatre.
Photograph: © Craig Schwartz Photography

Soft Power is a dazzling spectacle, mobilizing what Hwang and Tesori call the "delivery system" that enables musical theater to steal our hearts: sumptuous music; gorgeous, sometimes outrageous sets and costumes; stellar singing and dancing (Center Theatre Group 2018). This time, however, they serve a *creative vision* that upends whiteness and theater's Eurocentricity, allowing white audience members to see themselves from a Chinese perspective. *Soft Power* "explodes" conventional form and structure, said East West Players Artistic Director Snehal Desai (discussion with author, May 31, 2018). A framing play, set before the 2016 election, opens as playwright DHH pitches a TV show to Chinese film executive Xue Xing. DHH invites Xue and Xue's American girlfriend Zoe to a Hillary Clinton rally; Xue meets Clinton and emerges starstruck. When DHH goes home to Brooklyn, he is stabbed in the neck as he walks home (an incident that actually happened to playwright Hwang). On the brink of death, DHH conjures a musical fever dream in which Xue Xing and

Hillary Clinton find romance, and Xue inspires Washington politicians to adopt a non-violent, cosmopolitan world view. Witty meta-theatricality and intertextuality animate the dazzling spectacle, including visual quotations from *La La Land* and the waltz from *The King and I*. This time, however, the Asian man is the dreamboat and the tutor, not the tutee.

The musical creates a future when China has won "soft power." We see a critical version of the US as an amalgam of Hollywood, McDonald's, Las Vegas glitz, and Western frontier. Supporting this vision are the witty dialogue and the songs: right-wing senators, lovingly bearing their firearms, sing "Good Guy with a Gun"; "The Ballot Box" wittily explains the labyrinthine complexities of the Electoral College. The US appears as a dangerous country with no universal health care, where even children and the mentally ill carry guns.

Supporting this view of the US as "barbaric" is an all Asian American cast, with the exception of Alyse Alan Louis, who plays Hillary Clinton. Actors Conrad Ricamora (Lun Tha in the 2015 Broadway revival of *The King and I*; Oliver, the gay Asian hacker on *How to Get Away with Murder*) and Francis Jue, veteran of many of Hwang's plays, lead an ensemble of talented, young Asian American musical theater artists. They play characters from Xue Xing's daughter (powerhouse singer Kendyl Ito) to all the white characters, including Xing's unexpected protector, the redneck Bobby Bob (Austin Ku, in a blond wig), Randy Ray (Raymond Lee, also in a blond wig), ringleader of the conservative thugs, and Vice President Mike Pence (Lee, again). In the group production numbers, all Asian American actors wear blond wigs as they play white "Americans." As an Asian American weary of yellowface and whitewashing, I found their antic performances as blonds to be hilarious and deeply satisfying, a racialized turning of the tables.

Soft Power stages an unprecedented power reversal, in which we see the US from a "Chinese" perspective. When have we ever seen such a *creative vision* on the stages of a mainstream US theater? For minoritarian subjects, this can be gratifying; some white audience members have grumbled on social media that "China is no better" than the US. Hwang stated his intent to me:

> My goal was always to create that complicated feeling of watching stereotypical or inauthentic work which is also executed so artfully that it sucks us in nonetheless. I feel this experience is very familiar, particularly to audiences of color and women. Also, I'm interested in exploring appropriation, which is sometimes difficult for white audiences to understand; one typically hears white people say things like, "I don't mind when Japanese people dress up like cowboys, so why should they be upset?" But appropriation needs to be understood in the context of a larger power dynamic between cultures. The notion of a powerful China (which, let's face it, many Americans fear) appropriating and stereotyping a weaker America, helps to more accurately replicate that dynamic. Where it comes to audiences of color, I hope the experience of seeing SP [*Soft Power*]

proves empowering, validating the feeling of being dehumanized … that we've experienced most of our lives, and …proves that we can create something just as beautiful and moving as those works we may find problematic.

(D. Hwang, e-mail message, May 20, 2018)

Soft Power realizes Hwang's aims, in a historically unprecedented, genre-exploding production written from a perspective heretofore unseen on the stages of mainstream US theater.

As minoritarian artists, Smith and Hwang have battled structural hierarchies throughout their careers. Mobilizing progressive *creative visions* of possibility embodied through *creative labor* that showcases the artistry of people of color, and welcoming into the rehearsal room multiple points of view that can offer perspectives on race and power (*the work of creativity*) are some of the ways theater can constitute a progressive social force. *Creative vision, creative labor,* and a progressive *creative process* can enact *reparative creativity*: interventions that can remake our theatrical, psychic, and social worlds.

Notes

1 "Race" is the product of racism, as Angela Davis states in Smith's *Fires in the Mirror* (Smith 1993, 30). "Race" is both social construction and Maussian "social fact:" it assumes a taken-for-granted "reality" within our current episteme. Rather than reify individual attitude and skin color as "racism" and "race" respectively, I build on Foucauldian biopolitics, "racism as the state-sanctioned … vulnerability to premature death" (Gilmore 2007, 28) and "slow death:" "the structurally induced attrition of persons keyed to their membership in certain populations" (Berlant 2011, 102). That is, racism is far more than the Ku Klux Klan or intentional mendacity; it can occur as the long-term leaching of life (through disease, depression, incarceration, dispossession, racial profiling) from particular populations.
2 Scarlett Johansson in *Ghost in the Shell* is a recent example.
3 The proper name *Twilight* masks multiple incarnations: three principal versions of the play (world premiere at the Taper, Broadway version, and the touring/Samuel French production); the book *Twilight* (not the script of any particular production); and the film, which differs markedly from the theatrical versions.
4 I knew Smith from the National Program Committee of the American Studies Association for the two years preceding and including the Columbian Quincentennial. None of the submitted panels criticized the idea of "discovery." I was chosen as spokesperson of the faculty of color to raise this issue to the larger committee.
5 A history of African American women who are solo artists and playwrights—e.g., Beah Richards, Sonia Sanchez, Whoopi Goldberg—precedes Smith; I am not arguing that she is the first or only. Smith herself claims inspiration from works such as ntozake shange's *For Colored Girls*. Still, it remains all too rare to see a woman of color as the protagonist or as the solo performer on a Broadway stage or the stages of regional theatre.
6 In my recent book I wrote about *Yellow Face* in terms of both the politics of representation and Hwang's creative process, including the (solicited) notes I sent to dramaturg/producer Oskar Eustis and playwright Hwang (Kondo 2018).
7 The single exception was a scene where Lucas Caleb Rooney played an Asian American student.

Bibliography

Berlant, Lauren. 2011. *Cruel Optimism*. Durham, NC: Duke University Press.

Center Theatre Group. 2018. "Four Years, Two Breakfasts, and One Big Commission: Michael Ritchie and David Henry Hwang Discuss the Creation of 'Soft Power.'" *Center Theatre Group News & Blogs*, April 23, 2018. www.centertheatregroup.org/news-and-blogs/news/2018/april/four-years-two-breakfasts-and-one-big-commission (accessed April 3, 2019).

Chambers-Letson, Joshua Takano. 2006. "Reparative Feminisms, Repairing Feminism—Reparation, Postcolonial Violence, and Feminism." *Women and Performance: A Journal of Feminist Theory*, 16(2): 169–189.

Eng, David. 2011. "Reparations and the Human." *Columbia Journal of Gender and the Law*, 21(2): 561–583.

Gilmore, Ruth Wilson. 2007. *Golden Gulag: Prisons, Surplus, Crisis, and Opposition in Globalizing California*. Berkeley, CA: University of California Press.

Harvie, Jen. 2013. *Fair Play: Art, Performance, and Neoliberalism*. Basingstoke: Palgrave Macmillan.

Klein, Melanie. 1984. *Love, Guilt, and Reparation: And Other Works, 1921–1945*. New York: The Free Press.

Kondo, Dorinne. 1997. *About Face: Performing Race in Fashion and Theater*. New York: Routledge.

____. 2018. *Worldmaking: Race, Performance, and the Work of Creativity*. Durham, NC: Duke University Press.

Muñoz, José Esteban. 2006. "Feeling Brown, Feeling Down: Latina Affect, the Performativity of Race, and the Depressive Position." *Signs*, 31(3): 675–688.

Sedgwick, Eve Kosofsky. 2003. *Touching Feeling: Affect, Pedagogy, Performativity*. Durham, NC: Duke University Press.

Smith, Anna Deavere. 1993. *Fires in the Mirror*. New York: Anchor.

____. 1994. *Twilight: Los Angeles, 1992 on the Road: A Search for American Character*. New York: Anchor.

____. 2018. "A Conversation with Anna Deveare Smith." Lecture presented USC Annenberg School of Communications, Los Angeles, CA, February 15.

Spivak, Gayatri Chakravorty. 2003. *Death of a Discipline*. New York: Columbia University Press.

Wong, Alia. 2016. "How the Justice System Pushes Kids Out of Classrooms and Into Prisons." *The Atlantic*, December 28, 2016. www.theatlantic.com/education/archive/2016/12/anna-deavere-smith-shares-notes-from-the-field/511589 (accessed July 15, 2018).

Chapter 18

Artists of color/cross-racial casting

Donatella Galella

When people of color take on characters outside of their ethno-racial identities, they demonstrate the arbitrary creation of race. To take center stage, they often cannot overly emphasize the perils of ongoing prejudice plus power. But they also have the potential to dismantle the structures that shore up institutional racism. Although both theater and race are imaginary, they have real impacts. Neither scientific "essence" nor immaterial "illusion," "race," as defined by sociologists Michael Omi and Howard Winant is "a matter of both social structure and cultural representation" (Omi and Winant 1994, 54, 56). Anti-racist cross-racial casting practices wield possibilities to change systems and symbols.

In this epilogue, I historicize and theorize the racial paradigms of people of color playing ethno-racial identities separate from their own. After glossing nineteenth century minstrelsy traditions of blackface and yellowface, I show how, in the mid-twentieth century, people of color received more roles, yet sometimes appeared as interchangeable with each other. Rather than focus on casting people of color in classic productions such as Shakespearean dramas, I expand upon Dorinne Kondo's case studies of Anna Deavere Smith and David Henry Hwang, contemporary artists of color who envision cross-identity casting at the very outset of their creative works. Smith's *Twilight: Los Angeles, 1992* (1994) paired with Lin-Manuel Miranda's *Hamilton* (2015) exemplify color-blind multiculturalism, mobilizing actors of color to suggest an overcoming of race in ways that do not radically challenge white supremacy. Hwang and Jeanine Tesori's *Soft Power* (2018) paired with Qui Nguyen's *Vietgone* (2015) feature Asian American performers in white-face satirizing American white supremacy. These examples revise the national sociological scripts to which systemic racism relegates people of color. While Smith poses all experiences as valid and Miranda re-centers the white founding fathers of the United States, Nguyen, Hwang, and Tesori re-Orient hierarchy toward reparative racial justice that gives due attention to white privilege and to Asian Americans. Refusing a neat ending, I do not believe in a linear, liberal history in which conditions for people of color inevitably and necessarily improve as time goes on; I also do not view history as discrete in which one kind of casting mode wholly replaces another. Instead, I see cross-racial casting as a struggle over power—representation and the redistribution of roles.

Minstrelsy, interchangeability, and indeterminacy

In the early nineteenth century, United States-based racial minstrelsy featured white people (or immigrants who became white) stereotypically performing as people of color so as to indulge in the pleasures of otherness beyond bourgeois normativity and profit from the wages of whiteness (Ignatiev 1995; Lott 1993; Roediger 2007). Blackface minstrelsy helped to rationalize dominant white supremacy in the midst of slavery. This popular performance practice entailed blackening the body—particularly the face—with burnt cork, accentuating the lips, speaking and singing with a certain racialized and classed dialect, and dancing with great virtuosity. Blackface minstrelsy represented blackness in excessive ways as lazy, happy, and comical, as if enslaved people enjoyed living on plantations. These representations contained contradictions. Figures of Mammy versus Jezebel both desexualized and hypersexualized blackness, and they obscured sexual violence against enslaved black women. Minstrel shows also included performances of Shakespeare, train whistles, and Chineseness (Roediger 2007). When more people of Asian descent came to work low-status jobs in the United States, Orientalist performances justified policies of exploitation and exclusion. Yellowface involved yellow make-up, slanted eyes, mincing walks, Orientalist music, and the queue braid to portray Asians as foreign yet assimilable, threatening yet weak (Moon 2004; Metzger 2004; Lee 2010).

Anti-racist activists worked against this dominant racial paradigm with varying levels of success. Groups like the National Association for the Advancement of Colored People (NAACP) protested blackface minstrelsy as it moved from stage and radio to the visual mass medium of television, as in *Amos 'n' Andy* (1951). In the 1960s, the Oriental Actors of America picketed and brought legal cases against yellowface productions in New York City such as the 1968 revival of *The King and I* (1951) at New York City Center (Lee 2006).

As this kind of minstrelsy became less prevalent, some actors of color played characters with ethno-racial identities that did not conform with their own, and "titillating" yellowface did not disappear (Phruksachart 2017, 96). Shannon Steen contends that "depictions of blackness were increasingly attached to notions of authenticity and naturalness," hence casting more black actors to play black characters, while depictions of Asianness have taken longer to develop these values (Steen 2010, 44). For example, black musical performer Juanita Hall adopted Asian roles in *South Pacific* (1949) and *Flower Drum Song* (1958) (Edney 2010). Latina actress Rita Moreno embodied Asianness as Tuptim in the film version of *The King and I* (1956). Reflecting on transnational circulation and translation, Tamara C. Ho writes:

> As a Sino-Burmese immigrant in 1970s California, I learned about the country of my birth by watching a Puerto Rican actress playing a Burmese concubine who protests her servitude to an Asian patriarch by transposing a famous novel written by a white American woman.
>
> (Ho 2015, xvii)

Performance historian Brian E. Herrera offers the term "stealth Latino" to understand ambiguous Latinx racialization and dramaturgy in this time period: "'stealth Latino' performances exploit the uncertain or mixed raciality of Latina/o performers to amplify themes of racial distinction, legibility, and violation that are central to the dramatic narrative being performed" (Herrera 2015, 60). He documents Latino actors who took on Latino, black, Asian, Middle Eastern, Native Americans, and white roles, such as Ricardo Montalban who portrayed a Japanese kabuki performer in *Sayonara* (1957) as well as a Jamaican fisherman in *Jamaica* (1957). In turn, Asian Americans were sometimes cast in Latinx roles, like Nobuko Miyamoto who played a Puerto Rican in the movie of *West Side Story* (1961). Racial lines were not stable but in flux, as people of color seemed transposable. Furthermore, as Herrera suggests, many of these theatrical and filmic texts mediated anxieties about interracial intimacy and resonated with the ethno-racial indeterminacies of performers' identities.

Color-blind multiculturalism: *Twilight: Los Angeles, 1992* and *Hamilton*

Some contemporary artists of color use deliberate cross-racial casting to reveal the construction of race. The Latino troupe Culture Clash, like Anna Deavere Smith, interviews people and then performs those interviews, sometimes across different identities. *Kimchee and Chitlins* (1993) by Elizabeth Wong, similar to Smith's *Twilight: Los Angeles, 1992*, dramatizes tensions between Korean immigrants and African Americans with a chorus of actors who cross-racially portray Asian and black characters. In so doing, these kinds of theatrical productions might advance a dangerous racial paradigm of seeing color, seeing past color, and then equating all perspectives. When racism appears to be individual attitudes that could be altered if everyone simply listened to each other, the presence of performers of color playing across identities could denote that ultimately racism is not that severe and not a system. These color-blind multiculturalist dynamics of including people of color and erasing difference play out in Smith's *Twilight: Los Angeles, 1992* and Lin Manuel-Miranda's *Hamilton*.

   In her theatrical work, Anna Deavere Smith adjusts her voice, gesture, clothing, and affect with great precision to embody the people whom she has interviewed, illustrating the fashioning of identity. Her persona as a light-skinned African American woman mediates her performances of those racially like and unlike herself, revealing both herself and the other. Cherise Smith asks, "Is the artist's display of her dissimilarity a critical intervention in the re-presentation of identity, difference, and the politics of identity, or is it a strategy for reveling in difference in order to engage in liberal humanist homogenizing?" (Smith 2011, 158). I would answer: both. For *Twilight*, Anna Deavere Smith explores a range of perspectives on the police beating of Rodney King, the uprising in Los Angeles, and the second trial of the officers. For instance, she represents King's aunt, who says that she did not raise him with racial thinking, but then quickly follows up by insisting that they have friends of all colors. By including this monologue, Smith shows the contradictions of color-blind multiculturalism and garners sympathy for King.

She subsequently reenacts an interview with a white cop who defends the use of the chokehold as a more effective de-escalation tool than the baton blows against King's body; he seems logical, as he dismisses the deaths of black people due to the "upper body control hold" as "hysteria" (Smith 1994, 54–55). Smith implies that these competing narratives have equal claims to legitimacy. All sides matter. According to sociologist Eduardo Bonilla-Silva (2017), white Americans rhetorically use abstract liberalism to imagine the playing field as already level and therefore cover up and rationalize existing racial inequality. Smith's metaphor of "twilight" itself emphasizes ambiguity (Paterson 2015). In the final monologue, "Limbo," gang member Twilight Bey asserts, "I can't forever dwell in the idea, / of just identifying with people like me and understanding me / and mine" (Smith 1994, 255). In her performance, Smith embodies empathy and asks audiences to do the same. But in light of who has power, who needs to identify with and understand whom? The constellation of these curated interviews and the conclusion of inviting audiences to empathize with others propose that the end goal should be mutual understanding, not the equitable redistribution of resources and destruction of white supremacy. Smith also modeled an empathetic approach with the openness she provided to her interview subjects and to her dramaturgical interlocutors. Dorinne Kondo shares her experience of Smith's critical generosity and argues that Smith and Culture Clash stage "a (re)vision of history, a (re)vision of place, a (re)vision of race," yet "both may be enjoying mainstream success precisely because many audiences and funding agencies view the work as evidence that 'we can all get along'" (Kondo 2000, 107). Smith offers alternate ways of being and relating to one another. By presenting marginalized and mainstream voices in a sympathetic light and in her body, she appeals to people across the political spectrum.

Smith's following project, *House Arrest* (1997), has not received the acclaim nor attention of *Twilight*. Departing from her typical solo show format, she taught her mimicry methodology to a multiracial ensemble at Arena Stage in Washington, D.C. After conducting more than 500 interviews, Smith, with Kondo as dramaturg, assembled monologues into a narrative that explicitly called out the presidency as white patriarchy, such as Thomas Jefferson's rape of Sally Hemings, and the press as biased, navel-gazing storytellers that mediate what the public considers true. Given the lukewarm reviews and canceled regional theater productions, I wonder if the comparable success of *Twilight* relative to *House Arrest* indicates that, though both productions used cross-racial casting to suggest the arbitrariness of race and the commonality of humanity underneath, the latter alienated some spectators with its incisive critiques of the United States and how systems of inequality shape the news. Perhaps patrons expected Smith to reconcile all arguments and conform to the conventions of her earlier works.

Instead of having a woman of color play an assortment of white people and people of color, the multiracial cast of the popular Broadway musical *Hamilton* plays almost entirely white American historical figures. Drawing from Hip Hop, musical aesthetics, and Ron Chernow's founders chic[1] biography (Chernow 2005), Lin-Manuel Miranda created a compelling theatrical work that apparently remaps the patriotic narrative of United States history onto those too often left out of the narrative. The cast is key to this racial paradigm of color-blind multiculturalism. Herrera identifies multiple kinds of casting modes to comprehend the storytelling: (1) conceptual in having people of color play whites, (2) color-conscious in having white actors specifically play King George, (3) color-blind in having the ensemble take on a variety of cross-racial roles, and (4) compositional in having casting be part of the official script (Herrera 2018, 229–234). Miranda has contributed to the confusion by claiming both that "our story should look the way our country looks" (quoted in Weinert-Kendt 2015) and "[we] never threw around the terms 'colorblind' or 'color-conscious.' That's how it shook out" (qtd. in Ball and Reed, 2016, 20). His contradictory comments open up a variety of political interpretations.

Take for example the initial casting of black actor Daveed Diggs as the white Marquis de Lafayette. When he says, with Hamilton, "Immigrants: we get the job done," he makes visible the racialized labor upon which the United States runs (Miranda and McCarter 2016, 121). Some immigrants and descendants of immigrants have taken up this mantra at progressive marches after the 2016 US presidential election, as they stake their claim to Americanness. For many audiences of color, seeing Diggs rap with such dexterity as he contributes to the founding of the United States can be inspirational. But if Lafayette, a white Frenchman who came to North America with the intent of returning to France, counts as an "immigrant," then this category loses specific meaning. In this age of heightened xenophobia against American immigrants of color, this whitewashed definition elides those of Latin American and Asian origin who have made the United States their home, even as they are so frequently presumed as foreigners. Moreover, in the celebration of "Immigrants: we get the job done," immigrants gain value based on their labor, not their inherent humanity. Lafayette also repeatedly urges Washington to "fight for your land back," accepting the premise of settler colonialism (Miranda and McCarter 2016, 118). Furthermore, as a black performer, Diggs conjures up the legacy of slavery yet does not call out Hamilton as a trader and owner of enslaved people. Instead of focusing on actual historical people of color or indicting systemic white supremacy as foundational to the United States, *Hamilton* casts marginalized people in order to center whiteness (Monteiro 2016; Waldstreicher and Pasley 2018). This casting "showcases the nation as equal, diverse, and inclusive but only under the terms of emphasizing white history makers and softening the salience of race and racism" (Galella 2018, 372). Brandi Wilkins Catanese observes, "Very often, transcendence of racial issues is framed as both the tactic and the goal of contemporary racial politics. This is an objectionable strategy because, fundamentally, asking (usually nonwhite) people to transcend racial consciousness is usually just a more polite way of demanding that they 'get over it'" (Catanese 2011, 21).

Color-conscious criticality: whiteface in *Vietgone* and *Soft Power*

Twilight: Los Angeles, 1992 and *Hamilton* join a long tradition of cross-racial performances that argue for the shared humanity of people of color and white people—but whiting up can do more reparative work to make white privilege visible and then privilege people of color. Marvin McAllister documents a history of black people performing whiteness from plantation cakewalks to stand-up comedy routines. He identifies what he calls whiteface minstrels ("extra-theatrical, social performance in which people of African descent appropriate white-identified gestures, vocabulary, dialects, dress, or social entitlements") and stage Europeans ("black actors appropriating white dramatic characters crafted initially by white dramatists") (McAllister 2011, 1). Color-conscious use of whiteface reveals both the invention of race *and* persistence of racism. In the final part of the counter-minstrel show *The Shipment* (2009) by Young Jean Lee, black actors perform a dramatic upper-middle-class dinner party scene only to reveal that they were playing white characters. As whiteface minstrels, they challenge the audience's presumption that their racialized bodies equate with their characters. In *An Octoroon* (2014), Branden Jacobs-Jenkins adapts Dion Boucicault's famous mid-nineteenth century melodrama. Claiming that he could not find white actors willing to play overtly racist characters, Jacobs-Jenkins writes in a black actor to stand in for not only himself, but also the leading white protagonist and antagonist in *The Octoroon*. The actor-as-playwright transitions to stage-European by putting on bright white make-up and a blonde wig in front of the audience. Whiting up exposes how racial logic in processing racialized bodies is learned and how some performers have the luxury of turning down one-dimensional roles.

In her monograph on critical whiteness performances by African American artists from Douglas Turner Ward to Dave Chappelle, Faedra Chatard Carpenter writes, "these enactments of whiteness do much more than simply invert racial representations and/or reify revised racial hierarchies. As revisionist—and revisioning—tactics, these artistic expressions complicate how we perceive others as well as how we perceive ourselves" (Carpenter 2014, 29). Qui Nguyen's *Vietgone* and David Henry Hwang and Jeanine Tesori's *Soft Power* provide further examples of critical approaches to cross-racial casting that challenge yellowface. These stage productions unsettle whiteness, but they do not necessarily inspire white people to dismantle white supremacy. People with privileges are rarely willing to relinquish those privileges voluntarily. But *Vietgone* and *Soft Power* are also for people of color, Asian Americans in particular, to feed their hunger for reparations, just as Koritha Mitchell has argued that early twentieth century lynching plays were principally for black families to survive amid anti-black terrorism (Mitchell 2011).

In *Vietgone*, Qui Nguyen calls for an all-Asian American cast to talk in unexpected ways as the actors dramatize how his parents, Vietnamese refugees, met in Arkansas. Instead of having them speak with stereotypical Asian accents—dropping l's, for instance—Nguyen writes in African American Vernacular English: "Dayum son, there's alotta white people up in here" (Nguyen 2017, 48). He frames Asians as modern and African Americans as the core of American culture. In this particular quotation, the performer acknowledges that patrons at large professional non-profit theaters where *Vietgone* has been performed are typically majority white. Whites do not go unseen but are made cognizant of their own whiteness from the very beginning of the play. The white American characters do not speak seamlessly, as they make remarks like, "Yeehaw! Get'er done! Cheeseburger, waffle fries, cholesterol!" *Vietgone* denaturalizes who sounds "normal" by using what Carpenter calls "linguistic white-face"—"the self-conscious and often exaggerated manipulation of one's vocal qualities (including variables such as word choice, grammar, and timbre) for the sake of suggesting that the speaker is white or 'white identified'" (Carpenter 2014, 24). Fumbling with Vietnamese translations, the Asian American actors playing white characters estrange white Americanness and can prompt laughter at this fumbling. On the other hand, the Vietnamese characters portrayed by Asian American performers use rap to express themselves. In this passage, Nguyen's father Quang pushes back on a white hippie who opposed US intervention in the Vietnam War: "Never had someone try to shoot ya dead / Son, war's more than just some theory in your head" (Nguyen 2017, 58). Nguyen has previously used African American representation to embody Asianness. In *The Inexplicable Redemption of Agent G* (2012), another play about recuperating his parents' histories in Vietnam, he cast a black actor to play a version of himself who says that he feels black in his heart. This kind of cross-racial casting raises questions about cultural appropriation and cross-racial solidarity.

Both Nguyen and Hwang use a narrator to blur the line between fact and fiction. In *Vietgone*, an Asian American actor portraying the playwright avers that any similarities between characters and real people are "purely coincidental" (Nguyen 2017, 48). Raising metatheatrical awareness, these playwright-characters illuminate the mechanics of race and performance to encourage spectators to think critically. Although explicitly putting themselves in their works may appear self-indulgent, this tactic enables the playwrights to be self-reflexive, as they need to be taught lessons about Vietnam and China, respectively. When Nguyen interviews his father, Quang, he comes from an American perspective and keeps pressing on the Vietnam War. Meanwhile, his father wants to talk about falling in love, changing his son's diaper, and training in American military bases to help his people back in Vietnam. *Vietgone* acts as an uncomfortable corrective to liberal, US-based narratives. In addition, Quang wants Harrison Ford to play him in the story, whereas the playwright objects to yellowface, demonstrating that Asian Americans hold different points of view.

This part of the play is the only time when Quang speaks with a heavy Vietnamese accent, as if bringing the audience back to the real world before they leave the theater and reconsider the racialization of language and storytelling.

Soft Power similarly employs linguistic as well as physical whiteface to re-Orient racial hierarchy. When Chinese film producer Xue Xing commissions playwright-character David Henry Hwang to write a television show that will increase China's cultural influence, he speaks in English with a Chinese accent. But when the play turns into a musical told from a Chinese perspective, he sounds like he is from the United States. Meanwhile, in a kind of payback for Orientalist productions that mix up accents from all over Asia, the Asian American cast members indicate their performance of whiteness with an amalgam of white-identified accents: cowboy talk ("so git"), *Newsies* speak ("we gots to see his card"), and California surfer ("feeling the good vibes today?"), among others. White sidekick characters with names like Bobby Bob make up for Yum-Yum in *The Mikado* (1885). They wear blonde wigs, call attention to their round eyes, and insist, "everybody's strange who doesn't look like me." Although largely comical, the white Americans threaten and execute violence. In the performance, after Hillary Clinton loses the 2016 election, the ensemble dons American flag attire, dances white boy-band choreography circa 2000 while wielding weapons, and chants "Make America great again!" and "Chinese go home!" invoking early twenty-first century and late nineteenth century racist rhetoric.

Furthermore, Hwang and Tesori make apparent the symbolic violence of white supremacy by commenting on and reversing *The King and I*. Zoe, a white woman played by the only white actress in the cast, points out that the Richard Rodgers and Oscar Hammerstein II musical celebrates a white nanny teaching the King of Siam to be civilized, and it silences critiques of Orientalism with its seductive music. *Soft Power* the musical then imagines Xue Xing attempting to teach Hillary Clinton the fundamental limits of American democracy in a nation built on racism, capitalism, and hetero-patriarchy. Tesori's score conjures Rodgers's lush style and the choreography quotes *The King and I* as the couple bounds around the stage à la the number "Shall We Dance?" But in this alternate scenario without Yul Brynner, an Asian American actor plays the Asian man and the musical within the play is written in a speculative future when China dominates the global stage. Chinese supremacy has replaced white supremacy, as Chinese propaganda compels audiences to see the United States as racist, misogynist, homophobic, and anti-science, a revisioning that can discomfit the powerful and validate the minoritized. Hwang and Tesori at once move spectators to cling to the hope of democracy, critique the United States in contrast to China, and become conscious of how the very form of the musical emotionally manipulates them. By making clear the operations of art, race, and power as well as privileging Asianness, *Soft Power* offers Asian Americans the opportunity to feel seen and heard in a musical, and not from a debased, Orientalist position.

The stakes of cross-racial casting are high, as systemic racism continues to shape the roles people of color play in everyday life. In the theater, centering people of color and their creative critiques can shift who feels uncomfortable and who feels empowered to speak out against racial injustice.

Note

1 "Founders chic" cultural productions celebrate the Founding Fathers of the United States by chronicling their allegedly self-made accomplishments and repackaging this "great" man's history as cool, relatable, and modern.

Bibliography

Ball, Don and Josephine Reed. 2016. "Lin-Manuel Miranda: Immigrant Songs." *NEA Arts*, 1: 18–21. www.arts.gov/NEARTS/2016v1-telling-all-our-stories-arts-and-di versity/lin-manuel-miranda (accessed April 3, 2019).

Bonilla-Silva, Eduardo. 2017. *Racism without Racists: Color-Blind Racism and the Persistence of Racial Inequality in America*, 5th ed. Lanham, MD: Rowman & Littlefield.

Carpenter, Faedra Chatard. 2014. *Coloring Whiteness: Acts of Critique in Black Performance*. Ann Arbor, MI: University of Michigan Press.

Catanese, Brandi Wilkins. 2011. *The Problem of the Color[blind]: Racial Transgression and the Politics of Black Performance*. Ann Arbor, MI: University of Michigan Press.

Chernow, Ron. 2005. *Alexander Hamilton*. New York: Penguin.

Edney, Kathryn. 2010. "'Integration through the Wide Open Back Door': African Americans Respond to Flower Drum Song (1958)." *Studies in Musical Theatre*, 4(3): 261–272.

Galella, Donatella. 2018. "Being in 'The Room Where It Happens': Hamilton, Obama, and Nationalist Neoliberal Multicultural Inclusion." *Theatre Survey*, 59(3): 363–385.

Herrera, Brian Eugenio. 2015. *Latin Numbers: Playing Latino in Twentieth-Century US Popular Performance*. Ann Arbor, MI: University of Michigan Press.

___. 2018. "Looking at *Hamilton* from Inside the Broadway Bubble." In *Historians on Hamilton: How a Blockbuster Musical is Restaging America's Past*, edited by Renee C. Romano and Claire Bond Potter. New Brunswick, NJ: Rutgers University Press.

Ho, Tamara C. 2015. *Romancing Human Rights: Gender, Intimacy, and Power between Burma and the West*. Honolulu, HI: University of Hawai'i Press.

Hwang, David Henry and Jeanine Tesori. 2018. *Soft Power*. Los Angeles, CA: Ahmanson Theatre.

Ignatiev, Noel. 1995. *How the Irish Became White*. New York: Routledge.

Kondo, Dorinne K. 2000. "(Re)Visions of Race: Contemporary Race Theory and the Cultural Politics of Racial Crossover in Documentary Theatre." *Theatre Journal*, 52(1): 81–107.

Lee, Esther Kim. 2006. *A History of Asian American Theatre*. Cambridge: Cambridge University Press.

Lee, Josephine. 2010. *The Japan of Pure Invention: Gilbert and Sullivan's The Mikado*. Minneapolis, MN: University of Minnesota Press.

Lott, Eric. 1993. *Love & Theft: Blackface Minstrelsy and the American Working Class*. New York: Oxford University Press.

McAllister, Marvin. 2011. *Whiting Up: Whiteface Minstrels and Stage Europeans in African American Performance*. Chapel Hill, NC: University of North Carolina Press.

Metzger, Sean. 2004. "Charles Parsloe's Chinese Fetish: An Example of Yellowface Performance in Nineteenth-Century American Melodrama." *Theatre Journal*, 56(4): 627–651.

Mitchell, Koritha. 2011. *Living with Lynching: African American Lynching Plays, Performance, and Citizenship, 1890–1930*. Urbana, IL: University of Illinois Press.

Miranda, Lin-Manuel and Jeremy McCarter. 2016. *Hamilton: The Revolution*. New York: Grand Central.

Monteiro, Lyra D. 2016. "Race-Conscious Casting and the Erasure of the Black Past in Lin-Manuel Miranda's *Hamilton*." *Public Historian*, 38(1): 89–98.

Moon, Krystyn R. 2004. *Yellowface: Creating the Chinese in American Popular Music and Performance, 1850s–1920s*. New Brunswick, NJ: Rutgers University Press.

Nguyen, Qui. 2017. "Vietgone." *American Theatre*, February: 48–67.

Omi, Michael and Howard Winant. 1994. *Racial Formation in the United States from the 1960s to the 1990s*, 2nd ed. New York: Routledge.

Paterson, Eddie. 2015. *The Contemporary American Monologue: Performance and Politics*. London: Bloomsbury.

Phruksachart, Melissa. 2017. "The Many Lives of Mr. Yunioshi: Yellowface and the Queer Buzz of *Breakfast at Tiffany's*." *Camera Obscura*, 32(3): 92–119.

Roediger, David R. 2007. *The Wages of Whiteness: Race and the Making of the American Working Class*, 2nd ed. Brooklyn: Verso.

Smith, Anna Deavere. 2004. *House Arrest*. New York: Anchor.

____. 1994. *Twilight: Los Angeles, 1992: On the Road: A Search for American Character*. New York: Anchor.

Smith, Cherise. 2011. *Enacting Others: Politics of Identity in Eleanor Antin, Nikki S. Lee, Adrian Piper, and Anna Deavere Smith*. Durham, NC: Duke University Press.

Steen, Shannon. 2010. *Racial Geometries of the Black Atlantic, Asian Pacific, and American Theatre*. New York: Palgrave Macmillan.

Waldstreicher, David and Jeffrey L. Pasley. 2018. "*Hamilton* as Founders Chic: A Neo-Federalist, Antislavery, Usable Past?" In *Historians on Hamilton: How a Blockbuster Musical is Restaging America's Past*, edited by Renee C. Romano and Claire Bond Potter. New Brunswick, NJ: Rutgers University Press.

Weinert-Kendt, Rob. 2015. "Rapping a Revolution: Lin-Manuel Miranda and Others from *Hamilton* Talk History." *New York Times*, www.nytimes.com/2015/02/08/theater/lin-manuel-miranda-and-others-from-hamilton-talk-history.html (accessed April 3, 2019).

Part VII

Casting across identities

Chapter 19

Reaparecer

Elaine Ávila

Preface

Ping Chong's and Tavis Wilks's experiment in decolonizing theater questions the roots of racial violence by upturning otherness, witnessing the making of "a people" from many peoples, and stepping into heritages. I am inspired by my mentor Suzan-Lori Parks, collaborator Arvaarluk Kusugak, and colleague Claudia Rankine to do the same.

"Nobody can come from nowhere,"
says the Professor who specializes
in Indigenous land claims
and I burst into tears.
I am not nobody
I do not come from nowhere

Portuguese language allows double negation …
 Moreover, triple negation is also possible.[1]

On my mother's side, nuns destroyed letters
to hide a bastard lineage
on my father's, we "passed"
we erased language, custom and race
for the greater glory of fitting in.
A scholar proclaims us
the "invisible minority"[2]
But my people aren't nobody.
They aren't from nowhere.
After all
Portuguese whaling
exploration
and colonialism
mean our diaspora is
African, Chinese, Inuit, Musqueam,

South Asian, Dutch, to name a few.
At the Portuguese restaurant
the owner's brother
upon hearing about my play at the local college,
pulls everything out of his wallet
to share his stories with us,
his Portuguese citizenship card,
escudos—Portuguese money from before the EU,
a saint card of Queen Isabel from the parade
in Chino, California.

It proves everyone's stories matter, no matter how small or out of the way. [3]

I Skype into a reading of my play
the connection is so scratchy I can't hear much
except the Brazilian actress's commitment to
standing up to austerity
and everyone singing Grândola, Vila Morena
the great Portuguese song of solidarity
and revolution
wholeheartedly to the New York night.

Like any other immigrant force in the USA, ours too are part of this beautiful amalgamation of narratives that form the tapestry of this nation of foreigners … We have been culturally isolated from the world in many ways particularly during the 20th century, a consequence of decades of dictatorship, censorship, and repression. We stood "proudly alone," as Salazar would claim. [4]

The African-Canadian actor sings fado
and tells me I've got it right
about how we are afraid
to speak of what's hidden
in the songs:
slavery,
the black woman beaten
as she nurses the master's son—
but we will speak of her now
we will sing her song.

I've been moving away from that old-fashioned Eurocentric idea of the actor as an empty vessel to the understanding that we all bring our baggage into the room. Who is in the room affects what happens in the room. This is an idea that is at the heart of Indigenous dramaturgy—that lived experience counts; it fuels the imagination and the spirit; we are whole people in relationship creating things together for a community to share. Our experience matters. [5]

The South Asian-Canadian actress tells me
I've got it right
to question gas and oil
even if it hurts my career
and yes, women can be
the main character
we can be strong
and funny
and we don't have to be perfect.
The Musqueam actress looks
deeply into my eyes
understanding that I am
trying to honor my ancestors
and find where I come from
just like she is
and she reads the character
with such respect
I know I must keep on keeping on.

And as we started arriving in this country, as it happens to any given group of people that embarks on the journey, the process of assimilation is never easy. Most of our immigrants—as with pretty much any other group of migrants that chooses the US as a haven for opportunity and a better life—were coming from impoverished, humble backgrounds. Sadly, and in order to integrate ourselves, we often denied our origins, going as far as not speaking Portuguese to our children and even rejecting our roots. I know of a lot of Portuguese-American families where this was the case. Can you imagine how many stories were lost in the process? [6]

Portuguese professional actors tell me
they have never ever played a Portuguese character
and stories start pouring out of them
like fado music from their families' radios
saying we are here
we will lift our voices.

I know these people. They were the characters of my childhood, and the voice of fadista Amalia Rodrigues was the soundtrack. When we failed to fit in, to find a binding identity, we played our fado and heard our music and reminded ourselves we had voices too. [7]

Fall (cair)
Trust (confiar)
Confiar Cair
Cair Confiar

To be the ghost of Amalia … to pay homage to a voice I have listened to all my life … pulling from her spirit, her exquisite voice … I could feel her energy all around … I just had to fall into it, trust it. [8]

Fall (cair)
Trust (confiar)
Confiar Cair
Cair Confiar

No matter where I was, my identity lived somewhere else. [9]

We will reaparecer (reappear)
things are not as they parecer (seem)
we will aparecer (appear).

Notes

1 Duolingo (2019).
2 "Most often Portuguese fictional characters do not have a voice and therefore cannot defend themselves from racial and cultural slurs … If the Portuguese have any yearnings or feelings, readers rarely learn them" (Silva 2008: 26, 82).
3 Kitimat resident, on hearing that I wrote one of the first Portuguese plays to premiere in California, on a commission from Pomona College.
4 Diogo Martins, artistic director, Saudade Theatre, New York (email message to the author, December 15, 2018).
5 Kathleen Flaherty, dramaturg/director, Playwrights Theatre Centre, Vancouver (email message to the author, December 13, 2018).
6 Diogo Martins (email message to the author, December 15, 2018).
7 Paulo Ribeiro, actor, Vancouver (email message to the author, January 2, 2019).
8 Sara Marreiros, actor/fadista, Victoria (email message to the author, January 2, 2019).
9 Paul Moniz de Sá, actor/director, Vancouver (email message to the author, January 2, 2019).

Bibliography

Avila, Elaine. 2016. "Chasing Kitimat: Going Backwards to Move Forwards." *Howlround*, April 21. https://howlround.com/chasing-kitimat (accessed April 4, 2019).
Duolingo. 2019. "Double/Triple Negation in Portuguese." https://forum.duolingo.com/comment/22017957/Double-Triple-Negation-in-Portuguese (accessed January 14, 2019).
Silva, Renaldo. 2008. *Representation of the Portuguese in American Literature.* Amherst, MA: Tagus Press.

Chapter 20

Collidescope 2.0

Performing the "alien gaze"

Priscilla Page

Introduction

I teach at a large university in rural New England where the legacies of institutional racism and Black scholarship, art, and activism are both present. In my work, I use theater to facilitate dialogue about what happens on our campus and in our surrounding communities. When the opportunity presented itself to bring Ping Chong and Talvin Wilks to UMass Amherst as part of Art, Legacy, & Community, a two-year humanities-based program focused on the exploration of Black history and social transformation on our campus, I did not hesitate in joining my colleagues.

Collidescope 2.0 would become the culminating event for "Art, Legacy, and Community 2014–2016," a creative research endeavor led by Judyie Al-Bilali in collaboration with Gilbert McCauley, Megan Lewis, and me (all in the Department of Theater at University of Massachusetts Amherst). Our goal was to craft an array of offerings that brought together Amherst area families, college students, and professors in an exploration of "race" and politics from many perspectives. Unique to Art, Legacy, & Community is that, as a leadership team, we contributed expertise and our distinct perspectives informed by different cultural identities: Al-Bilali and McCauley are African American; Megan Lewis is white South African; and I am bi-racial Chicana. Our individual identities shape our shared commitment to racial justice and social transformation.

Art, Legacy, & Community: a creative research project

Al-Bilali was inspired to create this community-wide program based on her experience coming back to UMass Amherst in 2013 as a new professor, having previously received her BA and MFA from the school. She immediately saw a chasm between what she experienced as a student in the 1960s and the experiences of students of color on our campus during President Barack Obama's second term. As many people touted "new" ideas about a post-racial society and celebrated diversity, Al-Bilali witnessed divisions among Black students based on national identity and diasporic experience. She also saw that most young people did not know about the history of Black art and activism on our campus. UMass Amherst has one of the oldest Afro-American Studies departments in the nation that came to be, as they often did on US campuses, through the concerted efforts of Black students. Chancellor Randolph Bromery, the first Black chancellor in the Northeast (1971), and a cohort of radical Black faculty ushered in this wave of Black activism, art, and scholarship.

In the early planning stages of "Art, Legacy, & Community," Al-Bilali and I attended *Brooklyn '63*, [1] an Undesirable Elements (UE) production written and directed by Chong and Wilks that featured Brooklyn-based activists concerned with the sweeping gentrification of their neighborhoods. UE is a series of works that Chong and Wilks have developed over twenty years that assembles interviews with residents of a community or shared constituency group into a ritualized script of testimonial theater, "examining issues of culture and identity of individuals who are outsiders within their mainstream community."[2] UMass alumnus Stanley Kinard was one of the performers and he included the story of Black student activism at UMass in his narrative arc. We were excited about this connection and thought that our students could undertake a UE process with Chong and Wilks. But they were in the process of developing *Collidescope* at the University of Maryland and, as we continued to refine the vision for Art, Legacy, & Community, it became clear that bringing these artists to create *Collidescope 2.0* at UMass Amherst would match our goals.

Our multi-faceted work on Art, Legacy, and Community 2014–2016 began one year before Chong and Wilks arrived. We created a new course to support the research and production of the piece and developed a focus on research and writing in the existing devised theater class (both taught by Al-Bilali); co-produced a community-based education event with Women of the African Diaspora (of Amherst) and UMass student facilitators; staged readings of topical plays on three area campuses; and hosted guest lectures on Black art and activism at UMass.[3] Our goal was to introduce students to a multiplicity of artistic voices and alternative ways of creating theater and making community. We wanted to ground students in the idea of creative research so that they could better understand Chong's and Wilks's process of using research as a starting place for creative work. Lastly, all of our activities were connected to larger themes of race, culture, history, and politics as expressed in local, regional, and national contexts.

Our ultimate goal was to connect students to the rich cultural history of our region in order to invigorate their sense of self and community on our historically white campus. We structured our work to inspire a more progressive discourse regarding the social construction of "race" and how it impacts the region as a whole. We wanted our students to be encouraged by the knowledge of a long-standing and dynamic heritage of activism and creative accomplishment by people of color at UMass. This ongoing project was—and continues to be—challenging as the campus and the nation grapple with the institutional and systemic racism that are stitched into the fabric of our society.

Collidescope: "Upturning otherness"

Collidescope: Adventures in Pre- and Post-Racial America is an ongoing performance project through which co-creators Chong and Wilks explore the impact of racial violence in the United States and its effect on African American citizenship and agency, "utilizing found text, speeches, and testimonies" (Wilks 2016). Initially commissioned by the Department of Theatre at the University of Maryland and performed there in 2014, the project moved to the University of Massachusetts Amherst where it was performed as *Collidescope 2.0* in Spring 2016, and then to Wake Forest University as *Collidescope 3.0* in Spring 2017. In the Introduction to the UMass playscript, Chong and Wilks state, "[*Collidescope*] was developed as a collision course view of the legacy and psyche behind this history of racialized violence, racism and social injustice in America" (Chong and Wilks 2016, 3).

The audience experiences the play through the lens of intergalactic space travelers as they explore the question of violence toward and hatred of "the other" across a wide expanse of US history. In each iteration of the play, Chong and

Figure 20.1 "Epilogue: Hands Up, Don't Shoot" (Michael Brown Memorial section) from *Collidescope: Adventures in Pre- and Post-Racial America* at University of Maryland, College Park, 2014. Directed by Ping Chong and Talvin Wilks. Photo by Stan Barouh, courtesy of Ping Chong + Company

Wilks make casting choices mindful of plurality and in consonance with representations of race, ethnicity, culture, and nationality. They intentionally cross-cast actors against dominant culture's perceived notions of race and gender lines to emphasize the "alien gaze" through which US racial history is being observed. In essence, the aliens in the play—who examine racial violence on this planet—do not share the same sensibilities about race or gender that dominate the US cultural imaginary and, thus, do not see those markers in the same way. Instead, the aliens cast the actors available to them, who come from a wide range of identity positions, to re-create these moments resulting in what Wilks calls "upturning otherness" (Talvin Wilks, personal communication, September 30, 2018). The casting in Collidescope challenges expectations of who might play what role, often representing an element of "otherness" in order to draw the audience's attention to the dynamics of power at play regarding their own (and society's) assumptions of raced and gendered identities. As directors, Chong and Wilks attempt to step into the "alien gaze" as they make casting choices, which means, according to Wilks, "Being white doesn't mean an actor is any more equipped to play Thomas Jefferson than an actor of another race" (Talvin Wilks, personal communication, September 30, 2018).

From Undesirable Elements to Collidescope

Chong and Wilks first worked together in 1994 on the fourth production of Undesirable Elements at the Seattle Group Theatre. Over the many years of creative partnership, Chong and Wilks solidified a unique way of working; Wilks explains, "My initial role was to think of myself as a dramaturg in that process, but it always involved co-writing and co-interviewing. It was a co-collecting collaborative process" (Page 2018, 39). This collaborative process is a thread that follows into the Collidescope series. Another thread from UE is the concept of "the outsider" or those who are deemed "undesirable" by members of the dominant groups in our society.

Chong explains that his awareness of injustice developed at a young age. As immigrants to Canada in the 1940s, his parents discovered they could not continue their lives as artists. In Canada, they worked (barely surviving) on a potato farm. Later, they moved to New York City's Chinatown. His father worked hard to support his extended family in the strange and often hostile city. Reflecting on his life, Chong says, "My love of creativity came first, but the principles of social justice came to me very early. I was very aware of injustice as a young boy. As an artist-citizen, it is my job to make people aware of their responsibility to a just world."[4] Chong has taken this awareness into his visionary work as an acclaimed multi-media artist.

Talvin Wilks is a highly-accomplished director, dramaturg, playwright, and producer who has taken on the enormous task of documenting Black theater history in the US. Through his interviews with three generations of Black theater professionals from the 1960s forward, he has created a dynamic archive of Black theatrical tradition that he generously shares with young artists. His commitment to history and tradition is not static; rather Wilks carries it into the rehearsal hall whenever he embarks on a new project. He requires his collaborators to commit to a process of rootedness with their character work. He asks them to contemplate their characters' individual places in the wider scope of history. While rehearsing *Collidescope 2.0*, he linked history to practice when he asked the student cast members, "What do we do with our knowledge of racial violence in this country? How do we remember and, in fact, honor those who lost their lives to the brutalities of slavery, Jim Crow, and the current attack on the lives of young Black men?" As the students engaged these tough questions, Wilks reminded them to "Breathe slowly, in and out." Connecting through breath, across space and time, Wilks links his craft as a director to a much deeper spiritual practice that aims for true freedom.[5]

Chong's and Wilks's impulse to address gaping racial inequalities in our society manifested at the same time as the August 2014 uprising in Ferguson, Missouri, after police officer Darren Wilson shot and killed Michael Brown. They had a vision for a transformative theater project with an attention to process and collective creation. *Collidescope* (1.0) would later open at the University of Maryland in November 2014, just as a St. Louis County Grand Jury voted not to indict Wilson for the extrajudicial killing of Brown. Immediately after the play's opening in Maryland, Chong reflected on the purpose of *Collidescope*:

> Whenever I am asked to come and work with young people, I try to not only teach them the art of theater, but also something about citizenship, and something about the unofficial history, because we all know that every country writes an official history which is very different than the actual history.
>
> (Reed 2014)

Chong's and Wilks's lifelong cultivation of "diversity in praxis,"[6] individually and as co-creators for more than two decades, exemplifies an approach to theater-making where content and form are connected. They address issues of race and imbalances of power and they model *decolonial* practices while creating their work. I employ Ngũgĩ wa Thiong'o's ideas about decolonization as a way to signal Chong's and Wilks's move away from a system of dominance and subordination that is often replicated in rehearsal rooms (Ngũgĩ 1981). In some instances, theater directors choose to reside at the top of the creative pyramid, while actors, dramaturgs, designers, and technicians all fall in line below. In their rehearsals of *Collidescope*, I observed Chong and Wilks work against such a hierarchical model. Their work also connects with Ngũgĩ's notion of "decolonising the mind" in that they ask participants to question everything and challenge received notions of knowledge and power.

For Chong, *Undesirable Elements* and *Collidescope* are linked because, with both works, he posed the same question: "What is it to be considered different in society?" In *Collidescope*, Chong and Wilks show that African Americans "have always been forced to be the other" in the colonial, white supremacist, capitalist patriarchy that defines the US (Ping Chong, personal communication, October 16, 2018).

Not just a play

As they prepared to move *Collidescope* to UMass Amherst, Chong and Wilks began to describe it "as a framework to explore race that relied on the notions of both place and process" (Talvin Wilks, personal communication, September 30, 2018). The focus on place came about through conversations with Al-Bilali who asked them to incorporate scenes specific to UMass Amherst and our region. To that end, Chong and Wilks employed their process of interviewing local residents alongside place-based archival research. Similarly, students in Al-Bilali's devised theater course began researching place as part of Art, Legacy, and Community. The students' findings and the early drafts of scenes they wrote became the basis for two campus-specific scenes that ultimately became part of the UMass script.

Collidescope as process meant that the student actors were engaged as co-creators in writing and devising. In Maryland, students often led the conversations, which shaped rehearsal room experience—a central tenet of a decolonized theater practice. Wilks reflects on this process:

> We encouraged the students to ask for what they needed in each process. In Maryland, this resulted in a special session for students of color to address perceived notions of aggression and plain ignorance amongst their peers; the uncertainty actors felt when speaking across race and ethnicity; the question of the absence of black women's voices inside of the history we were exploring; and the need for respect in the room. We learned that we could not assume that we were all just having a good time. Through this process, we learned that casting across difference empowered some actors and had the potential to minimize the voices of others. Our casting choices privileged and then counter-privileged each actor from scene to scene.
>
> (Talvin Wilks, personal communication, September 30, 2018)

For these students, acting in *Collidescope* was stepping into a shared heritage by playing historical characters such as Fannie Lou Hamer, Paul Robeson, and James Baldwin. The students demanded respect in the rehearsal process because the subject matter was so meaningful and, at times, volatile. Throughout the *Collidescope* process, Chong and Wilks acknowledged that the stakes were high for everyone and that there were different implications for each person in the room.

Chong and Wilks continued to refine their collaboration with the actors at UMass. They applied lessons learned from the cast at the University of

Figure 20.2 "Scene 6: Politics and Race in America" (Fannie Lou Hamer section) from *Collidescope 2.0* at the University of Massachusetts-Amherst, 2016. Direc-ted by Ping Chong and Talvin Wilks.
Photo by John Solem, courtesy of Ping Chong + Company

Maryland regarding cross-racial and cross-gender casting choices as well as the intentional and historically accurate use of racial epithets, racialized violence, and gendered violence. They developed a series of questions for the UMass cast that zoomed in on the themes of the play, such as: "What does the term 'post-racial' mean to you?" and "If you could ask any question about race relations in America, what would it be?" (Wilks 2015). Chong reflected, "It was a process of continual discovery for all involved" (Ping Chong, personal communication, October 16, 2018).

Moving through these questions and the challenging material in the script, Chong and Wilks discussed the courage required of the actors involved in this work. In their article "From Safe Spaces to Brave Spaces," social justice edu-cators Brian Aroa and Kristi Clemens note that the creation of so-called safe spaces can have the unintended consequences of silencing some participants while privileging others (Aroa and Clemens 2013). Chong and Wilks, similarly, asked the cast members to commit to the making of *brave space*. According to this notion, actors are encouraged to be brave and actively generate the kind of space that they need in order to engage in difficult dialogues and accomplish the challenging work. Embedded in Chong's and Wilks's approach live, for me, the implicit questions: Who determines what is safe and how do harmful dynamics of power get replicated in the request for safe space? And how does the creation of a safe space help or hinder the artistic process? If everyone involved commits to making brave space, then there is an agreement about process that moves to equalize all players.

What follows are specific examples from the productions and rehearsal processes at the University of Maryland, UMass Amherst, and Wake Forest University, which illustrate a de-colonial, collaborative way of working that attempts to undo the very ideas about power and domination in the rehearsal room that the play similarly upends on the stage. As was clear from the outset, *Collidescope* was indeed a process and not just a play.

Staging the alien gaze

Wilks explains the role of the alien gaze as a method of examining the construct of race:

> The conceit is that the aliens are learning by constructing, they are experimenting with the concepts of race in order to understand them. The process is conscious and unconscious since we as the creators are making specific choices that may seem arbitrary initially but, as the piece progresses, become revelatory because they challenge the way we are used to witnessing and constructing race *(seeing and hearing)*. One particular scene that stands out in this way is one of the very first "re-enactments," *Scene 1: On the Eve of the American Revolution.*
>
> Based on an actual petition of liberty by freedmen and slaves to the Boston Commonwealth in 1775, the collection of voices (signatories), is clearly a group of men from various cultures and backgrounds—slaves from the Caribbean and West Indian colonies as well as recent African descendants and Black Brahmin (original black families, i.e., colonists) who may have served as indentured servants but were never slaves—all identifying as black men or *men of colour*. The construction of the scene offered us an opportunity to research and explore the polyglot accents and cultures of this unique collection of men representing class and religious distinctions, providing a greater understanding of the many peoples who constituted this population at the time. So the scene, although a collection of *"Blacke"* men, demands a diverse representation, which is in a way how the *alien gaze* functions as a device. It has been a scene where we have cast Asian, East Indian, Latinx, African, and African American students to more closely convey this sense of a cultural multiplicity, an opportunity to display the diversity of this gathering leading us to a grouping of individuals that seems truer to the understanding of the original collective. In this way, the *alien gaze* challenges an audience's notion (according to a national imaginary) of how we would expect to see and hear this group of men— now played by men and women of varied backgrounds; and, in so doing, we are witnessing the making of "a people" from many peoples. The

roster of signatories from the original document—Pharaoh Shores, Jack Pierpont, Nero Funelo, Brister Sienser, Chester Joie, Felix, and Sambo Freeman—reflect a diversity of origin (albeit slave names) who, in their own words, self-identify and protest:

"The petition of A Great Number of Blackes, detained in a State of slavery in the Bowels of a free and Christian Country, Humbly showeth that your Petitioners apprehend that they have in Common with all other men, a Natural and inalienable Right to that freedom, which the great Parent of the Universe hath Bestowed equally on all mankind ..." (Chong and Wilks 2016, 15).

The scene begins with a call to prayer; as a Muslim man prays, another man reads the latest rallying cries of Patrick Henry, a slave owner, "Give me freedom, or give me death." Not missing the hypocrisy, they collectively lament their shared struggle, although one man acknowledges that some of them are "free" already. To that, the reply comes, "a free black man is not free either." In this "re-enactment" we experience a historical debate by blacks in the shadow of the revolutionary debate portrayed by a group of students of color.

(Talvin Wilks, personal communication, January 8, 2019)

One student, Robyn Sutton-Fernandez, who performed in this scene in the UMass production, shared this perspective:

As an experienced actor, I had never taken on roles that changed my perspective regarding how I see myself as a woman, person of color, and how I identify as an American. I walked into the process feeling very nervous about the various roles I was asked to play. I had so many questions: How do I step into the shoes of a free, educated Black man fighting for racial equality with the knowledge that Black women were excluded from those rights? How do I portray a so-called Christian white man who believed that slaves were savages and only fit for servitude? What identity do I create for an unidentified Black man who was lynched and whose body disappeared in 1918? And, can I truly embody Fannie Lou Hamer, whose strength and perseverance played a vital role in the Civil Rights movement? I was aware that Ping and Talvin included each character because of their distinct voices and the complexities of how those characters saw themselves as Americans. I realized that I had to allow myself to be truly open and feel every emotion that came to me in the rehearsal process. Each feeling, whether it was anger, hurt, frustration, or emptiness, allowed me to bring each character to life.

(Robyn Sutton-Fernandez, personal communication, December 10, 2018)

Another significant point in understanding how the notions of "upturning otherness" and "alien gaze" manifested is to recognize that casting is an open process each time. *Collidescope* assembles and responds to the differing dynamics that each collection of students brings to the process, not pre-determined by the creative team. The majority of roles are determined by the individuals who show up and the curiosity with which the aliens view our society. For example, the "re-enactment" of "Scene 11: Baldwin's Nigger," based on text taken from the video of a meeting between James Baldwin and Dick Gregory at the West Indian Student Centre in London (1968), has been explored differently for each production based on how the cast responded to and devised this scene: at UMD, Baldwin was performed by Moriamu Akibo, a young female actor of Nigerian descent; at UMass, Baldwin was performed by a chorus of six actors— African American, Latinx, white, Asian, male and female; and ultimately, at Wake Forest, Baldwin was performed by an African American woman, Justice Von Maur. As the culminating scene before the epilogue, the resonance and power of Baldwin's voice fulfills the specific journey taken by each collective of actors.

On the creative process at Wake Forest University, Wilks noted, "While we were very clear about the [cross-identity] casting by this third iteration, we still encountered students who faced challenges in their embodiments of otherness" (personal communication, September 30, 2018). Student actor Serena Daya was cast as Civil Rights activist Fannie Lou Hamer and felt conflicted about creating this portrayal. She shared, "I struggled to embody Fannie Lou's essence. I am not a Black woman. I am a reasonably privileged Asian woman. I don't know the struggles of Black women in our society, and especially not Black women in Fanny Lou's time" (personal communication, September 2018). Daya kept working on the portrayal and stayed committed to the role: "My job was to find myself in Fanny Lou and be authentic." Wilks noted that everything changed for Daya when she found her voice through this portrayal. She wrote about her breakthrough with this character:

> Fanny Lou's voice was distinct. She was sick and tired of being sick and tired. That resonated with me. I don't remember how I got to Fanny Lou's voice, but I remember when it landed. I thought about how I could get Fanny Lou's voice to resonate with the very back of the theatre. I visualized my voice punching the back wall. Not just reaching it—but delivering a deft right hook to the back wall. And then it came out of me. Fanny Lou's voice. It needed that oomph of the right hook.
>
> (Serena Daya, personal communication, September 30, 2018)

It is likely that Daya arrived at this portrayal because of the brave space that was created in the rehearsal room and the explicit goal of performing across difference in the play. And again, these roles are not just about the staging of otherness—they carry the responsibility of witnessing history and how these individuals had previously been seen by society. As stated by Chong, upturning otherness is a "metaphor for the fact that we are all in this together for better or worse." He shared:

Figure 20.3 "Scene 10: On the Eve of the American Civil War" (The Civil War/
Secession Ball section) from *Collidescope 3.0* at Wake Forest University,
2017. Directed by Ping Chong and Talvin Wilks.
Photo by Ken Bennett, courtesy of Ping Chong + Company

I was invited to give a lecture about my work at the art museum at the
University of Illinois where I presented *Baldwin/NOW* and an African
American professor asked, "Why would a Chinese man want to create
piece inspired by Black Lives Matter?" My answer was, "Because I am
either part of the problem or part of the solution, because I am an American and this is an American problem not just a Black and White problem,
because I am an outsider and an outsider's perspective can be constructive

and possibly more objective, because I am a human being and this is a human problem."

(Ping Chong, personal communication, October 16, 2018)

Conclusion

The piece ends with a warning, in a voiceover from an Alien, which embodies both the content and philosophy of creating the full work:

> *Homo sapiens*, human beings, mankind or whatever they like to call themselves, see themselves as a superior species, possessed of a rational and reasonable nature. Based on our brief survey we beg to differ. We maintain that pathological and irrational characteristics increasingly rule the species to their detriment. Will this species have the capacity to make radical change in its behavior or will it persist in its self-denial in recognizing the darker aspects of its nature? As travelers through intergalactic space, it is not for us to say. We can only depart from this curious world without conclusion. When and if we pass this way again eons from now, we will certainly review our present assumptions and compare our future notes to see if in fact our assumptions were true or false, that is if the species survives its self-destructive impulses.
>
> (Chong and Wilks 2016, 117)

Collidescope 2.0 at the University of Massachusetts Amherst was an experiment in decolonial theater-making. Chong and Wilks privileged agency for the actors and utilized the creative contributions of everyone in the room. They established a space of power-sharing and challenged notions of dominance and subordination. Chong reflected on the nature of the project in Maryland: "The show's really about citizenship and the promise of the Constitution. It's about the promise of what this nation says it is, and what it isn't for so many people in this country."

As *Collidescope* moved to Amherst in Spring 2016, anti-Mexican sentiment was rising and Republican candidates were fomenting xenophobic and racist fears. Our campus was one of many whose computers and printers were hacked by white nationalists who sent images of swastikas to our library and other administrative offices. Months later, Chong and Wilks were in residence at Wake Forest to hold auditions, which fell on the eve of the election of Donald Trump as president. Wilks shared, "Someone came in the next day and reported that there were racialized attacks the night before. Black people were accosted with racial epithets and told to 'go home,' accompanied by shouts of 'It's our time now. It's Trump time now'" (personal communication, September 30, 2018). In an incredibly disheartening way, *Collidescope* demonstrates that the "past is prologue." However, at its core is the potential for learning, growth, and connection. With *Collidescope*, Chong continues to ask, "What does it mean to be an American? Who determines who is an American? And, what does citizenship mean? Yes, race is part of the issue; and, in the end, it is also an issue of power, an issue of class, and an issue of human failings" (personal communication, October 16, 2018).

Acknowledgment

This chapter would not have been possible without Talvin Wilks' generosity of time and the sharing of material from his archive on the *Collidescope* process.

Notes

1 Kumble Theater for the Performing Arts, Brooklyn, New York, May 2013.
2 For more information about the history of UE, see www.pingchong.org/undesirable-elements.
3 These events were supported and archived by Lewis and myself (greater details, descriptions, and a comprehensive list are housed on our website: https://artlegacycommunity.weebly.com).
4 This biography was crafted with information from Josephine Reed (2014) and my personal interview with Chong in advance of the Rand Theater Lecture at UMASS Amherst (Ping Chong in discussion with the author, Spring 2016).
5 This biography was crafted from personal knowledge and the introduction to my piece of Wilks for the *SDC Journal* (Page 2018).
6 Wilks uses this term to signal an active and ongoing commitment to diversity that addresses racial inequality through the production of critical multicultural theater rather than superficial efforts that "celebrate difference" and while avoiding concrete conversations about racist practices embedded in our society.

Bibliography

Arao, Brian, and Kristi Clemens. 2013. "From Safe Spaces to Brave Spaces." In *The Art of Effective Facilitation: Reflections From Social Justice Educators*, edited by Lisa M. Landreman, 135–150. Sterling, VA: Stylus Publishing.

Chong, Ping, and Talvin Wilks. 2016. *Collidescope 2.0: Adventures in Pre- and Post-Racial America*. Unpublished manuscript.

Ngũgĩ wa Thiong'o. 1981. *Decolonising the Mind: The Politics of Language in African Literature*. London: James Currey.

Page, Priscilla. 2018. "Talvin Wilks: Director, Dramaturg + Playwright of Images." *SDC Journal*, Spring: 36–43.

Reed, Josephine. 2014. "Interview with Ping Chong." Artworks Podcast, NEA, December. www.arts.gov/audio/ping-chong (accessed April 4, 2019).

Wilks, Talvin. 2015. Rehearsal notes on Collidescope Devised Process, UMass Amherst. Unpublished manuscript.

———. 2016. Collidescope UMass Phase Development. Unpublished manuscript.

Chapter 21

The spatio-temporal logics of *Collidescope*'s welcome table

Brandi Wilkins Catanese

I spent part of my time working on this essay in the midst of a federal government shutdown precipitated by an authoritarian leader's insistence that our federal government spend billions of dollars to construct a wall separating the United States from Mexico, materializing a vision for an America that is isolationist, that ignores humanitarian crises (in some instances precipitated by US foreign policy), that disappears children from their families in ways that terrifyingly echo the disappearing acts of dictatorial regimes in other regions of the Americas. It is an America that prioritizes building walls of exclusion rather than tables of welcome. It is a manifestation of energies that were consolidating at the same time as the 2016 production of *Collidescope 2.0: Adventures in Pre- and Post-Racial America* at UMass Amherst. What was then nascent to some eyes (but transhistorically routine to others) is now fully in bloom. While it is the America that has always been, it is not the America that many of us are trained to recognize. This is what pre- and post-racial America really looks like.

What *Collidescope*—in its ongoing process and its localized outcomes— demonstrates quite clearly is the fact that performing race, or heritage, or inherited history with an eye toward inclusion is both a spatial and a temporal project, where the abstract ideal of harmonious collaboration must confront the material constraints of time and place within which the collaboration is attempted. In what follows, I will undertake a radial analysis that explores the relation between Daniel Banks's formulation of the welcome table, the script of *Collidescope 2.0*, and Priscilla Page's embedded reflection on the "not just a play" experience of working on the show at UMass Amherst in order to advance our thinking about the opportunity that the welcome table paradigm offers to move our theaters (educational and otherwise) toward a more emphatically anti-racist practice.

Materializing the table

My point of departure is to take seriously the metaphor of the welcome table. In his generative essay, Daniel Banks begins with a triangulation of music, theater, and social practice: after an epigraph that quotes the opening stanza of the spiritual "I'm Gonna Sit at the Welcome Table," Banks situates his critical conceit of said table in relation to James Baldwin's unfinished play, *The Welcome Table*, itself at least partly inspired by Josephine Baker's unconventional practices of homemaking, through which she intentionally built an international, interracial kinship network that welcomed people from all backgrounds into her fold and her personal space via formal adoption and practices of radical hospitality. If we linger for a moment with each of these, the complex stakes of the welcome table framework begin to emerge. Rather than an easy metaphor, it is a boldly challenging one.

First, the lyrics of the spiritual position the welcome table in a certain but as-yet unrealized future. The welcome table is a site of redressive abundance for people caught in the grip of slavery, whose quadruply articulated claim of space and place implicitly names both the lack of welcome the singer experiences in the present and also the inevitability of change. In the context of the song, it is an aspirational space that challenges the racial and political status quo. While many understand the "one of these days" refrain to reference the afterlife, making the promise of the welcome table a metaphysical eventuality rather than a social and material transformation, that longer spiritual horizon need not be understood solely as an accommodation to the injustices of the here and now. For one reason, there is a version of this flexible song that progresses from claiming this welcome table to an avowal of truth to power, as singers first assert access to the table ("I'm gonna sit"), then to the sustenance that the table will provide ("I'm gonna feast on milk and honey"), and then to a rearticulation of shared history: "I'm gonna tell God how you treat me ... one of these days" (Southern Gospel Revival n.d.).[1] The singer's subaltern narrative of the path to accessing the table will challenge the logics of exclusion that have historically prevented access to the table and its resources, and force a reckoning with inequality rather than a normalization of it. Testifying about the abuses of the present issues a powerful declaration of the singer's access, not just to the welcome table and its resources, but also to an audience with a higher power than that of the people who currently control the structures that produce and sustain inequality. Whether one subscribes to the Christian framework implicit in this song or not, the audacity of this promise to tell is clear. In the same version of the song, the next verse pushes this inversion of power to its conclusion, naming a broader social transformation that cannot be understood as separate from the material circumstances of the present: "All God's children gonna sit together ... one of these days," which will further instantiate the reshaping of social interaction and resource allocation. The manifestation of the welcome table will affect not just the disenfranchised, but everyone. It will require a reordering of practices of sociality to account for all members of the community.

In the life cycle of this presumably nineteenth-century song, its message of faith and justice has been deployed in multiple contexts, most significantly recirculating in conjunction with civil rights activism of the 1950s and 1960s, which grounded the lyrics in an unambiguously immediate temporality. Rather than milk and honey, freedom singers named the spoils of the welcome table more immediately as access to full citizenship rights: declarations that "I'm gonna be a registered voter" and "I'm gonna sit at the Woolworth counter" were performative utterances that aligned with the performative power of sit-in demonstrations and other collective social actions through which activists were helping to build a new world together (National Museum of American History n.d.). The lunch counter sit-ins, for example, literally tested the concept of the welcome table, challenging white citizens to change or to reveal the violently racialized limits of the American South's legendary hospitality and vision of community. As the archive reveals, many white citizens chose the latter path.

To cite James Baldwin as another influence on the framework of the welcome table as a model for inclusive casting practices is to engage the challenges of the present without the guaranteed optimism of the future. Baldwin wrote multiple drafts of *The Welcome Table*, all of them as an expatriate (or exile?) who reflected on America while refusing to subject himself to its daily denials of access to all that the welcome table represents. Like the original spiritual, Baldwin's *The Welcome Table* was in some ways a prospective document rather than a reflection of the present. The very fact of his exile status suggests that the welcome table as a model for American interaction faced multiple obstacles—it was a thing that could be realized neither now (Baldwin's lifetime) nor here (in the United States). Baldwin's life in France was an expression of that impossibility, and also of the irrepressible imperative to at least try to create that space of welcome, for oneself and for others, that both Baldwin's and Josephine Baker's life choices attempted to actualize.

As we can see across these lyrical, dramatic, and biographical terrains, constructing and populating a welcome table is an act of will, and an act of conscious opposition to the dominant social order. Constructing it, granting access to it, and maintaining the resources that make it a meaningful social site all require claims to a space that can house such a radical construct.

Gathering at the table

James Baldwin himself might function as the ligature that easily connects Banks's "The Welcome Table" to *Collidescope 2.0*: his massive creative and critical legacies inspired both Banks and the collaborative team of Ping Chong and Talvin Wilks to develop works that challenge racial complacency in applied ways. Banks's essay proposes a way of acting upon our responsibilities as art-makers in a complexly racialized America to make space for all, and the *Collidescope* project develops "a collision course view of the legacy and psyche behind this history of racial violence, racism, and social injustice in America" (Chong and Wilks 2016, 2). *Collidescope 2.0* presents a vertiginous, multimedia, non-linear jaunt through histories of racial violence and oppression, and is structured around a conceit that further emphasizes the locational politics of deploying a welcome table approach to performance: to properly estrange audience members from biases that might overdetermine expectations about what they will see and the bodies that should deliver the story, preshow stage directions dictate that "The audience enters through a long hallway into the theater. The hallway is lit; there is an alien sound ambience to signify entering another reality. When they are in the theater they are technically in the Alien spacecraft" (Chong and Wilks 2016, 7). Therefore, despite the play's title, all of the action of the play occurs not exactly in pre- and post-racial America, but rather on a spacecraft where the racial rules of the United States cannot over-determine meaning or belonging, and more specifically, what we collectively allow ourselves to know about pre- and post-racial America.

In this way, *Collidescope 2.0*'s representation of racial conflict across time literalizes a critical performance tradition that Daphne Brooks has identified as afro-alienation, whereby social agents "defamiliarize[e] their own bodies by way of performance in order to yield alternative racial and gender epistemologies" (Brooks 2006, 5). As Priscilla Page's essay highlights, intentional casting across racial lines produced opportunities not just for actors who identified as black or African American to help disrupt racial and gender epistemologies, but for students from other racial backgrounds to do so as well. Thus, despite the production's centering of manifestations of anti-blackness in US history, the diverse group of students who gathered to develop this work in each of the three college settings where it has been produced have been welcomed into a process that required them to develop a relationship to that history as their own, regardless of their positioning as racialized subjects within that history. Just as Banks's essay described instances of inclusive casting in which actors who did not appear to be historically accurate legatees of particular narratives were able to somehow disclose (or have disclosed) their "invisible" but salient relationships to the racialized past, *Collidescope 2.0* performers found their way toward unexpected kinship with historical figures, whether through helping to depict the range of black experiences (from enslavement to relative Brahmin privilege) in Revolutionary War-era Boston or by experiencing a sense of transformation akin to Anna Deavere Smith's admonition that "if you say a word enough, it becomes you … manipulating words has a spiritual power," and feeling a right to forcefully declaim Fannie Lou Hamer's words even as a person whose different racial positioning as a self-identified Asian woman yielded protection from some of the indignities that Hamer's story contained (Martin and Smith 1993, 51). Recognizing and resisting the ways that dominant historical narratives have encouraged most Americans to distance themselves spatially, temporally, and thus politically from these aspects of our shared past allows *Collidescope 2.0* participants to help turn audience members into passengers on that Alien spacecraft that refuses to invest in the laws of (racial) time and space that construct much of American theater.

James Baldwin's vision of a welcome table appears at the beginning of Banks's essay but does not show up in *Collidescope 2.0* until nearly the end of the work. In the play's final substantive historical scene, titled "Baldwin's

Nigger," the audience hears excerpts from a speech Baldwin delivered in London in the 1960s that include striking meditations on what is at stake in an honest articulation of our contorted, shared racial inheritance. Merely at the level of language, the scene invites audiences into an oppositional way of thinking about race and belonging in a US context. At the top of the scene, Baldwin relates an exchange with a black British man of West Indian heritage who asked multiple questions in a vain attempt to get Baldwin to claim a place of belonging other than (prior to) the United States. Reflecting on that failed conversation, Baldwin notes, "…something that one has that one wants to resist, yes, and also to use…is the fact that, like it or not, I am an American. … I was formed in a certain crucible" (Chong and Wilks 2016, 92). However, laying claim to his status as an American is not at all a capitulation to a simple nationalist pride. Rather, Baldwin asserts, "what one does realize is that when you try to stand up and look the world in the face, like you had a right to be here. When you do that…[you] have attacked the entire power structure of the Western world" (Chong and Wilks 2016, 92). To take one's place at the welcome table is to participate in the project of dismantling the American racial order that we know. In the UMass production, six performers of varying racial and gender identities perform this Baldwin speech, and the optics of this casting choice reinforce the message contained in Baldwin's words. Despite the dishonest taxonomies that are used to separate people into categories of privilege and abjection, we are locked into relation even with those who are the "them" to our "us." Rather than offering a heartwarming leap toward reconciliation, coming to a diversely populated welcome table "like you [have] a right to be here," simultaneously possessing and being the object of a forthright, historically informed gaze, makes a critical demand for accountability.

Baldwin's words are the last to ring in an audience's ears before *Collidescope 2.0*'s epilogue, which forcefully reminds audiences of the alienation device that has structured the work. The table to which they have been invited to consider and recognize their implication in America's history of racial violence is suspended in another time and place, one from which it is possible to reflect on the representation of that history somewhat dispassionately. An alien voice-over in the epilogue names race as "a troubling pathology" endemic to humankind, reflective of "self-destructive impulses" that "rule the species to their detriment" in defiance of the scientific knowledge that exposes the contextual insignificance of the physiological differences that structure and ostensibly justify inequality in our societies (Chong and Wilks 2016, 97). These words speak most obviously to the violent histories that have been represented across the play's eleven scenes, but also serve as a final reminder that the audience's interpretations of what they have seen an ensemble of racially diverse performers do should allow for the ethical resonance that racially dissonant casting choices might provoke.

Locating the table

As Page's essay makes clear, *Collidescope* has been performed to date at three different universities: University of Maryland (1.0), UMass Amherst (2.0), and Wake Forest University (3.0), all of which are historically—and for the most part remain predominantly—white institutions.[2] When the work premiered at University of Maryland in 2014, its opening coincided with national outcry over a grand jury's failure to indict Michael Brown's murderer in Ferguson, Missouri, a city only 10 miles from Josephine Baker's birthplace of St. Louis, whose atrocious practices of discrimination helped propel her away from the United States toward a place where she could eventually construct the welcome table that she wanted to occupy in her lifetime. By contrast, the work's performance run at UMass came as the 2016 election season was gaining momentum most especially through the deployment of xenophobic rhetoric that was a virulent backlash against the supposed postracial significance of Barack Obama's presidency. Attending to the time and place of these productions is critical because the racial "message" of the works will always grate against what Banks (following Shakespeare scholar Ayanna Thompson) refers to as the "sociologies of viewing" that those times and places will instill in audiences.

One of the most distinctive features of Banks's welcome table ethos is its emphasis on activating the ethical and analytical faculties of audiences. In order for inclusive casting practices to fulfill their potential of offering abundance to all participants in a theatrical endeavor, they must exist in relation to invitational communication with prospective audiences and the broader communities from which they are drawn; and, furthermore, must offer processing space after the production itself. The welcome table refuses—or at the very least, drastically pushes back—the diegetic framing of performance meaning making, and those who are welcomed to and receiving sustenance at the table are not only performers given expanded access to performance opportunities, but also audience members who must welcome the opportunity to have their interpretive faculties challenged by forging "a dialogue…to provide accurate historical information about the stories being told and to introduce new language to describe their sociologies" (Banks 2013, 8).

Page's description of *Collidescope 2.0* as a capstone moment in the larger UMass Theater Department initiative "Art, Legacy, and Community 2014–2016" provides a context for understanding how the politics of place inflect the welcome table framework. The decision to develop scenes for *Collidescope 2.0* that "place a lens on a series of historical events in the Western Massachusetts area … as a way to investigate the rich history of student and community activism within the Amherst/African American community" serves as an invitation to both performers and audience members alike to reimagine the university, their places within it, and the role of the region in constructing some of the racialized ideologies that the production hopes to challenge (Chong and Wilks 2016, 2). The space of the production becomes a place to levy criticisms of things like how we "do diversity" within the neoliberal university, such as a preference for convening yet "another student forum on race … / another student forum on race … / another student forum on race …" (Chong and Wilks 2016, 58), rather than providing material resources to address the structural issues that have plagued multiracial campus communities for decades and more. Deploying the Theater Department's resources of time, space, and materials toward emphatically inclusive performance aesthetics and historical storytelling that centers legacies of local student activism in the face of institutional negligence is an effort to disrupt inertia concerning matters of racial equity in the campus context. This creative practice models and invites all audience-participants (whether students, faculty and staff, or administrators) to hold UMass Amherst history in ways that they have not yet, and to engage imaginatively and differently with student desires to create a campus community that holds expressive space for all of its members.

The elegiac beginning and ending of *Collidescope 2.0*, which invoke the murders of Trayvon Martin and Michael Brown, respectively, make clear that welcome tables are hard won spaces, difficult to construct and find homes for, and challenging to maintain. The urgent need to create what Page invokes as brave space for coalitional engagement with our shared American past is quite clear, but so too is the precarity of these undertakings. Josephine Baker's grand welcome table, housed within the villa Les Milandes for three decades, was financially impossible to maintain and, even across the Atlantic, she became a victim of the foreclosure phenomenon that impedes the intergenerational transfer of wealth and material legacy within black communities. Likewise, the different welcoming homespace Baldwin created for himself in France in St. Paul-de-Vence was demolished in piecemeal fashion to make space for "19 'grandly' chic apartments with 'a panoramic view of the sea,'" marketed by Sotheby's, slated to be ready for occupancy in the spring of 2019 (Zaborowska 2018). And in our current context, the American regional theater community is in the midst of a moment ripe with potential for transformation, as nearly two dozen new Artistic Directors at LORT theaters were projected to be hired between 2017 and 2019, with the opportunity to articulate visions for a twenty-first-century American theater that engages our integrated society proactively rather than reactively, as an asset to be explored, rather than a liability to be managed. Diversification of artistic leadership would shift dynamics at the many tables that comprise the American theatrical apparatus, but this outcome is by no means guaranteed. If those responsible for deciding on the next generation of leaders do not themselves critically engage with the histories of exclusion that have created a collection of "major" American theaters whose leadership does not reflect the communities within which the institutions are housed, we will have more of what LeRoi Jones (later known as Amiri Baraka) referred to in a quite different context as "the changing same" (Jones 1998, 180). It will be incredibly easy to make empty contributions to a rhetoric of inclusion, with "one of these days" as an implicit subtext that cynically accommodates the status quo. The ability to both create and protect the spaces where welcome tables may be set remains freighted with dynamics of social and economic power that artists and audiences must skillfully navigate together.

Notes

1 It is important to note that, as with other communally authored spirituals, multiple versions of the song circulate, not all of whose lyrics articulate the political and ethical challenges that this one does.
2 Per demographic data from each institution's website, UMD College Park's student population is approximately 49% white (which is not a majority, but is by far the largest single racial group on campus), Wake Forest is approximately 70% white, and UMass Amherst is approximately 72% white.

Bibliography

Banks, Daniel. 2013. "The Welcome Table: Casting for an Integrated Society." *Theatre Topics*, 23(1) (March): 1–18.

Brooks, Daphne. 2006. *Bodies in Dissent: Spectacular Performances of Race and Freedom, 1850–1910*. Durham, NC: Duke University Press.

Chong, Ping and Talvin Wilks. 2016. *Collidescope 2.0: Adventures in Pre- and Post-Racial America*. Unpublished manuscript.

Jones, LeRoi. 1998. *Black Music*. New York: Da Capo Press.

Martin, Carol, and Anna Deavere Smith. 1993. "Anna Deavere Smith: The Word Becomes You: An Interview." *TDR*, 37(4) (Winter): 45–62.

National Museum of American History. n.d. "Our Story: Students Sit for Civil Rights." https://amhistory.si.edu/ourstory/pdf/freedom/lunchcounter_songs.pdf   (accessed January 9, 2019).

Southern Gospel Revival. n.d. "Welcome Table." https://sifalyrics.com/southern-gospel-revival-welcome-table-lyrics (accessed January 9, 2019).

University of Maryland, College Park. n.d. "Enrollments by Gender and Race/Ethnicity." www.irpa.umd.edu/CampusCounts/Enrollments/enroll_by_raceandgender.pdf (accessed January 9, 2019).

UMass Amherst. n.d. "Diversity Matters: Data." www.umass.edu/diversity/data-policies (accessed January 9, 2019).

Wake Forest University. n.d. "Campus Life: Diversity." https://admissions.wfu.edu/campus-life/diversity (accessed January 9, 2019).

Zaborowska, Magdalena J. 2018. "The Last Days of James Baldwin's House in the South of France." *Literary Hub*, April 27. https://lithub.com/the-last-days-of-james-baldwins-house-in-the-south-of-france (accessed January 10, 2019).

Afterword

Daniel Banks

> To declare one's identity is to write the world into existence.
> —Edouard Glissant (1989, 180)

i.

The world is a different place than it was when I completed work on the "The Welcome Table: Casting for an Integrated Society" at the end of 2012—and even more so since Claire and I proposed this book. There have been literal and meta-phorical shots heard around the world with an increase in anti-bias and anti-vio-lence work and movements—specifically Black Lives Matter, founded in July 2013, and the recent version of Me Too (#MeToo), which ignited in October 2017[1]—with people paying the price for rampant discriminatory, abusive, and illegal behaviors. And yet, for some people, this behavior is a manifestation of such systemic bias, discrimination, and abuses of power that they (perhaps more quietly now) still ask, "What's the big deal?" The answer to that question might be, as Liesl Tommy reminds us in her preface to the volume, "representation matters." As evidence of that assertion, in recent years many US theatre-based, grassroots initiatives have grown and thrived, such as The Kilroys, The Jubilee, The Artists' Anti-Racism Coalition, the Theatre Folks of Color Facebook group curated by The Crew, Urban Bush Women's Summer Leadership Institute (that has existed since 1997), and my company DNAWORKS' Welcome Table Initiative, among others.[2] Institutions are also widely employing strategies ("the Rooney Rule," British Film Institute's "Diversity Standards"[3]) and consulting with organizations (artEquity, Indigenous Direction, and the People's Institute for Survival and Beyond) to further the work of equity, access, and opportunity.

I wrote the original article because, as a director in both commercial and educational spaces, I was disheartened that the term "non-traditional casting" was still used to describe casting that was, in fact, historically accurate. The term belied a biased view of history at work in many areas of the field. Offering an alternative to "non-traditional" casting, in 1990 a group of European heritage artists wrote a *New York Times* op-ed in support of the protest, initiated by

David Henry Hwang and B. D. Wong, over the casting of Jonathan Pryce in *Miss Saigon*. In the letter they called for "non-biased" casting (perhaps my new favorite among casting terminologies)—although, arguably, all casting is biased, the question being, "What does a particular bias make possible or not possible in terms of performance and representation?" (Bartlett et al. 1990, H9).

In rehearsals, classes, and workshops I often propose that the most political action a person can take in the US is to be culturally specific (and, for me, ethnicity, color, heritage, gender, sexuality, class, region, ability, and age are unique—and intersecting—cultural groups, in that members of these constituencies have specific ways of knowing and being in the world). Cultural specificity challenges the colonial projects of assimilation and acculturation. To be culturally specific is to be at risk in a country that has built itself socially and economically on the virtues of submitting (or dedicating) oneself to a new, mainstream, "American" culture. Brandi Catanese writes of the "melting pot" theory of US culture: "the methods by which this amalgamation occurs are incendiary, and violently obliterate any distinct traces of what came before" (Catanese 2012, 8). This violence is the price of attaining privilege by aligning oneself with a dominant culture. Therefore, to be *visibly* culturally specific, and not phenotypically of that dominant group, has its own price—it is to be a reminder of that violence as well as the social and spiritual loss that accompanies the divestiture of identity and self.

ii.

> To cast any play is to engage in a practice that is both artistic and ethical.
> —Brian Herrera (2017, 33)

Claire Syler and I did not originally intend the sections of this book to be driven by cultural identity; nor was it our intention that the contributors to each section identify with the same identity group. We imagined that the book might be structured along known casting practices, such as color conscious casting, multi-ethnic casting, and integrated casting; recent formulations such as "courageous casting," Patricia Ybarra's "coalitional casting" (Ybarra 2015), Brian Herrera's "culturally analogous casting" (Herrera 2017, 29); and concepts that we had not yet encountered.

But, as Ann Elizabeth Armstrong describes in her chapter about emergent theory, people presented themselves with passionate narratives about the intersections of how they identify and how they are identified by others. They described the casting practices that they employ for the specific types of theatre they create and the politics in which they are embroiled as a consequence of living in a country that created itself on the backs of assimilation and acculturation. And, so, the challenges of casting *in* a segregated country have dictated the aesthetic conversations surrounding casting *for* an integrated theatre.

Approaching this situation as theatre artists first, saying "yes, and …", we accepted the emergent structure, which has allowed us to view similarities and differences across case studies and worldviews. Here I share some of the synergies among book sections as an index of practices and daily concerns in a largely un- or under-represented cross-section of US theatre—a map of the deeper discourses available to the field when terms such as "non-traditional" and "colorblind" casting are left behind.

Several chapters refer to the concept of "curating" or "casting the room"— calling out the imperative for relevant culture bearers to be *in leadership* positions whenever cultural narratives are told. This principle echoes the words adopted by the Disability Rights movement in the 1990s, "Nothing about us without us," and is a clear measure of a producing organization's commitment to the communities served by such productions, both on and off the stage.

Closely related to this question of culture bearers is the necessity of an actor's cultural competence. What emerges from certain chapters is that, for some practitioners—but not others—and in certain situations, this approach can open doors to casting people in culturally specific roles from outside a given cultural group if there are no actors with cultural competence available from that group. As discussed in the sections on casting both Middle Eastern and Native American drama, the alternative would be to forego presenting the work, thereby depriving multiple communities of the ability to experience an author's work and cultural narrative.

Several of the case-studies implicitly call for an interrogation of the capitalism of institutional theatre—a system that often values individual accomplishment over collective achievement. From my experience working around the country, many theatres are currently reframing their concepts of artistic excellence to include measures of how fully a project or company represents the attendant local community/ies. Most of the projects and companies discussed in this book are not funded at the level of larger arts organizations. Many of the large companies receive funding dedicated to representing those very same communities and constituencies, yet often fall short of doing so at the level of that specific funding.[4] This approach to grant allocation often siphons off resources from culturally specific organizations, creating a vacuum of representation and opportunity.

There are recurring tropes of the cultural liability of "stereotype," "minstrelsy," and "passing," each of which threatens the sustainability of a cultural identity and its stories. Arguably, minstrelsy is the fundamental US theatre form, with and against which all our entertainment industries are in dialogue; US casting controversies are therefore invariably embedded with vestiges of Black-faced minstrelsy.[5] Across industries, people from dominant cultural groups have historically played (and directed) people of all cultural identities— and still often do; while actors of historically marginalized groups only have access to roles that the Mobius loop of (industry ↔ cultural imaginary) determines matches their phenotypes and abilities. Disabled actors, as Carrie Sandahl details in her chapter, are frequently called to fulfill roles of "disappearance," making sure that disability does not trigger "audience's social anxieties and fears around issues such as loss of bodily autonomy" (89).

Finally, contributors in several chapters discuss the "problem of the pipeline," pointing out the challenge in filling casts of actors from a particular identity if training programs do not accept these actors or if potential actors are discouraged from entering the industry before they even apply for training. The metaphor of the "pipeline" holds on multiple levels, in that a pipeline often carries a precious resource that has usually been mined and is surrounded by the exploitation of land and people. In addition, the ways in which some training programs frame the rich opportunity to accept students from a wide variety of backgrounds connect to W. E. B. Du Bois's timeless question from his 1903 work *The Souls of Black Folk*, "How does it feel to be a problem?" (Du Bois 1994, 1).

In these and numerous other ways, the intersectionality among the case-studies emerges, either by the authors' direct acknowledgment or through the juxtaposition of narratives from the field.

iii.

Words are spells in our mouths.

—Suzan-Lori Parks (1995, 11)[6]

The chapters in this book, given that they illuminate the cultural breadth of US theatre, could be easily described in terms of "diversity" and "inclusion," according to the ways that these terms are leveraged in the field. A challenge of these terms, however, is that they do not address equity or access to opportunity; and they are rarely applied equally to everyone (some constituencies are "unmarked" in this conversation in that they are not discussed as "diverse"). I propose that equity means *power sharing*; furthermore, that "diversity," as a concept, does not call for this redistribution of resources. In fact, it is precisely a *lack* of power that is embedded in the term "diversity"—the power to apply this term to a particular group, the power to claim credit for "including" someone from that group into their space, the power to disinvite, the power to decide what a person can and cannot do once they are present, when they can do it, how much they get paid, with whom they will be working, and under what conditions. Angela Pao offers, "Inclusion always carries the possibility or risk of containment" (Pao 2010, 136). Like "inclusion," "diversity" is divested of power, agency, and self-determination.

In short, "diversity," as a deployable concept, redirects attention away from the person or group of people in power. The Artists' Anti-Racism Coalition proposes, "Let's stop using words like diversity and start saying 'anti-racism' … In this work, in reclaiming our humanity and working towards a more just and liberated world, we have to be really intentional about our language and anti-oppression" (Clement 2019). For an organization (or an industry) to shift the conversation from diversity and inclusion to power sharing and equal places at the table is to change that organization's cultural ecosystem from monocultural to pluri-cultural. This adjustment happens not by changing who works at the organization, but rather by who is responsible for establishing the organization's cultural ethos and norms. Representation *and leadership* matter.

Rooted in the dilemma of equitable casting is the power of the director (and producer). Over twenty-five years ago, in the volume *Upstaging Big Daddy* (1993), to which this book owes a debt, director and educator Ellen Donkin challenged theatre professionals to "rethink the role of the director":

> A director's personal style is one element among many in the complex system called mode of production, which sees to it that whatever is produced ultimately reproduces "dominant ideology." The way we direct is part of that system, and we need therefore to become conscious of our own processes.
>
> (Donkin and Clement 1993, 81)

Since discussions of casting often focus on the process's product, such conversations—like the concepts of "diversity" and "inclusion"—often mask the people responsible for the power of decision-making if they are not named. Donkin instructs, as do many of this book's chapters implicitly and explicitly, "If a director doesn't think through where she stands politically, she is likely to wind up serving the interests of a dominant ideology, whether she intends to or not" (Donkin and Clement 1993, 6). This is true of all the decision-makers in the process of casting, who are themselves consciously or unconsciously "contained" by systemic structures of inequity and discrimination.

iv.

Uh Huh? But How Do It Free Us?

—Sonia Sanchez[7]

By contrast, the "welcome table" proposes a model of representation that is plural, coalitional, and connected to community, one that can *move the artistic and ethical center* of theatre's power relationships.[8] Rather than supplanting one dominant ideology with another, the welcome table seeks a model of collaborative consensus building and power sharing. My hope is that, after experiencing a welcome table, people will be inspired to create their own tables; and that these satellite movements can then call on each other for support, catalyzing—as discussed by Claire in her introduction— coalitions/networks of belonging and simultaneous action.

I'd like to end with the words of Glenda Dickerson (1945–2012), a revolutionary who, when people gathered, would ask them, "On whose shoulders do you stand?" Perhaps if people who have suffered the alienating impact of assimilation and acculturation had a clear(er) connection to their forbearers or a deeper experience of cellular memory, they would find more in common with people whose lives manifest this strength through expressive culture and ritual. I invite the reader both to embrace and engage in the cultural specificity of Dickerson's statement as well as to seek the relevance in their own experience:

> Lost memory, submerged charges, silenced voices, forgotten dreams. These were the colors I wore. How weary I was of personifying in true color "the other." How I longed not to have to explain myself. What would I not give to announce and not apologize. Where was the language that spoke of the kind of liberation I had in mind—a way of living or operating that is not solely defined by what we are transgressing, resisting, or deconstructing? Perceiving oneself as seen by others leads to self-consciousness, not self-awareness. Where was the eye that turned inwards and was pleased? How do we define ourselves when we are living someone else's vision, women living on the edge of time? How could we learn to exalt the culture of the African-American woman from Africa to America, to trumpet our grandmothers' voices?
>
> (In Donkin and Clement 1993, 157)

I acknowledge all the contributors to this volume for their courageous and world-building work. And I pay homage to the elders listed in the Acknowledgments who dared to ask—for equity, for a seat at the table, for clarity about why access to opportunity was being denied, and for the field to recognize *equitably* the culturally specific institutions that are denied resources.

Part of achieving equity is a genuine willingness to listen to and consider one another's truths, especially if doing so is "uncomfortable" (2). An oft-repeated heuristic in examining questions of equity and access is: for someone who has lived with unexamined or unacknowledged privilege for their entire lives (along any identity line), equity is likely to feel like oppression, in that a redistribution of privilege can feel like personal loss rather than a just, ethical, and humanitarian gain. The alternative is to refocus that aversion to loss and ask, "How do it free *all* of us?"

Notes

1 The original "Me Too" campaign was initiated in 2007 by Tarana Burke, as compared to the "hashtag" version started by actress Alicia Milano (see Vagianos 2017).
2 DNAWORKS is a thirteen-year-old arts and service organization dedicated to dialogue and healing through the arts. See www.dnaworks.org.
3 See www.bfi.org.uk/supporting-uk-film/diversity-inclusion/bfi-diversity-standards.
4 See, for example, the recent data collected by the Artists' Anti-Racism Coalition regarding the "gender and ethnicity of the artists who had been produced at the ten largest non-profit theatres in New York City over the last ten years" in comparison with the demographics of the city (Clement 2019).

5 This is the formulation I use to expose the vectors of power and the willful construction of this deleterious representational "strategy" (Banks 2006).
6 Used by permission of Theatre Communications Group.
7 The title of an early play by legendary writer Sonia Sanchez. According to Sanchez, the title is incorrect in the several volumes in which it is printed. What appears here is Sanchez's correct title (Sonia Sanchez, personal communication, February 18, 2018.)
8 Borrowing both from Herrera (2017) and Ngũgĩ wa Thiong'o's concept of "moving the center" (Ngũgĩ 2008).

Bibliography

Banks, Daniel. 2006. "Unperforming 'Race': Strategies for Reimagining Identity." In *A Boal Companion: Dialogues on Theatre and Cultural Politics*, edited by Jan Cohen-Cruz and Mady Schutzman, 185–198. New York: Routledge.

Bartlett, Robin, Victor Garber, Craig Lucas, Terrence McNally, Ellen Parker, and Larry Kramer. 1990. "Miss Saigon; We Still Need Affirmative Action." *The New York Times*, September 2, H9.

Catanese, Brandi Wilkins. 2012. *The Problem of the Color[blind]: Racial Transgression and the Politics of Black Performance*. Ann Arbor, MI: University of Michigan.

Clement, Olivia. 2019. "Meet the Collective of Theatremakers Working to Undo Racism in the American Theatre." www.playbill.com/article/meet-the-collecti ve-of-theatremakers-working-behind-the-scenes-to-undo-racism-in-our-industry (accessed January 7, 2019).

Donkin, Ellen and Susan Clement. 1993. *Upstaging Big Daddy: Directing Theater as if Gender and Race Matter*. Ann Arbor, MI: University of Michigan.

Du Bois, W. E. B. 1994. *The Souls of Black Folk*. New York: Dover Publications.

Glissant, Edouard. 1989. *Caribbean Discourse: Selected Essays*. Charlottesville, VA: University Press of Virginia.

Herrera, Brian. 2017. "'But Do We Have the Actors for That?': Some Principles of Practice for Staging Latinx Plays in a University Theatre Context." *Theatre Topics*, 27(1): 23–35.

Ngũgĩ wa Thiong'o. 2008. *Moving the Centre: The Struggle for Cultural Freedoms*. London: James Curry.

Pao, Angela C. 2010. *No Safe Spaces: Re-casting Race, Ethnicity, and Nationality in American Theater*. Ann Arbor, MI: University of Michigan.

Parks, Suzan-Lori. 1995. "Elements of Style." In Suzan-Lori Parks, *The America Play and Other Works*. New York: Theatre Communications Group.

Vagianos, Alanna. 2017. "The 'Me Too' Campaign Was Created by a Black Woman 10 Years Ago." *Huffpost*, October 17. www.huffingtonpost.com/entry/the-me-too-campaign-was-created-by-a-black-woman-10-years-ago_us_59e61a7fe4b02a 215b336fee (accessed April 4, 2019).

Ybarra, Patricia. 2015. "A Message from TAPS Chair, Dr. Patricia Ybarra," December 4. www.brown.edu/academics/theatre-arts-performance-studies/news/2015-12/message-taps-chair-dr-patricia-ybarra (accessed April 4, 2019).

Index

Page numbers in italics refer to figures. Page numbers in bold refer to tables. Page numbers followed by "n" refer to notes.

Abaga 65, **65**, 68, 69
abstract liberalism 193
Academy Awards *see* Oscars
access to opportunity 3, 51, 52, 86, 122, 162, 225, 231, 233
accountability 53, 54, 224
acculturation 25, 229, 233
Actors' Equity Association (AEA) 8, 12, 13, 15, 27n2, 40, 51, 52, 63, 66, 97, 147, 155
actors of color 13, 24, 52–53, 76, 190, 191; archetypes 45–47; cross-cultural casting 22; *Death of a Salesman* 40–45, *41, 43*; ethnicity, hiding 39; and expectations of viewers 17–18; *Hamilton* 190, 194–195; *Kung Fu* 184–185; *Macbeth* 5, 7, 36–37, *38*, 46–47; in multilingual plays 122; *Octoroon, An* 195; performance of Shakespeare 19, 21, 36–37, 39; sense of community, creation of 46; *Shipment, The* 195; tradition 19, 21; *Twilight: Los Angeles, 1992* 178, 179–182, *181*, 190, 192–193; and visual information of audience 19; *Yellow Face* 183; *see also* race
actor training programs: and disabled students 88, 90, 93–94; and Middle Eastern Americans 74–75
Adams, Maurianne 42
advocacy, actor-led 51, 52, 53–54
African Grove Theatre 19
African heritage actors 5, 17, 19, 24, 25, 76; *see also* actors of color
afro-alienation 223

Ahmanson Theatre 185, *186*
Aidoo, Ama Ata 39
Aker, Melis 62
Al-Bilali, Judyie 207, 208, 212
Aldridge, Ira 21, 26
Alexander, Elizabeth 179
Al-Hakim, Tawfiq 62
Allen, Paula Gunn (Lakota) 163
Alliance for Inclusion in the Arts (AIA) **8**, 16, 97
Alliance Theatre 19–20
Alsultany, Evelyn 78, 79
American Indian Community House 149
Americans with Disabilities Act (ADA) 107
American Theatre magazine 151
Amos 'n' Andy 191
Andorra 18
And So We Walked 168n3
Anthony, Chris 154
Apothetae, The 92
Arab Americans 58, 76, 77, 78, 80; *see also* Middle Eastern American theater
archetypal casting 77
archetypes, and actors of color 45–47
Armstrong, Ann Elizabeth 5, 9, 229, 131
Aroa, Brian 213
Art, Legacy, & Community program 207–209, 212
artistic relationships within community 20–21
Artists' Anti-Racism Coalition 228, 231, 233n4
Artists Repertory Theatre 168n3
artrepreneurs 177

arts education, for children with disabilities 94
Asher, James 77
Asian American Performers Action Coalition (AAPAC) **8**, 13, 15, 18
Asian Americans 60–61, 174, 176, 191, 192; *Kung Fu* 184–185; *Soft Power* 185–188, *186*, 190, 195, 197; *Twilight: Los Angeles, 1992* 180; *Vietgone* 195–197; *Yellow Face* 182–184
assimilation 25, 74, 76, 205, 229, 233
Association for Theatre in Higher Education 5
audience 5, 27, 168; *Collidescope* 209, 222–223, 224; and color-blind casting 33, 34; and cross-racial casting 193; development 34; dialogue with 19, 20–21, 23; and disabled actors 89, 90, 231; engagement 20, 21, 126–127, 132, 133, 136–140; ethical and analytical faculties of 225; expectations of 17–19, 20; and multilingual plays 121, 126–127, 129, 132, 135; participation 23, 138; sharing the hypothesis 23, 24; visual information of 19
auditions 39, 61, 63, 80, 118, 122, 123
Austin, J. L. 14, 26
authenticity 58–59, 174; and creativity 58, 70; and cross-racial casting 182; and disabled actors 86, 91, 96; and Middle Eastern American theater 7, 57, 58; and Native American theater 165; and whitewashing 51
Autobiography of an Ex-Colored Man (Johnson) 17
Autry Museum of the American West 147
Ávila, Elaine 9, 203

Baby Blues, The 149
Bailey, Pearl 18
Baker, Josephine 12, 27, 221, 222, 225, 226
Bakhtin, Mikhail 118
Baldwin, James 12, 45, 221, 222, 223–224
Band's Visit, The 80
Banks, Daniel 4, 5, 7, 9, 37, 131, 132, 220–221, 222, 225, 228
Baraka, Amiri 39
Barbot, Matthew 50
base roll 158n9
Belluso, John 100, 103, 104–105, *104*, *106*

Bengal Tiger in the Baghdad Zoo 75
Benshoff, Harry M. 76
Berger, John 13, 17
Bettis, Hilary 50
Big River 92
Bird, Gloria (Nez Perce) 164
blackface 91, 173,176, 190, 191, 230
Black Lives Matter 217, 228
Black Panther 173
Blaine-Cruz, Lileana 53
Blitzstein, Marc 17
Blumenbach, Johann 14
Body of Bourne, The 103, 104–105, *104*, *106*
Bogdan, Robert 103
Bonilla-Silva, Eduardo 193
Booth, Susan 20, 21
Boucicault, Dion 195
Bourne, Randolph 103, 104, 105
Bracy, John 42
Breakdown Services 93, 97–98
Brecht, Bertolt 64, 102, 103, 121
Broadway 18, 39, 61, 80, 86, 92, 96, 176, 177, 194
Broadway League 12, 167
Bromery, Randolph 208
Brooklyn '63 208
Brooks, Avery 40, *41*, *43*
Brooks, Daphne 223
Brooks, E. B. (Sami, Algonquin) 154
brown, adrienne maree 132, 133, 134
Brown, Carlyle 139
Brown, Jocelyn 15
Brown, Kevin 120
Brown, Michael 211, 225, 226
Bruno, Christine 8, 85
Burch, Susan 104
Burke, Tarana 233n1
Butler, Judith 14, 26

Call Me Mehdi **65**, 66, 69
Capparell, Stephanie 40
Carbon Black 159
Carlson, Marvin 118
Carpenter, Faedra Chatard 195, 196
Carradine, David 184
CastAndLoose Live! 49–50, 53, 54, 54n1, 54n2
casting notices 49–50, 53
Casting Society of America (CSA) 87
Catanese, Brandi Wilkins 9, 28n7, 194–195, 220, 229

Center Theatre Group 179, 185, *186*
Césaire, Aimé 39
Chacón, Jorge 50
Chaney, James 137
Channing, Carol 18
Chappelle, Dave 195
Charlton, James 101, 105, 106, 110
Chekhov, Anton 64, **65**, 66
Chernow, Ron 194
Children of a Lesser God 86
Childress, Alice 39
Chong, Ping 9, 203, 207, 208, 209–210, *209*, 212–213, *213*, 216–218, *217*, 222
chorus in multilingual plays 121, 125, 128–129, 134
Christmas Carol, A 19, 20, 86
Civil Rights Movement, veterans of 137–138
Clark, Brian 100
classroom casting 22, 34–35
Clemens, Kristi 213
Clements, Marie 149
Coburn, James 185
collective writing 102
Collidescope: Adventures in Pre- and Post-Racial America 9, 211–212, 225; alien gaze 210, 214–216; and Baldwin 221, 222, 223–224; brave space 213–214, 216, 226; *Collidescope 2.0* 9, 207, 208, 212–214, *213*, 215–216, 218, 220, 222, 223, 224; *Collidescope 3.0* 209, 216–218, *217*, 225; focus on place 212; as process 212, 215–216; upturning otherness 209–210, *209*, 215; and welcome table 220–227
Colón-Zayas, Liza 50
color-blind casting 8, 13, 15, 33–34, 35, 38–39, 76, 194; *see also* race
color-blind multiculturalism 190, 192–195
color-conscious casting 15, 176, 194, 195–198
colorism 44
Coltrane, John 39
Coming Home **65**, 66, 68, 69
community building, and multilingual theater 123, 131–132
community engagement, and multilingual plays 126–127
Compression of a Casualty **65**, 68, 69
Cost of Living 86
Cradle Will Rock, The 17–18
Crazy Rich Asians 173

creative labor 9, 176, 177, 179, 184, 188
creative process *see* creativity
creative vision 9, 176, 177, 178, 179, 184, 186, 187, 188
creativity 188; and authenticity 58, 70; and disability 95; Native 163–164, *164*; reparative 177, 179, 188; *Twilight: Los Angeles, 1992* 178–182, 179–182, *181*
Creeps 104
cripface 86, 91, 173
cripping up (disability) 86, 90–92
cross-cultural casting 22
cross-cultural projects 118
cross-gender casting 183, 213
Crossing Mnisose 168m3
cross-racial casting 9, 13, 52, 177, 190, 213, 223; context, intent, impact of casting 174; *Hamilton* 190, 194–195; *Kung Fu* 184–185; *Octoroon, An* 195; *Shipment, The* 195; *Soft Power* 185–188, *186*, 190, 195, 197; *Twilight: Los Angeles, 1992* 177, 178–182, *181*, 190, 192–193; *Vietgone* 195–197; works of David Henry Hwang 182–188; *Yellow Face* 182–184
Cruz, Gilbert 50
Cruz, Migdalia 50
cultural community development 135
cultural competency 69–70, 79, 153, 155, 230
cultural imaginary of disability 101, 103, 104, 105
cultural knowledge 9, 75, 79–80, 152, 154
culturally conscious casting 7; archetypes 45–47; and audience development 33, 34; classroom casting 34–35; *Death of a Salesman* 40–45, *41*, *43*; intention *vs.* reception of production 35; *Macbeth* 36–37, *38*, 46–47; *see also* race
culturally specific theater 26
cultural specificity 63, 229
culture bearers 152, 154, 156, 230
Culture Clash 192, 193
Curious Incident of the Dog in the Night-Time, The 87
curriculum 22, 23, 93, 94, 139

Dabis, Cherien 79, 80
Darvag Theater Group 63, 71n4
Davidson, Gordon 179
Davis, Angela 188n1
Davis, Clinton Turner 15

Deaf West 86, 92
Death of a Salesman 7, 37, 40–45, *41, 43*
decolonising the mind 211
decolonization, and contemporary Native
American theater 160; advancement of
professional standards for Native
American artists 165–166; elevation
of contemporary Indigenous stories
162–165; Indigenous theatrical praxis
160, *161*, 168; reclamation of theatrical
space 161–162; sustenance of Native
American artistic community 166–167
Defoe, Ty (*Giizhig*) 9, 145, 154
Del Carmen, Guadalís 50
"De Nua" 128
Dern, Laura 98n3
Desai, Snehal 186
Detroit Repertory Theatre (DRT) 23–24
devised theater 22
Dickerson, Glenda 232–233
Dickson, Joy 154
Diggs, Daveed 194
directors 135; capacity to overwrite the
script 52–53; of color 53; with cultural
knowledge 75; role of 232
disability 8, **8**, 85–87, 100; as asset 95;
-centric theater companies 92; civil
rights model of 101; as complicated
thing 102–103; cultural imaginary of
101, 103, 104, 105; disabled characters
89; hidden history of 104–105; and
higher education 93–94, 105–107;
history 102–103; language, in press
material 96; medical model 94, 95;
narrative prosthesis 89, 103;
nondisabled actors playing disabled
characters 90–91, 92; *One Day: On the
Road to the ADA* 107–109; relaxed
performances 97; representation of 89;
as social construct 100, 103; and social
history/economics 103–104; social
model 94, 108; sympathetic notion of
101; theatrical left 101–102
Disability Rights Movement (DRM) 103,
105, 108, 230
disabled actors 85–87, 88, 230–231;
choosing roles/plays for 95; cripping up
86, 90–92; critiquing 92; database 93,
94; demand for 88; health-related issues
of 97; interventions to increase
participation of 95–97; involvement in
decision-making 96; lack of

disability-specific roles 89, 90; locating
95; mentorship of 97; multiple identity
groups 96; non-unionized 97;
overcoming obstacles 90; performing
non–specific roles 89–90; pipeline
92–94; presence, effect of 89–90;
work, seeking out 95
disabled playwrights 100, 102, 103–105, 107
Distant Thunder 154
diversity 24, 26, 52, 78, 167, 231–232
diversity wheel (Woodson)
135, *136*
DNAWORKS 21, 228, 233n2
documentary theater 178
Donkin, Ellen 232
double consciousness 42
Douglass, Frederick 25
Down in Mississippi 139, 140
Doyle, Kevin **65**
Du Bois, W. E. B. 21, 42, 231
Dunn, Carolyn (Muscogee/Cherokee/
Choctaw) 159

East West Players 185
Ebert, Roger 91
Eco, Umberto 134–135
Ecstasy: A Water Fable 75
El Guindi, Yussef 7, 62, **65**, 75, 80
Emeka, Justin 7, 36, *38, 41, 43*, 53
emergence, definition of 132
emergence paradigm 132
emergent strategy 132, 133, 229, 230;
adaptation 133–134; for audience
engagement 136–140; and casting
132–134; fractal 133; Freedom
Summer Ambassadors 139, 140;
interdependence and decentralization
134; iterative practices 134; and open
work 134–135; possibilities, creation of
134; resilience and transformative
justice 134; *Walk with Me: Freedom
Summer Walking Tour* 138–139, 140; *see
also* multilingual theater
Emory University Center for
Ethics 20
Erdrich, Louise (Anishinaabe) 163
Ervin, Mike 100, 104, 105
ethnically specific theater 26
Eustis, Oskar 177, 179
Evita 50, 51
Évora, Cesária 126
extended dramaturgy 132, 136–140

Eyring, Teresa 12, 26

Face Value 182, 184
Faculty Research Network 23
Farcas, Stephanie Barton 97
FastHorse, Larissa (Sincagu Lakota) 168n3
Ferreira, Eunice S. 9, 117, *121, 125*, 131, 132, 133, 134, 135, 136
Ferris, Madison 92, 96
Fichlander, Zelda 52
Flower Drum Song 191
for colored girls 188n5
for-profit theaters 51, 87
Foucault, Michel 177
Freedom Summer 1964 137–138
Freedom Summer Ambassadors 139, 140
Freeman, David 104
Frisch, Max 18
Funckes, Carol 105–106, 110
funding 26, 76, 177, 230

Gabrielino-Tongva people 150
Galella, Donatella 9, 190
Gallaire, Fatma 62
Gao Xingjian 121, 134, 135
Geiogamah, Hanay (Kiowa Delaware) 148, 159, 165
gender 34, 63, 85, 178, 181, 183, 184, 210, 223
Gift Theatre, The 95
Glancy, Diane 149
Glass Menagerie, The 37, 45, 86, 92, 96
Glissant, Edouard 228
God of Carnage 20
Golden Thread Productions 7, 60, 61–62, 72; ReOrient 2009 65–69, **65, 67–68**; ReOrient Camp 62; ReOrient Festival of Short Plays 7, 62–65, 70; ReOrient Forum 62
Gomez, Terry (Comanche) 159
Gooding, Cuba, Jr., 91
Goodman, Andrew 137
Graves, Joseph 14
Griffin, Sean 76
Grossman, Edith 119
Guevara, Zabryna 54n2
Guirgis, Steven Adly 27n4, 51

Hall, Juanita 191
Hamer, Fannie Lou 216, 223

Hamilton: An American Musical **8**, 122, 190, 194–195
Hamilton, Anne 23
Hamlet 39
Hammerstein, Oscar II 197
Hanania, Ray 73
Hanney, Bill 50
Hansberry, Lorraine 39
Happiest Song Plays Last, The 75
Harjo, Joy (Creek) 165
Harrell, David 85
Haugo, Ann 149, 158n5
Hedayat, Sadegh 62
Hello Dolly 18
Henk, Annie 50
Hernandez, Laura 108, *109*
Herrera, Brian Eugenio 5, 7, 49, 81n2, 192, 229
heteroglossia 118–119
higher education, disabled students in 93–94, 105–107
Highway, Tomson 148
Hill, Kevin P. 50
Hip Hop Theater 22
History of Bowling, The 104, 105
Ho, Tamara C. 191
Hogan, Linda (Chickasaw) 166
Holly, Ellen 26
Hollywood 73, 74, 76, 77
Hollywood Diversity Report (2018) 79
Homebody/Kabul 80
House Arrest 177, 193
Houseman, John 17
Hughes, Langston 17
Hwang, David Henry 9, 61, 176, 177, 182–188, *186*, 190, 195, 196, 197, 229
Hyman, Earle 26
hyperlinked dramaturgy 128–129, 134

I AM PWD campaign 97
Ibrahim, Denmo 75
identity(ies) 14, 19, 40, 190, 208, 230; Arab American 77; Asian American 182–188; cultural 40, 73, 207, 229, 230; disability 96, 100, 102; and emergent strategy 135; gender 34, 210, 224; hybridity of 9, 203–206; intersectionality 96; Middle Eastern 60, 72–73; Native American 150, 152, 153, 160, 165, 166; and race 15, 38; and visual information 18

I Heart Hamas 77
Iizuka, Naomi 22
Illinois State University **8**, 149
imagination 155, 174, 176
Imarisha, Walidah 174
immigrants 61, 70, 73–74, 120, 194,
  204, 205
I'm Not a Serial Killer **65**, 66
inclusion 24–25, 26, 37, 52, 85, 86, 87,
  147, 166, 180, 222, 223, 225, 226,
  231–232
Indiana Rep 149
Indigenous theater *see* Native American
  actors; Native American theater;
  Native Voices at the Autry (NVA)
Individualized Education Plans (IEPs)
  94–95
Inexplicable Redemption of Agent G, The 196
institutional theatres 52, 53, 230
integrated casting **8**, 20, 21, 24, 26, 51–52
Integration Showcase **8**, 51
interdisciplinary innovation 137
intersectionality 96
In the Heights 51
Ives, David 61

Jablon, Marc *43*
Jacobs-Jenkins, Branden 195
Jajeh, Jennifer 77
Jamaica 192
jazz musicians 39–40
Jensen, Sharon 16
Jobrani, Maz 80
Johansson, Scarlet 85
Johnson, James Weldon 17
Johnson, Katie 139
Jones, LeRoi 226
Jubilee, The 228
Jue, Francis 187
Just Lucky I Guess (Channing) 18

Kahn, Michael 25
Kalke, Celise 20
Katasse, Frank Henry Kassh (Tlingit) 152,
  154–155, *156*
Kean, Thomas 19
Kennedy, Adrienne 39
Khoury, Jamil 70, 78, 80
Kilroys, The 228
Kimchee and Chitlins 192
Kinard, Stanley 208
King, Bruce 149

King, Martin Luther, Jr., 85
King, Rodney 179, 192
King and I, The 183, 185, 191, 197
Klein, Melanie 177
Kondo, Dorinne 9, 176, 190, 193
Kopić, Kristina 93
Krislov, Marvin 40
Kruger, Barbara 13
K-12 public education system, disabled
  students in 94
Kung Fu 177, 184–185
Kushner, Tony 61, 80
Kusugak, Arvaarluk 203
Kwei-Armah, Kwame 20–21

La Jolla Playhouse 154
Lang, Bill 149
language, casting 1–2, 9–10, 13, 14,
  15–16, 18, 19, 24–25, 27, 203–204
Larsen, Nella 17
Last Airbender, The 51
Latino American theater 60, 61, 192
Lebank, Ezra 137
Lee, Bruce 184, 185
Lee, Canada 26
Lee, Wen Ho 183
Lee, Young Jean 195
Lenk, Waylon (Karuk) 154
Leon, Kenny 53
Lerner, Motti **65**
Let Me Down Easy 177
Lewis, John 137
Lewis, Megan 207
Lewis, Victoria Ann 8, 93, 94, 100
liberal arts institutions 126, 132
Lights! Camera! Access! 98
linguistic whiteface 196, 197
Linnaeus, Carl 14
literary translation *see* translation, and
  multilingual plays
Littlefield, Edward (Tlingit) 154
Longmore, Paul 89, 102, 103, 105
Lorde, Audre 164
LORT (League of Resident Theaters)
  system 148, 149, 157, 166, 226
Los Angeles uprisings (1992) 179, 192
Luster, Milfordean 23
lynching plays 195

McAllister, Marvin 195
Macbeth 5, 7, 36–37, *38*, 46–47
McCauley, Gilbert 207

MacDonald, James 104, 105
McNally, Terence 61
Mamet, David 61
Manahatta 168n3
Mandvi, Aasif 80
Manning, Lynn 100
Mansour, Mona 62
Man Who Came to Dinner, The 39
Marks, Victoria 107
Mark Taper Forum **8**, *104, 106*, 149,
    178, 180, *181*
Marriage Proposal, A 65, **65**, 66, 68
Marriott Theatre 51
Marshall, Jack 19
Martin, Douglas 103
Martin, Trayvon 226
Matlin, Marlee 91, 92
Mattar, Sandra 74
M. Butterfly 61, 182, 185
Measure for Measure 152
Mee, Charles 22
melting pot theory 229
metapragmatics 132–133, 134, 135
Me Too campaign 228, 233n1
Metwally, Omar 80
Miami University, Ohio 9, 132, 137,
    140n3, 149; Native American Women
    Playwrights Archive 158n6
Middle East: definition of 60; depiction of
    Middle Easterners/Middle Eastern
    Americans 76, 79; diversity of 60, 62,
    63; monolithic perceptions of 62
Middle Eastern American/North African
    Americans (MENA) *see* Middle Eastern
    American theater
Middle Eastern American theater 7,
    57–59, 72–73; academia and actor
    training 74–75; artistic home, creation
    of 60–62; casting needs of multiple
    plays 64; cultural factors 73–74; cultural
    knowledge and embodied practices
    79–80; lack of material 78–79; pro-
    blems in industry 76–78; ReOrient
    2009 65–69, **65, 67–68**; ReOrient
    Festival of Short Plays 7, 62–65, 70;
    sins of omission 75
Middleton, Clark *104*
Midsummer Night's Dream, A 37
Mihesuah, Devon A. 162
Mikado, The 197
Miller, Arthur 40–45, *41, 43*
Miller, Wentworth 18

Minard, Duane (Yurok) 154, 155
minstrelsy 91, 191, 195, 230
Miranda, Lin-Manuel 190, 192, 194
Miss Saigon **8**, 176, 182, 229
Mitchell, David T. 89
Mitchell, Koritha 195
mixed-race casting 13
Mohler, Courtney Elkin (Santa Barbara
    Chumash) 9, 159
Monologist Suffers Her Monologue, The **65**
Montalban, Ricardo 192
Mora, Luis Eduardo 50
Moreno, Rita 191
Moses, Bob 137
Moses, Daniel David 149
Motherfucker with the Hat, The 27n4, 51
Mouawad, Wajdi 75
Moura, Ana 128
multiculturalism: color-blind 190, 192–195;
    and race 178
multilingual theater 8–9, 115–116,
    117–118; audience and community
    engagement 126–127; bilingual actors
    118; chorus 121, 125, 128–129, 134;
    closing ritual 126; ensemble 122–123,
    124, 133–134, 135; heteroglossia
    118–119; hyperlinked dramaturgy
    128–129, 134; intentionality and
    consistency in casting 122; lobbying
    127; as local and global 129–130;
    multiple dimensions 135; play, finding
    119–122; rehearsal 123–126; research
    experiment 125; staging 127; transla-
    tion 119, 125, 128, 129; tripartite actor
    121; *see also* emergent strategy
Museum of Contemporary Art Chicago 97
musicals 185–188, *186*, 190, 195, 197
Music Man, The 39
Muslims 79; *see also* Middle Eastern
    American theater
mythos of casting 5

Nagle, Mary Kathryn (Cherokee) 168n3
Najjar, Michael Malek 7, 72
narrative prosthesis 89, 103
National Association for the Advancement
    of Colored People (NAACP) 191
National Disability Theatre 92
National Endowment of the Arts
    (NEA) 88
National Theatre of the Deaf 92

Native American actors 149–150,
150–151; advancement of professional
standards for 165–166; apprenticeship
157; community, sustenance of
166–167; pipeline 165–166;
self-identified 166; skill development
151, 156; tribal background of 149,
165, 166; workshops for 153–154, 156
Native American theater 9, 145–146, 151,
159–161; call to action 167–168;
companies, and land base 166;
creativity 163–164, *164*; culture
bearers 152, 154, 156; elevation of
contemporary Indigenous stories
162–165; pan-Indian portrayal 150;
professional standards for Native
American artists 165–166; reclamation
of theatrical space
161–162; sustenance of Native
American artistic community
166–167; *see also* Native Voices
at the Autry (NVA)
Native Voices Artists Ensemble 156, 157
Native Voices at the Autry (NVA) **8**, 9,
147, 159, 160, 162, 165–166; apprentice system 157; beginnings 148–149;
casting the room 152–155; complicated
issues 149–150; Los Angeles 155; *Off
the Rails* 152–154, *153*; productions
149; space, creation of 147–148; *They
Don't Talk Back* 152, 154–155, *156*
New Arab American Works 72
Newman, Harry 13, 14, 16, 18,
21–22, 27
New World Theatre 149
New York City Center 191
New York Shakespeare Festival **8**, 24
New York University 17
Ngũgĩ wa Thiong'o 211
Nguyen, Qui 190, 195, 196
Nielsen, Kim 104
Nightingale, The 27n4
9 Parts of Desire 75
Nobuko Miyamoto 192
non-biased casting 229
non-profit theaters 51, 52, 53, 196
non-traditional casting 13, 33, 52–53,
228, 230; and expectations of viewers
17–19; and language 15–16; rethinking
tradition 19–22
Non-Traditional Casting Project (NTCP)
8, 13, 15, 52

No One as Nasty 104
Noor Theatre 72
North Shore Music Theatre 50
No Such Cold Thing **65**
*Now Look What You Made Me
Do* 149
Nussbaum, Susan 100, 104

Obama, Barack 12, 207, 225
occupational therapy, for disabled
students 94
Octoroon, An 195
Off the Rails 152–154, *153*, 168n3
Of Mice and Men 100
Oklahoma! 74
Oliva, Judy Lee 149
Omi, Michael 190
One Day: On the Road to the ADA
107–109, *109*, 110; reenactment,
casting 107–108; role preparation
108–109
one-person show *see* solo performance
open work 134–135
Oregon Shakespeare Festival (OSF) 149,
153, 154, 168n3
O'Reilly, Kaite 90, 108
Oriental Actors of America **8**, 191
Orientalism 174, 182, 183, 191, 197
Orphan Sea, The 8–9, 117, 119, 120–122,
121, *125*, 131, 133, 137; audience and
community engagement 126–127;
choral movement *124*; chorus 121,
125, 128–129, 134; ensemble, casting
122–123, *124*, 133–134, 135;
hyperlinked dramaturgy 128–129,
134; open work 134–135; rehearsal
123–126
Oscars 90, 91, 92
Other Voices Project **8**
Our Town 39

Page, Priscilla 9, 207, 220, 223,
225, 226
Paley, Petronia *41*
Pao, Angela 16, 23, 24, 231
Papp, Joseph 24, 52
Parks, Suzan-Lori 61, 203, 231
Parsi, Novid 62
passing 72, 76, 230
Passing 17
PENN State Center Stage 149
People's Theater 102

performativity, theory of 14
Performing Arts Center (Anchorage, Alaska) 155
Perseverance Theatre 154, 155
Phamaly 92
P.H.*reaks: The Hidden History of People with Disabilities 103
Pilgrims Musa and Sheri in the New World 75
Ping Chong + Company **8**
Pinkleton, Sam *186*
pipeline problem 92–94, 165–166, 231
playwrights 78, 79, 196; and color-blind casting 76; disabled 100, 102, 103–105, 107; Latinx 50; and multilingual plays 118, 120; Native American 147, 148–149, 151, 152, 162, 163
Playwrights Center 149
Porchlight Theatre 51
Portland Center Stage at the Armory (PSC) 168n3
power 9, 135, 176, 177, 178, 179, 181, 185, 187, 188, 190, 210, 211, 231
pre-show discussions 21
Prison Break 18
Project Am I Right? 50, 53, 54
Pryce, Jonathan **8**, 176, 229
Public Theatre, The 149
Pyretown 104

race 5, 19, 178, 188n1, 190, 208; and audience 33–34; categories 14, 16; as discourse 14; and genetics 37–38; racial violence 209, 210, 211, 224; recognition of 37–40; redefinition of 40–45; and Shakespearean performance 19, 21, 34; transformation of 45–47; *see also Collidescope: Adventures in Pre- and Post-Racial America*; cross-racial casting
race-blind casting 13
race-conscious casting 13
racialism 14, 25, 37
racism 14, 25, 37, 177, 178, 182, 183, 188n1, 190, 192, 194–195, 198, 209
Radio (film) 91
Raffo, Heather 75, 80
Raisin in the Sun, A 34
Ramón, Ana-Cristina 167
Rankine, Claudia 203
Rauch, Bill 154
Real Pepsi Challenge, The (Capparell) 40

rehearsals 39, 45, 46, 70; *Collidescope* 211, 212, 214, 216; cross-racial casting 178, 179, 180; multilingual plays 117, 118, 119, 121, 123–126, 128, 134
Reinholz, Randy (Choctaw) 9, 147, 148, 149, 152–154, *153*, 155, 159, 160, 165, 168n3
relaxed performances 97
ReOrient 2009 65–69; cast list by play **68**; plays **65**; projected casting grid **67**
ReOrient Camp 62
ReOrient Festival of Short Plays 7, 62–65, 70
ReOrient Forum 62
reparative creativity 177, 179, 188
repertoire of collective action 6
Ricamora, Conrad 187
Richard III 19, 100
ritualized repetition of social norms 14
Rodgers, Richard 197
Romeo and Juliet 37
Roosevelt, Franklin Delano 17
Rosenberg, Lynne Marie 49–50, 53–54, 54n1
Ruderman Family Foundation 93
Ruined 75
Russell, Harold 91, 92

safe spaces 213–214
Said, Edward 174
Said, Najla 77
Sanchez, Sonia 232, 234n7
sanctioned ignorance 21, 22
Sandahl, Carrie 8, 88, 230–231
San Francisco State University 60, 61, 62
Sawyer, R. Keith 132
Sayonara 192
Schwerner, Mickey 137
Scorched 75
Scott, Jean Bruce 9, 147, 148, 159, 160, 165
Screen Actors Guild-American Federation of Television and Radio Artists (SAG-AFTRA) 97
sensory friendly performances 97
Shaheen, Jack G. 74, 79
Shakespearean performance 33, 34, 39; and actors of color 19, 21, 34, 36–37, 39; *Hamlet* 39; *Macbeth* 5, 7, 36–37, *38*, 46–47; *Measure for Measure* 152; *Midsummer Night's Dream, A* 37; *Richard III* 19, 100;

Romeo and Juliet 37; *Tempest,
The* 34, 39; and universality 39
Shalhoub, Tony 80
Shamieh, Betty 62, **65**, 73, 80
shange, ntozake 39, 188n5
Sherman, Howard 50
Shipment, The 195
Silk Road Rising 72
Silverman, Leigh *186*
Sixteen Wounded 80
Skidmore College 9, 117, 120, 122,
    130, 133
Smith, Anna Deavere **8**, 9, 177, 178–182,
    181, 188, 188n5, 190, 192, 223
Smith, Cherise 192–193
Smith, Linda Tuhiwai (Mâori) 162
Snyder, Sharon L. 89
social media 49, 50, 51, 53, 54
societal segregation 24
sociologies of viewing 17, 19, 21, 25,
    131, 135, 225
"Sodade" 126
Soft Power 177, 185–188, *186*, 190,
    195, 197
solo performance 179–182, *181*, 188n5,
    192–193
South Pacific 191
Soyinka, Wole 39
*Speaking in Tongues: Languages at Play in
    the Theatre* 118
special education, for children with dis-
    abilities 94
Spiderwoman Theater 149
Spivak, Gayatri 21
Spring Awakening 86, 92
Staggenborg, Suzanne 6
stealth Latino 192
Steen, Shannon 191
Steinbeck, John 100
Steppenwolf Theatre 96
stereotypes 5, 9, 69, 191, 230; Asian
    American 183; disability 89, 96, 101,
    103; Middle Eastern American 72, 77,
    78; Native American 162
Stocking, Ann *104*
Stoppard, Tom 61
*Stories from the Indian Boarding
    School* 157
Stroker, Ali 92
structural racism 178
students: classroom casting 34–35; of
    color 22, 108, 207–208, 212, 215;

disabled 89, 90, 93–95, 105–107;
    involving in play selection and
    casting 22; Middle Eastern American
    75; and multilingual plays *see* multi-
    lingual theater; Native American
    see Native American theater; and
    race 34
Studi, DeLanna (Cherokee)168n3
Svich, Caridad 8–9, 22, 115, 117, 119,
    120, 121, *121*, 122, 123, 124, 125,
    125, 127, 128, 130, 131, 133, 135
Syler, Claire 4, 33, 228, 229
systems theory 131

Talented Ones, The 58–59
Tamam **65**
Tavares, Sara 128
Taylor, Drew Hayden 149
Taylor-Corbett, Lynne 154
Taylor-Corbett, Shaun (Blackfeet) 154
team-teaching 23
Teenage Dick 87
television shows, writers of 79
Tempest, A 39
Tempest, The 34, 39
Teo, Mei Ann 9, 173
Tesori, Jeanine 185, *186*, 190, 195, 197
Teuton, Christopher B. (Cherokee
    Nation) 163
Thanksgiving Play, The 168n3
Theatre Communications Group (TCG)
    12, 21, 26, 38
Theatre Folks of Color Facebook 228
TheatreWorks 51
Theobald, Betsy 149
They Don't Talk Back 152, 154–155, *156*
Thompson, Ayanna 7, 15, 17, 19, 33,
    39, 131
Thornton, Michael Patrick 96
Time of Your Life, The 74–75
Tobar, Héctor 179, 180
Tommy, Liesl 228
Topdog/Underdog 61
translation, and multilingual plays 119,
    125, 128, 129
Trinity Rep 19
tripartite actor 121, 134, 135
Turchi, Laura 34
Twilight: Los Angeles, 1992 **8**, 9, 190;
    color-blind multiculturalism 192–193;
    cross-racial casting 177,
    178–182

Undesireable Elements **8**, 208, 210, 211–212
University of California, Los Angeles (UCLA) 107, 108, 159
University of Illinois 217
University of Maryland 209, *209*, 211, 225
University of Massachusetts Amherst (UMass Amherst) 9, 207, 208, 209, *213*, 215, 216, 218, 220, 224, 225–226
University of Missouri-Columbia 120
University of Redlands 107, 108, *109*
university training programs, and disabled students 93–94
Unsex Me Here 104, 105
Urban Bush Women, Summer Leadership Institute 228

Van Sickel, Eli 91
Verfremdungseffekt 121
Vietgone 190, 195–197
Villegas, Lauren 50, 53–54
Visnor, Gerald 148
Vogel, Paula 61

Waheed, Nayyiah 173–174
Wake Forest University 209, 216–218, *217*, 225
Walcott, Derek 39
Walker, Alice 44
Walk with Me: Freedom Summer Walking Tour 138–139, 140
Wallace, Naomi **65**
Ward, Douglas Turner 195
Washington, Booker T. 25, 40
Water by the Spoonful 75
waterscape play 122
welcome table 4, 5, 7, 12–28, 220–226
Welcome Table, The 12, 221–222

Welles, Orson 17
Western College for Women 137, 138, 140n2, 140n3
West Side Story 192
whiteface 182, 190, 195–198
white supremacy 2, 190, 191, 194, 195, 197
whitewashing 49–51, 53–54, 176, 184, 194
Whose Life Is It Anyway? 100
Wilks, Talvin 9, 203, 207, 208, 209, *209*, 210–211, 212–213, *213*, 214–215, 216, *217*, 218, 219n6, 222
Williams, Robin 98n3
Williams, Tennessee 45, 96
Wilson, August 6, **8**, 22, 25, 34, 38–39, 61, 76
Wilson, Darren 211
Winant, Howard 190
Wise, Tim 28n7
Wolf, Sara Kishi 108
Wong, B. D. 229
Woodburn, Danny 93
Woodson, Stephani Etheridge 135
Wortman, William 149, 158n6

Ybarra, Patricia 229
Yeghiazarian, Torange 7, 58, 60, **65**, 72, 78, 79, 80
yellowface **8**, 91, 182, 184, 185–188, 191, 195–198
Yellow Face 9, 177, 182–184
Yellow Robe, William S., Jr. (Assiniboine) 149
Youssef, Bassem 74, 81n1

Zahedi, Caveh **65**, 66
Zayas, José 120

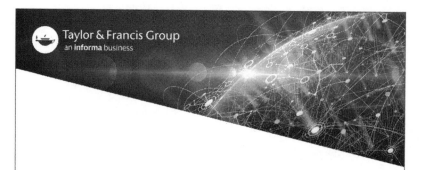